LOOKING BENEATH THE SURFACE

Looking beneath the Surface

THE STORY OF ARCHAEOLOGY IN NEW JERSEY

R. ALAN MOUNIER

RUTGERS UNIVERSITY PRESS

New Brunswick, New Jersey

LIBRARY OF CONGRESS CATALOGING-IN-PUBLICATION DATA
Mounier, R. Alan.
  Looking beneath the surface : the story of archaeology in New Jersey / R. Alan
Mounier.
    p. cm.
  Includes bibliographical references (p.) and index.
  ISBN 0-8135-3145-4 (cloth : alk. paper) ISBN 0-8135-3146-2 (pbk. : alk. paper)
  1. Indians of North America—New Jersey—Antiquities. 2. New Jersey—
Antiquities. 3. Excavations (Archaeology)—New Jersey. I. Title.
E78.N6 M68 2002
974.9'01—dc21

                                                                    2002023713

British Cataloging-in-Publication data for this book is available from the British
Library.

Manufactured in the United States of America

To the memory of Ernest C. Stanmire Jr. (1924–1998),
patriot, Renaissance man, and friend

CONTENTS

ILLUSTRATIONS

ACKNOWLEDGMENTS

In reflecting on my experiences in writing this book, I am keenly aware that this effort could not have been accomplished without the help of many people. The roster of friends and colleagues who have aided me is a long one indeed. Charles Bello, Jean Jones, Dr. T. Cregg Madrigal, Edward Rutsch, Bill Sandy, and Dr. Richard Veit answered the call for published materials and bibliographic information. Dr. Ilene Grossman-Bailey generously provided a copy of her doctoral dissertation, which I found to be a valuable source of information. Charles Bello and Richard Veit, along with Jack Cresson, Dr. Patricia Hansell, and Donald Pettifer, read various drafts of the chapters and offered helpful suggestions. Charles Bello played a further critical role in assembling many of the photographs that illustrate this work. Karen Flinn and Gregory Lattanzi provided archival photographs from the New Jersey State Museum. Edward J. Lenik also sent a photograph. Argorie Ingraham, Toni Sapello, and Dale E. Wettstein showed remarkable patience in dealing with my requests for custom photographs; their competent help is greatly appreciated.

Joseph R. Arsenault shared much useful information about sites in southern New Jersey. He also generously loaned artifacts for examination and photography; in addition, he prepared the handsome maps. Jack Cresson has always been eager to help with data and insights—at once subtle and profound—garnered from his many years of independent research. He also very generously provided me with numerous examples of replicated artifacts and the unpublished results of his various studies in experimental archaeology. Alan E. Carman and my dear sister, Alice Mounier, contributed original artwork. Mr. Carman and F. Dayton Staats also very graciously opened their respective collections for photography. Dr. Michael Gregg kindly arranged access to the library of the New Jersey Historic Preservation Office. Glenn Wershing offered information about sites in northern New Jersey. Landis Eaton and Larry Randolph helped with information about discoveries in the central portion of the state. Ron Brook scanned a lengthy typescript in preparation for word processing. Very detailed editing by Gretchen Oberfranc greatly improved the quality of the text.

My daughters, Sara, Marianna, and Jessica, have been supportive in many ways. My wife, Jerilyn, read and commented on several chapters; but more important, she provided constant encouragement and, at times, gentle nudging toward attainment of the final goal.

LOOKING BENEATH THE SURFACE

Introduction

This book tells the story of archaeology in New Jersey. It is a chronicle about an ancient past that is full of unrecorded events and the lost memories of now nameless, faceless people, whose mouths are stopped with dust. Possessing no system of writing, New Jersey's earliest residents left only a silent record: arrowheads that no longer kill, pottery long since dashed to pieces, and hearthstones turned cold by the passage of time. Such things are the stuff of archaeology.

Archaeology is a study of nuances, made even more subtle by the rapid decay of organic remains. As a rule, only the most durable of human creations —items of stone and pottery—survive the ravages of time. To complicate matters, the onslaught of our own culture and the undisciplined tunneling of greedy collectors have further diminished the stock of cultural materials that the ancients left behind. The task of the archaeologist is to gather and interpret these scraps for the benefit of science and the public generally.

By and large, archaeology originates with things in the ground. To extract those things usually requires digging; it is necessary, in a literal sense, to look beneath the surface. But digging up relics is a trivial pursuit if the only outcome is a collection of artifacts, however attractive or valuable they may be. Understanding what those relics mean in human terms is another matter altogether. The archaeologist must search for the mundane relationships, the deeper meanings, and the hidden mysteries of ancient life. Who were the people who created the items we now find? When and how did those people live? How did they integrate their lives with the natural and spiritual worlds? The goal of understanding the unwritten human past can be satisfied only through the careful analysis and interpretation of archaeological discoveries. That is the real challenge—and the real value—of archaeology. In this light, the phrase, "looking beneath the surface," assumes a profound, if figurative, significance.

In this book I attempt to tell the story of archaeology as it has unfolded, and as it continues to unfold, in New Jersey. By intent, I have not called this account *The Archaeology of New Jersey*, and not simply because that title is already twice taken (Cross 1941, 1956). It is inaccurate to portray our current knowledge as definitive, except in a most ephemeral way. I prefer to talk about what we *think* we know rather than what we can state as a matter of certainty. Our knowledge is never complete, never immutable. Every new archaeological investigation holds the potential to change our view of the past. As with any other science, new discoveries can cause even the most fervently held beliefs to fall precipitously into disfavor.

Each chapter of this book, although designed to stand alone, relates closely to the others. The first chapter, "Setting the Stage," provides necessary background information, describing what archaeology is and what it is not. I also summarize the currently recognized archaeological cultures in chronological sequence. To put into context how those cultures evolved and why they varied from place to place and from time to time, I provide an account of the transformation of the physical environment over the past 15,000 years. Archaeological dating methods are briefly noted. In addition, I review the fascinating history of archaeological research in New Jersey, focusing in particular on the hot-blooded controversies concerning "glacial man" and the "Trenton argillite culture." Finally, I look briefly at the important role of experimental archaeology.

The next three chapters treat particular subjects—artifact types, archaeological settlements, and burial practices—in considerable detail. The title of chapter 2, "What in the World?" is borrowed from a television program produced by the University of Pennsylvania in the 1950s, which featured artifacts from around the world, together with commentary by leading archaeologists and anthropologists. This chapter is essentially an encyclopedia of the kinds of artifacts that are found in New Jersey and the surrounding region. Although we tend to think of our aboriginal ancestors as living an austere, Stone Age existence, they enjoyed a remarkably well-rounded material culture, devising all of the technologies necessary for their survival from the materials provided by nature. Understandably, their textiles and carved wooden bowls and masks have disappeared, along with a myriad of other perishable possessions. One senses that their material and spiritual worlds were intimately entwined.

Chapter 3, "A Good Place to Live and Work," delves into the nature of aboriginal settlement in New Jersey. All cultures integrate the activities of daily life into a system of settlements. We have our farms and factories, our cemeteries and places of worship, our villages, suburbs, and large cities. Although their settlements differ from ours in form, content, and geographic extent, New Jersey's aboriginal occupants also arranged themselves on the landscape in thousands of villages and camps. In fact, we now occupy many of the same locations.

The fourth chapter, "Of Life and Death," deals with ancient burial practices as revealed by archaeological research in New Jersey. Without the careful work of the archaeologist, who would know that cremation was first practiced here almost 10,000 years ago! Prehistoric skeletons have been found in all parts of the state. Most ancient cultures apparently developed fairly simple burial customs, but elaborate mortuary cults arose from time to time. Some of the related graves contain many well-made offerings, frequently obtained from far-off corners of the continent. Some late prehistoric cemeteries also reveal trade goods that reflect dealings with Europeans. The analysis of skeletal remains can provide important information about the stature and health of ancient populations. Finally, the careful burial of dogs demonstrates the special relationship that developed anciently between humans and canines.

The last chapter, "A Journey of Archaeological Exploration," summarizes 21 archaeological investigations from various parts of the state, arranged in cultural-chronological order. Although the record of archaeological investigation in New Jersey is too lengthy to summarize in detail, these vignettes offer an overview of the wide variety of prehistoric archaeological sites in our state. Just as important, these summaries illustrate the accomplishments of dedicated individuals who have sought to know the past and to communicate that knowledge to the world of science and to the rest of society.

In writing this book, I have attempted to present only factual information and to document my sources thoroughly. When I express opinions, they are clearly stated as such. Without unduly slighting more recent works, I have drawn heavily on older publications because they contain a wealth of information that most readers would have difficulty finding otherwise. Besides, many of these works, now long out of print, offer insights that appear nowhere else.

Key to Site Numbers

1. 28-CM-25
2. 28-CM-28
3. 28-CU-79
4. 28-GL-15
5. 28-GL-123
6. 28-GL-139
7. 28-GL-170
8. 28-GL-171
9. 28-MO-125
10. 28-OC-100
11. Abature
12. Abbott Farm
13. Bell-Browning
14. Bell-Philhower
15. Bevan
16. Blue Hole
17. Boni Farm
18. Cadwalader
19. Canton
20. Cherry Hill
21. Dark Moon
22. East Point
23. Fairy Hole Rock Shelter
24. Fralinger
25. Furnace Brook Rock Shelter
26. Goose Island
27. Great Piece Meadow
28. Gruno Farm
29. Harding Lake Rock Shelter

30. Harry's Farm
31. Hartung Rock Shelter
32. Havins
33. High Bridge
34. Koens-Crispin
35. Larchmont
36. Lenhardt
37. Lumberton
38. Miller Field
39. Minisink
40. Pahaquarra
41. Pennella
42. Plenge
43. Raccoon Point
44. Red Valley
45. Rosenkrans Ferry
46. Salisbury
47. Savich Farm
48. Scott
49. Skyline Rock Shelter
50. Steel
51. Stow Creek Cache
52. Tuckerton Shell Mound
53. Turkey Swamp
54. Ware
55. West Creek
56. Williamson
57. Woodbury Annex
58. Zierdt

FIGURE I. Map of sites noted in the text. Courtesy of Joseph R. Arsenault Environmental Consulting.

I must admit that my bibliographic selections were also biased by my admiration for the pioneers of New Jersey archaeology. Charles Conrad Abbott, Ernest Volk, Alanson B. Skinner, Max Schrabisch, and Dorothy Cross are immortal icons. Herbert C. Kraft, for decades the mainstay of modern archaeology in New Jersey, has himself now passed into immortality. Anyone with a genuine interest in New Jersey archaeology owes a great debt of gratitude to these departed scholars.

I have attempted to provide solid information about archaeological sites from every corner of New Jersey. Even so, the results are somewhat uneven. Most of the state's heavily urbanized areas have contributed little to the record of archaeological research, because rapid industrial, commercial, and residential development has overlaid or destroyed prehistoric sites. Accordingly, most archaeological research has focused on what are now, or were formerly, the rural and suburban parts of the state, where investigations are less hindered by buildings, pavement, and the bustle of city life. On the whole, however, the accumulated record is imposing.

Although archaeology encompasses all of the human past, in this work I do not probe the historical period. For the rich record of historical archaeology in New Jersey, I recommend Richard Veit's *Digging New Jersey's Past* (2002). It is an excellent companion volume.

Archaeology is an intrinsic element of our shared cultural heritage. It belongs to all the people. With this in mind, I have purposely focused on archaeological sites that have disappeared from the landscape or that are currently protected from unauthorized digging. I have not given exact site locations, for obvious reasons. If this book encourages readers to involve themselves in archaeology—and I hope that it will—I urge them to do it properly. As will be seen in numerous examples throughout this book, serious students of archaeology need not be professionals. But they must conduct themselves responsibly as stewards of the past. To do otherwise is nothing less than the criminal and selfish destruction of our irreplaceable patrimony. The future of the past is in our hands.

1

Setting the Stage

*Archaeology is not finding things but finding out
about things; it is essentially detective work.*

———

WALTER SHEPHERD (1965)

We begin with an introduction to the nature of archaeology, the sequence of
archaeological cultures, and the ancient environments in which aboriginal cultures developed. We shall look briefly at the ancient and modern-day landscapes, along with the history of archaeological research in New Jersey and the
role of experimental studies. Readers with limited experience in archaeology
will gain an understanding of concepts used throughout the book.

WHAT IS ARCHAEOLOGY?

When my daughter was about five years old, her teacher asked her about her
family. Part of the exchange went something like this:

"Sara, what does your father do for a living?"

"He's an archaeologist."

"That's interesting! Please tell us what he does."

"He fixes trucks!"

Though erroneous, her response made sense. Sara had never witnessed my
professional work but had watched me repair my old truck on many occa-
sions. I am constantly amazed to find out that many people, perhaps most, do
not really know what archaeology is all about. But before we define what archaeology is, we should take a moment to review what it is not.

Archaeology is not paleontology, which is the study of fossils, and it is not geology, which is the study of rocks and minerals. So if you are introduced to an archaeologist and start chatting about the latest dinosaur discovery or the beautiful crystals you saw at the curio shop, don't be too surprised if you receive a dazed look in response—or upwardly rolling eyes.

In reality, however, archaeologists do know quite a lot about such things —and a whole lot more. The fundamentals of geology are necessary to identify the materials from which implements, utensils, and weapons were made and to understand the natural and cultural processes that affect the development of the landscape. The archaeologist must have a basic knowledge of fossils, which sometimes appear in cultural assemblages, of anatomy, because skeletons and refuse bones are sometimes found, and of physics, mathematics, land surveying, map making, ecology, and so forth. Eclectic knowledge is the hallmark of a good archaeologist.

Contrary to popular opinion, archaeology is seldom as glamorous and certainly never as adventurous as movies and novels would have us believe. I have had any number of acquaintances who were quickly disabused of their illusions about archaeology by spending a few hot, sweaty hours of fruitless searching while swatting deerflies and stumbling through a nearly impenetrable stand of scrub oaks in the Pine Barrens of southern New Jersey. Having endured an "adventure" of this sort, one aspiring Indiana Jones told me that he had just decided to look for an "inside" job!

Archaeology is not merely the collecting of relics. That is part of the job, to be sure, but frequently a small part, and sometimes it is not archaeology at all. How can this be?

Archaeology is the study of human behavior in the past tense. It is a science that is accomplished by examining the physical evidence of human activities, namely, the artifacts and cultural features left by the people in question. An *artifact* is anything made and used by humans. In virtually all cases, artifacts show modifications resulting from use or design. A cobble that served as a hammerstone will show battering merely as a consequence of that use. Formal artifacts, such as axes, arrowheads, and pottery, reflect a conscious design intended to serve a particular purpose: chopping wood, taking game animals, or cooking. Usually artifacts are portable objects. *Cultural features*, on the other hand, are aggregations of artifacts, such as caches (stockpiles) or hearths, or structural elements, such as refuse pits or houses. Features, by and large, are not transportable, although many of their constituent elements may be.

FIGURE 2. A stone hearth. Probably used for roasting shellfish, this feature is a platform of fire-broken rocks, one course deep, and measuring about 5 × 7¹/₂ feet (1.5 × 2.3 m). Photograph by the author.

The places where archaeological things occur are known as *sites.* A site may be described simply as a location that contains evidence of past human behavior, that is, artifacts or features or both. A site may be simple or complex depending on its specific history. Sites consist of *components,* which are expressions of a particular culture or group at a particular point in time. The simplest sites are those that were occupied only once by a single group of people. Sites of this kind are known as single component sites. Locations that were revisited are called multicomponent sites because they bear evidence of occupation by more than one cultural group or by the same group of people on more than one occasion. One of the archaeologist's tasks is to sort out the various components represented at the sites under consideration.

There are thousands of sites in New Jersey alone, and some means must be devised to differentiate among them. This task is accomplished by assigning each site a unique name or identifying number. Sites may be named after a property owner or a prominent landmark. The Lange Farm site in Gloucester County, for example, commemorates Pat and Marge Lange, a generous couple who gave generations of collectors and archaeologists permission to search their fields for relics. The Mile Hollow site near Bordentown was named after a peculiar topographic feature. Some sites, such as the Tuckerton Shell Mound, are identified descriptively.

To avoid confusion and redundancy, agencies that keep registers of archaeological sites usually identify them by a unique designation as well as by name. In New Jersey, all officially recorded sites are listed according to a system devised by the Smithsonian Institution. Each site is given a three-part code name: a two-digit number, followed by two letters, followed by a serial number. The first number coincides with the position of the state in an alphabetical listing of all the states. New Jersey is twenty-eighth on the list (because Alaska and Hawaii entered the Union after the system was initiated); so the first two-digit number for all sites in New Jersey is 28. Next comes an abbreviation for the county—CA for Camden, MO for Monmouth, and so on. Finally, an appended serial number represents the order in which the site was logged by the registrar. Following this system, Site 28-GL-15, the Lange Farm, is the fifteenth site registered in Gloucester County, New Jersey.

Just as some form of shorthand is necessary to differentiate among sites, archaeologists employ classification to simplify discussions about particular kinds of artifacts. Rather than referring descriptively to an artifact according to its form, dimensions, material, and presumed cultural affiliation, archaeologists often allude to a type name, for example, a Koens-Crispin point or Riggins Fabric-Impressed pottery. With a little exposure, anyone with an interest quickly forms a mental image of an artifact—and its place in a cultural-temporal framework—based on its typology, just as most people can easily differentiate between a 1917 Model T and a 1965 Ford Mustang.

While useful as archaeological shorthand, typologies can sometimes assume a reality that never existed anciently. Artifact attributes often exhibit a continuum that bridges the distinctions between named types. Based solely on surface texture or paste, many potsherds could easily be classed as belonging to more than one type. In addition, some artifact forms occur repeatedly in different cultural-temporal contexts. For instance, small triangular stone points appear at various times in prehistory, and these occurrences can be separated by thousands of years on a single site. Obviously an individual triangular point cannot be the product both of an Archaic culture, perhaps 5,000 years old, and of a Late Woodland culture having an antiquity of 1,000 years or less. Even so, there is a tendency, especially among the uninitiated, to pigeonhole artifacts into named types. That is the tyranny of well-established typologies. To borrow a phrase from the venerable Charles C. Abbott (1908:6), typology "is a most valuable servant, but a bad master!" For this reason, it is critical to interpret the artifact in its context and not merely as an isolated cultural expression.

The value of artifacts and cultural features lies in the clues they provide about otherwise unrecorded lives and times. If the aim of artifact collecting is simply to amass objects, then the work is not archaeology, because the effort does not contribute directly to an understanding of past human behavior. In reality, the archaeologist is not collecting artifacts at all but rather gathering archaeological data, the evidence that places archaeological finds into a meaningful context. As Abbott (1909:63) observed nearly a century ago, "The conditions under which an object is found [are] of more importance than the character of the object itself."

The archaeologist seeks to place discoveries into a context that is defined in space, time, and culture. To the archaeologist, space means geographic or terrestrial location. It has nothing to do with celestial space, although future researchers may well deal with the archaeology of twentieth-century space exploration! The archaeologist wants to learn the geographic range of the people under study. Our focus here is New Jersey and its various regions.

The dimension of time is of concern because it is important to know the chronological relationships among artifact assemblages and the people who made and used them. Time is measured in both relative and absolute terms. The superimposition of one set of artifacts upon another gives a sense of their relative ages. The remains of earlier cultures generally appear deeper in the earth than those of later groups, although it is always possible that plowing or mixing from other, later activities, including erosion and natural soil movement, may have disturbed the layers. When groups of apparently related artifacts consistently appear together in many sites within a region, they may be classed as elements of a particular cultural epoch, period, or horizon. These units have finite, although sometimes poorly defined, boundaries in time.

Chronological relationships can also be ascertained in more precise terms by specialized tests, such as radiocarbon (C^{14}) dating, which measures the latent radioactivity in organic materials. By this means, substances such as charcoal, bone, shells, and even human tissues can be dated with some accuracy, now often within a century or less. Therefore, by inference, C^{14} dating allows artifacts and cultural features that are associated with organic materials to be placed in time. Inorganic artifacts that have been subjected to heat, such as potsherds or hearth rocks, can be dated directly by another radiometric test, known as thermoluminescence dating. This approach is usually less accurate than the C^{14} method and is employed only infrequently. Yet another technique is dendrochronology, or tree-ring dating. By matching the patterns of growth rings observed in pieces of wood, this technique can define a prolonged cultural sequence if enough wooden specimens of overlapping ages survive and if at least some of the tree rings can be assigned to a particular date. This method is seldom used in the eastern United States for want of comparative samples. (See Michels 1973 for a description of various archaeological dating techniques.)

Despite advances in dating techniques, archaeological chronology remains somewhat imprecise. Even the results of the so-called absolute tests, such as radiocarbon dating, contain inherent errors. Consequently, laboratories never report a single date as definitive. Rather, the calculated ages are expressed within a certain range. A typical reading might be 1,000 ± 100 years ago (or B.P., before the present), which means that the sample probably dates between 900 and 1,100 years ago. But there always remains at least a small chance that the actual date might fall beyond the calculated range. Added to this possibility are uncertainties in correlating "radiocarbon years" with calendrical dates or in associating cultural materials with substances submitted for age analysis. Furthermore, artifacts of particular types often vary in age from place to place. For these reasons, time is best viewed in general terms from an archaeological perspective.

The last dimension of archaeological context is culture, which can be defined as a system of ideas and practices that have evolved among a particular group of people for coping with the problems of day-to-day living. An important aspect of culture is that it passes from one generation to the next. Each new generation does not have to rediscover a successful way of life; younger members receive it from their elders through the medium of culture. For this reason, ancient people who may be entirely unknown to history can be identified archaeologically by their shared cultural traits. They can also be distinguished from other groups of people having different cultural traits. As already mentioned, archaeologists seek to place these cultures in time and space.

Cultural ideas and practices may evolve in response to environmental, social, or technological changes. For example, there is good evidence from the New Jersey coast that rising sea levels changed marine habitats so that, over time, shellfish consumption among the Indians shifted from oysters to clams. The earliest intensive exploitation of shellfish in New Jersey apparently occurred more than 3,000 years ago, when oysters were collected vigorously. Within a thousand years or so, rising sea levels had destroyed or moved prime oyster habitat, and that change, possibly accompanied by heavy collecting pressure, led to exploitation of other mollusks, notably hard-shell clam (quahog) and conch. This trend, now made very clear by work in Cape May County

(Mounier 1997), was foreshadowed by an excavation at the Tuckerton Shell Mound in 1939 (Cross 1941:39–40).

Marshall Becker (1988, 1999) has presented convincing evidence that maize (corn) farming among the historic Lenape of the lower Delaware Valley was primarily an economic adaptation to social changes brought about by contact with Swedish colonists, who were ill prepared to feed themselves. Once the Europeans shed their dependency on native produce, the Lenape gave up market gardening and returned to their traditional foraging economy. Becker's research is particularly interesting because it shows a clear knowledge of horticulture among the Indians but a decided preference for the age-old tradition of foraging.

Cultures can also change in response to technological innovation. Every so often, someone devises a new and better solution to an old problem. It may be a more efficient way to launch a projectile or perhaps a better way to cook a meal. The introduction of the bow and arrow about 1,300 years ago and the incipient production of ceramics about 3,000 years ago are examples of profound technological innovations that are clearly reflected in the archaeological record.

Aspects of culture may be tangible or intangible. Religion and social organization are metaphysical aspects of culture that are more or less invisible archaeologically. The more durable cultural trappings—such as stone tools and pottery—are the ordinary stuff of archaeology because they can survive for thousands of years in the earth. Yet it is important to realize that all aspects of culture are inextricably intertwined; for this reason, nonmaterial elements of culture may be inferred from the shreds and tatters of material culture. For instance, ancient religious practices and social hierarchies can be conjectured from the arrangements of graves and the offerings that the burials sometimes contain.

Archaeological remains need not be ancient to be informative. Every day of the year, for example, police detectives use archaeological techniques to solve crimes. That is, they interpret the behavior of criminals on the basis of physical evidence: fingerprints, weapons, or other clues left at the crime scene. Because this book deals with the archaeology of the prehistoric era—that period of time for which there are no written records—the examples cited are mostly ancient. (See Veit 2002 for an engaging account of historical archaeology in New Jersey that picks up the record in the seventeenth century and brings it up to the modern era.)

During the late nineteenth century and the first half of the twentieth, professional archaeologists were to be found mostly in colleges and large museums, where they engaged in teaching and independent research. Their research interests frequently focused on the "high cultures" or "classical civilizations" of the Old World or of Central and South America. In today's highly bureaucratized world, many archaeologists make a living by consulting to developers or government agencies, which must satisfy regulations based on environmental law. Others, whom I call "archaeocrats," are employed by the federal and state governments to prepare regulations and to oversee the work of consulting archaeologists. To serve in any of these capacities, archaeologists are required to have both advanced academic degrees and specialized training.

Although work opportunities have swollen the ranks of professional archaeologists in recent years, amateur archaeologists are far more numerous, as they always have been, at least in the non-urbanized portions of the country. To be sure, one need not be professionally employed in archaeology to make a positive contribution. All that is required is a genuine desire to understand and record the past. A passion for collecting interesting, pretty, or valuable artifacts for personal gain does not fill the bill. The varied writings of Louis A. Brennan (1963, 1973, 1974), Charles F. Kier Jr. (1949, 1954, Kier and Calverley 1957), F. Dayton Staats (1978, 1986, 1987, and so on), and George Morris (1974, 1986, 1988, Morris and Reed 1990, Morris et al. 1996), among others, make clear the important contributions of the unsung avocational archaeologist.

In reality, the distinction between professional and amateur archaeology is specious. The real distinction is between archaeologists—whether professional or amateur—and looters. Louis Brennan (1973:13–18) used to call productive amateurs "public archaeologists" or "citizen archaeologists." The looters he called "abominable pot hunters" or "archaeological pirates." I often call them "rat-holers" because their desultory digging resembles mindless tunneling by rats. Brennan (1973:15) characterized the public and citizen archaeologist as "anybody who wants to do archaeology and is willing to learn and abide by the rules. He is anybody from seven to seventy . . . who plies a trowel or shovel knowledgeably and with sober archaeological intent." These are people who, "adhering to professional standards and aspiring to a professional breadth of knowledge, conduct independent investigations with the intent of making new and original contributions to knowledge."

By contrast, Brennan (1973:16) condemned the looters: "The archaeological pirate is interested only in finding and looting sites, and he searches them out like Jack Horner probing for plums in his pie. . . . Site looting is a long-

FIGURE 3. A neatly excavated site. Archaeology depends upon the careful recovery of artifacts and data. Courtesy of Charles A. Bello, Cultural Resources Consulting Group, Inc., Highland Park, N.J.

established tradition going back before there was an American archaeology, and it has the same status in the public view as rabbit- and squirrel-hunting." In other words, the public tends to view this activity as an innocuous hobby. In reality, science and public heritage are at stake. Brennan lamented the crass ignorance of the pot hunters and the damage they do to our shared heritage:

> When they steal from the American past, they also rob themselves . . . [because] artifacts (spearheads, stone axes, pottery, etc.) are more exciting to find, more satisfying to own, and more completely owned when they are recovered with the total assemblage and within the cultural context to which they belonged in the life of their makers and users. By themselves, artifacts are mere trinkets and curiosities. It is the scientific information about them, acquired by proper digging, that gives them their sheen of value. (1973:17)

Brennan's scorn and sorrow are as justified today as they were when he recorded his thoughts some thirty years ago. Once disturbed, archaeological sites cannot be re-created. As the archaeologist Hester Davis (1971) wrote, "You can't grow a new Indian site." Each site is a fragile and nonrenewable resource. Once a site has been opened and its original contexts disturbed, whatever it might have told us is lost forever if no one keeps a disciplined, accurate record. That is why real archaeologists—professionals and amateurs alike—take pains in planning their excavations, in digging, and in analyzing their finds.

The popular image of archaeologists has them coaxing ancient secrets from the soil with trowels, dental picks, and sable brushes. This perception is certainly true enough, and it contrasts starkly with the roughshod rat-holing of relic miners, who often leave the ground looking like the shell-pocked battlefields of World War I. Even so, there are circumstances under which less dainty technology can be usefully employed in the service of archaeology. Some sites lie deeply buried beneath tons of modern fill, which is best removed— under supervision, of course—by bulldozers or backhoes (Burrow et al. 1999; Tull and Slaughter 2001). In short, archaeologists try to use tools that are appropriate to the circumstances encountered in the field.

Fieldwork constitutes but a fraction of the archaeologist's work. The remainder, which often requires significantly more time, involves laboratory procedures—cleaning, cataloging, and analyzing the finds—and reporting. No archaeological project is complete without adequate interpretation and dissemination of findings.

Publicizing archaeological information is important for the growth of scientific knowledge. It is equally valuable, and perhaps more so, as a means to educate the public about its heritage. As with history, knowledge of archaeology can add immeasurably to the appreciation of one's state, city, or neighborhood. Pride of place is important to the vitality of communities, and archaeology can be instrumental in instilling that pride.

Archaeology is also valuable because it demystifies the past and corrects misconceptions. For instance, there is a persistent but mistaken belief that native peoples were natural-born conservationists. Although they were well attuned to their surroundings, the Indians apparently had no sense of environmental protection as this concept exists today. In fact, because they killed game animals in such large numbers, early prehistoric hunters may have played a role in the extinction of the large mammals of the Pleistocene epoch (Haynes 1973). I was once in the company of rifle-toting Eskimos who attempted to dispatch an entire herd of caribou in one fell swoop. Only a lack of marksmanship and a limited supply of ammunition prevented them from achieving their bloody goal. The concepts of ecological waste and conservation are not imprinted in the minds of native peoples and, evidently, never have been.

Another false notion is that aboriginal populations lived in a pristine environment, unspoiled by their daily actions. In fact, archaeology amply demonstrates that portions of the landscape were fouled by prehistoric economic activities. For instance, shellfish cannot be gathered and processed in bulk without making a stinking mess. While they were being formed, the huge shell dumps at Absecon, Keyport, and Tuckerton must have been utterly offensive to all creatures except for scavengers and flies! Many other aspects of aboriginal life—cooking, flint working, pottery making, as well as hunting and fishing—have left detectable imprints on the surface of the ground or within it. Indeed, the trash of ancient societies comprises the very sites that archaeologists now seek to excavate and interpret. Without trash, there can be no archaeology.

It is certainly true that environmental alterations by aboriginal populations differ from those wreaked by more modern industrial societies. With the possible exception of the Pleistocene extinctions, the ecological effects of ancient life generally proved less damaging and less persistent than those of historic cultures. No form of aboriginal pollution can match the staying power of a spent atomic fuel rod! Nevertheless, pollution and wholesale landscape modifications existed anciently as now, because humans—in fact, all organisms—simply cannot survive without affecting the environments in which they live.

Archaeology is a medium of education. Archaeological societies exist in all states, including New Jersey, for the purpose of encouraging archaeological research and disseminating knowledge about the past. These societies embrace the labors of dedicated amateurs as well as professional archaeologists. Such groups provide an outlet for interested parties to engage in constructive archaeological research and to benefit from the camaraderie of like-minded souls. Later chapters will highlight the contributions made to the prehistory of New Jersey by amateur and professional archaeologists, "whose hands uncover and preserve the work of countless others" (Streeter 1982).

ARCHAEOLOGICAL CULTURES IN TIME

Archaeological cultures are defined on the basis of distinctive artifact assemblages that occur repeatedly in particular places or settings and at particular periods of time. Archaeologists label these cultures by descriptive terms—Paleoindian, Archaic, and Woodland—which substitute for the unknown names of the peoples whose remains appear in archaeological sites. These names also apply to the periods of time during which the cultures predominated. The accumulated data respecting these cultures in time are known collectively as culture-history. In the following list of cultural-historical periods, all dates are approximate years before the present (B.P.).

12,000 – 8,000	Paleoindian
8,000 – 6,000	Early Archaic
6,000 – 5,000	Middle Archaic
5,000 – 3,000	Late Archaic
3,000 – 2,000	Early Woodland
2,000 – 1,100	Middle Woodland
1,100 – 500	Late Woodland

The prehistoric archaeology of New Jersey has been ordered within a general cultural-historical framework that has been applied over the years to the entire eastern United States. The basic outlines of this framework have remained unchanged since the publication of James Griffin's *Archeology of the Eastern United States* (1952), in which subregional summaries of the development of aboriginal culture were divided into the following categories: Paleoindian, Archaic, and Woodland.

The Paleoindian Period (ca. 8,000 – 12,000 B.P.)

The Paleoindian period is characterized by small, apparently mobile bands of hunters whose distinctive toolkit included "fluted" projectile points in a variety of forms. The name derives from the practice of thinning the basal section of the blade on one or both sides by the removal of long, slender flakes, thus creating one or two flutes. The flakes are sometimes called channel flakes or fluting flakes, and their discovery on a site is indicative of an early presence.

There are several styles of fluted points, and they have a continentwide distribution. In the Southwest and High Plains, Paleoindians used fluted points to kill large mammals, such as mammoths, mastodons, and an extinct form of bison (Willey 1966:37–50; Wormington 1957). In the East, direct associations with megafauna are generally absent, although the bones of caribou (*Rangifer tarandus*), dating to 12,500 B.P., have been found with a fluted point in the Dutchess Quarry cave in Orange County, New York (Funk, Walters, and Ehlers 1969). A tooth of the extinct giant beaver (*Castoroides*) was found in the Fairy Hole Rock Shelter in Warren County, New Jersey (Cross 1941:148), and rumors of clandestinely dug fluted points from the same site have surfaced (Glenn Wershing, pers. comm.). Sadly, the secretive work of looters may have

FIGURE 4. A fluted point and channel flake. Courtesy of Charles A. Bello, Archaeological Society of New Jersey.

yet again deprived the world of another significant discovery. Cultural and faunal remains of Paleoindian age have not been reported elsewhere in New Jersey.

In addition to fluted points, a host of related lithic implements, such as scrapers, knives, and perforators, were used for scraping hides, working wood or bone, drilling holes, and so forth. Stone tools predominate simply by reason of survival; but a variety of bone artifacts are also known, and items fashioned from perishable materials probably augmented a varied assemblage of tools, weapons, and personal gear. (See Marshall 1982 for a detailed treatment of the Paleoindian period in New Jersey.)

Because of the association of Paleoindian cultures in the West with now extinct Pleistocene mammals, the term "Big Game Hunters" came to be applied to Paleoindian populations as a whole (Willey 1966:37–51). Elsewhere in North America, direct faunal evidence for this association is lacking, and it is supposed that Paleoindians survived by hunting and gathering a variety of naturally occurring resources. Indeed, the discovery of fish bones, hawthorne seeds, and acorns with Paleoindian artifacts demonstrates that, from the earliest times, humans did not live by steak alone (McNett, McMillan, and Marshall 1977; Marshall 1982:34; Stanzeski 1998:45).

In New Jersey, Paleoindian remains in the form of fluted points and other specialized artifacts—such as formal scrapers and graving tools—have been found in a variety of locations. But these finds are among the least well represented cultural expressions (Marshall 1982; Mounier, Cresson, and Martin 1993; Stanzeski 1998). Many of the sites connected with these early people are believed to have been lost beneath sinking shorelines as a result of the postglacial rise in sea levels.

The Archaic Period (ca. 3,000 – 8,000 B.P.)

Emerging out of the Paleoindian tradition, the Archaic period was first described by William A. Ritchie in New York State. Ritchie (1932) defined the Archaic period as "an early level of culture based on hunting, fishing, and the gathering of wild vegetable foods, and lacking pottery, the smoking pipe, and agriculture" (also see Ritchie 1965:31). Among archaeologists, the term *Archaic* is now generally taken to mean a period of time or a stage of cultural development characterized by a hunting and gathering economy based upon the seasonal exploitation of natural resources by relatively small, mobile bands. Chronologically later than the Paleoindian period, the Archaic represents a continuous cultural adaptation to new environments emerging in post-Pleistocene times. The more efficient Archaic adaptations are thought to have allowed (or to have given rise to) population growth, but without recourse to horticulture.

The material remains associated with the Archaic period illustrate these adaptations. Hunting was carried out with a wide variety of flaked stone projectile points, chiefly of stemmed or notched styles. Spears or javelins armed with such points were probably propelled by hand or by means of an atlatl or spear-throwing device, as indicated by the discovery of stone weights or "bannerstones." Fish may have been speared, but net fishing is certainly implied by the existence of notched and, rarely, perforated stone sinkers. Advances in woodworking technology are manifested by the appearance of stone axes (which are often grooved for fixing a handle), celts (ungrooved axes or chisels), and gouges. Stone knives, scrapers, choppers, perforators, drills, hammerstones, and abraders served as fabricating or general utility tools. A well-developed bone and antler industry is represented in the Archaic toolkit at certain out-of-state sites (Ritchie 1965:47ff.), but such items have rarely survived in archaeological contexts in New Jersey. By Late Archaic times, bowls carved from soapstone and talc foreshadowed the development of a ceramic

FIGURE 5. Early and Middle Archaic bifaces. Upper row (left to right): Kirk Corner-Notched point; four Palmer points; a Stanly point; and a basally notched biface. Bottom row: bifurcate base points. Photograph by the author.

technology. In New Jersey, as elsewhere on the Atlantic seaboard, the Archaic period has been divided into subperiods (Early, Middle, and Late) on the basis of changes in material culture and inferred social organization.

The earlier Archaic cultural expressions are mostly broad-bladed bifaces, some of which are stemmed or notched near the base. Others have bifurcated bases (Coe 1964; Broyles 1966, 1971; Dincauze 1971; Ritchie and Funk 1971). Many bear serrated blades. The Palmer, Kirk-Stemmed, and Corner-Notched types are among the best-known Early Archaic bifaces.

The distribution of the cultures at the early end of the time scale is somewhat spotty. Organic remains rarely survive, but at the West Creek site in Ocean County, members of the Archaeological Society of New Jersey found several cremated burials associated with bifaces that resemble Kirk Corner-Notched points. Dating close to 10,000 B.P., these are the earliest burials yet reported in New Jersey (Stanzeski 1996:44 – 45, 1998:43).

The bifurcate-base LeCroy points are examples of Middle Archaic bifaces. Also appearing in Middle Archaic times are long, slender contracting-stemmed bifaces in the Morrow Mountain–Poplar Island–Rossville continuum, which transcends the Middle and Late Archaic periods and endures into Woodland times. The chronology is somewhat confused, but bifurcated projectile points appeared in the Southeast and Middle South about 9,000 years ago. These

FIGURE 6. Contracting-stemmed bifaces. These bifaces fall within the Morrow Mountain–Poplar Island–Rossville typological continuum. Photograph by the author.

forms seem to have evolved into narrow, stemmed styles about 1,000 years later. If the origination in the South is accurate, the appearance of similar points in New Jersey probably occurred somewhat later. The more common expressions of later Archaic cultures appear at sites across the region about 5,000 or 6,000 years ago.

Very late in the Archaic period broad-bladed bifaces—sometimes called "broadspears"—make their appearance. These are forms that apparently originated in the Southeast about 4,000 years ago. There are a number of varieties, which seem to overlap in time. These bifaces and related artifacts are elements of a cultural tradition sometimes called the Susquehanna tradition, because the defining traits were first recognized in the valley of the Susquehanna River (Witthoft 1949, 1953; Ritchie 1965:135). Often, broadspears were made from argillite, chert, or rhyolite imported from distant quarries.

Associated with these broadspears are atlatl weights, carved soapstone kettles, and an emergent form of pottery that resembles the stone containers. Later on, narrow, stemmed, or gently side-notched bifaces reappear. These bifaces are known as fishtail bifaces for their piscine (fishlike) outline. Because this suite of artifacts appears near the end of the Archaic period, this era is

FIGURE 7. Broken and reworked broadspears. The second biface from the left in the upper row shows a snapped blade characteristic of use as a knife. The two central pieces in the lower row have been reworked into perforators. Photograph by the author.

sometimes called the Terminal Archaic period. Others refer to it as the Transitional period because the appearance of early pottery seems to reflect a technological transition into the subsequent Woodland era (Witthoft 1949:10–11, 1953; Ritchie 1965:149–177).

In New Jersey a peculiar Late Archaic mortuary cult, known as the Koens-Crispin complex, appeared as early as 4,500 B.P. This complex emphasized cremation burials and the bestowal of lavish grave goods in the form of bannerstones (atlatl weights), celts, broad-bladed bifaces, fossils, and other exotic artifacts. This complex seems to have been located primarily in what is now Burlington County, although similar (but probably earlier) remains have been found well to the northeast in Monmouth County (Hawkes and Linton 1916; Cross 1941:81–90, 117–127; Regensburg 1971; Burrow 1997). The Koens-Crispin complex is apparently related to other mortuary cults from a similar period elsewhere in the Northeast (Ritchie 1959, 1965:149–177; Dincauze 1968).

The Woodland Period (ca. 500–3,000 B.P.)

The advent of pottery making about 3,000 years ago ushers in the Woodland period, which endured through successive stages of development (identified as

FIGURE 8. Fishtail points. Photograph by the author.

Early, Middle, and Late Woodland) into the sixteenth century. Archaeology says little about the period between A.D. 1500 and the arrival of Europeans in the early decades of the seventeenth century. This era is sometimes known as the Proto-historic period, meaning the time just prior to the beginning of recorded history.

The three subdivisions of the Woodland period are based upon the perception of differences in material culture, population sizes, and systems of settlement. The earlier subperiods, not as well known from archaeological remains as the Late Woodland, are sometimes lumped into a single category, Early-Middle Woodland. Occasionally, the Middle and Late Woodland are grouped together as "late prehistoric cultures."

There appears to have been a collapse of the native population just on the eve of the European onslaught, quite possibly induced by European diseases against which the natives had no immunity (Witthoft 1963:64; Ramenofsky 1987). Just like trade goods, these diseases apparently were diffused widely, infecting populations that had never stood face to face with white men.

In general terms, the Early Woodland is represented by material survivals of the preceding Late Archaic period, to which was added the fabrication of ceramic vessels. These early vessels commonly duplicated the flat-bottomed forms of the stone bowls produced in Late Archaic times and even contain fragmented pieces of soapstone (which may have been derived from stone vessels) as a tempering agent in the clay or "paste." Some of the ceramics bear the impressions of matting, basketry, or cordage, which have not survived directly. The manufacture of flat-bottomed ceramics proved to be relatively short-lived. An alternate form, the conoidal (conelike) vessel, which also originated about 3,000 years ago, survived in a variety of refinements until the end of aboriginal times.

Associated with the ceramic pieces were a variety of stemmed and notched projectile points and other lithic implements. Grooved axes and celts represent woodworking tools. Typical flaked stone tools and weapons consist of stemmed and notched bifaces, of which the fishtail, Hellgrammite, and Meadowood varieties are most diagnostic (Kinsey 1959:116–117; Ritchie 1961:35, 39; Hummer 1994). Fishtail bifaces, which are quite common, are relatively long, slender, but somewhat thick points with broad notches that form a waist at the root of the stem. Hellgrammite points are similar, except that they are usually thinner, more triangular in general form, and usually serrated along the blade. They are much less common than fishtails on most sites.

Also characteristic of Early Woodland contexts are Meadowood points, distinctive, very thin triangular bifaces, sometimes bearing squarish side-notches close to the base (Ritchie 1961:35–36). Most often rendered in Onondaga chert from New York State, these points, along with gorgets (perforated stone tablets) and pendants, are associated with an early burial cult known as the Meadowood complex. The Middlesex complex is another Early Woodland manifestation that is exclusively represented by graves, some with elaborate offerings of copper artifacts, stone pipes, and other items that appear to be related to the Adena culture from the Midwest.

Middle Woodland pottery is frequently represented by a conoidal form on which a surface texture derived from net impressions or crisscrossed cord markings predominates. Net-impressed pottery is commonly associated with broad-bladed bifacial points, knives, and other implements rendered in argillite, rhyolite, and other imported lithics. The most common biface form is known as the Fox Creek point, though most of these implements were probably knives rather than projectile points. The association of Fox Creek points and net-impressed pottery, which is particularly well documented in New Jersey at the falls of the Delaware near Trenton, is referred to as the Fox Creek culture (Ritchie and Funk 1973). In New Jersey, this expression is sometimes referred to as the Abbott phase, named for the prevalence of related artifacts at the Abbott Farm site (Williams and Thomas 1982). Fox Creek sites, generally small in size, occur elsewhere throughout the region (Mounier 1991;

FIGURE 9. Fox Creek and Jack's Reef bifaces. At left is a primary quarry biface of the Fox Creek culture. Two broken specimens are at center and two reworked bifaces at right. At upper right is a Jack's Reef Corner-Notched point. Scale is in inches. Photograph by the author.

Mounier and Martin 1992), but the details and significance of this distribution remain obscure.

At the Abbott Farm, the Fox Creek culture appears to have developed a strong economic dependence upon fishing, which was especially oriented toward the exploitation of spring fish runs. Fishing was no doubt integrated with other subsistence pursuits that are not so readily observable in the archaeological record. At other locations in New Jersey, the economic foundations of the Fox Creek culture remain poorly understood.

Although net-impressed pottery is considered to be the hallmark of Middle Woodland culture, other wares were also produced during this period. Conoidal vessels impressed with straight or crisscrossed cord markings are known, but they tend to be confused with earlier or later wares, except when found in association with other distinctive artifacts. Peculiar decorations that follow intricate zoned patterns appear on flared-mouth vessels at the Abbott Farm but rarely elsewhere (Cross 1956:144–147; R. Stewart 1998:266–274).

Another Middle Woodland cultural complex that is present but not strongly represented in New Jersey is the Kipp Island phase (Ritchie 1965: 232–253) or Webb phase (Thomas and Warren 1970), which is identified by the presence of triangular and pentagonal bifaces of the Jack's Reef type (Ritchie 1961:26–27). The associated pottery is often of a corded or cross-corded variety. The mortuary furnishings and other exotic artifacts that characterize this phase in New York and Delaware are apparently lacking at sites in New Jersey. The use of high-quality jasper bifaces and other lithic tools predominates. The Kipp Island phase in New York is seen as a cultural complex related in as yet obscure ways to the Fox Creek phase (Ritchie and Funk 1973). In New Jersey, items relating to both phases sometimes occur in small numbers on the same sites, but the cultural affiliations of the two remain vague (Mounier and Martin 1992; Jack Cresson, pers. comm.).

Beyond the cultural sphere of the Abbott Farm, obvious indications of Middle Woodland settlement are sparse. The Salisbury site along the Delaware River in Gloucester County has yielded numerous lithic artifacts of Jack's Reef origin, although they were not recognized as such at the time of discovery (Cross 1941:56–57 [pl. 16b, nos. 4, 6, 9; pl. 17a, nos. 7, 10, 13–17; pl. 19]). Substantial Fox Creek settlements are represented in collections from sites along the back bays on the Atlantic shore in upper Cape May County. Small sites in the interior of the coastal plains were temporary encampments, possibly of people shuttling between riverine and coastal aquatic resources or prospecting for unexploited niches in the hinterlands. Small Middle Woodland camps are also scattered among the rock shelters of northern New Jersey (Cross 1941:146; Hotchkin and Staats 1983).

Except for Fox Creek and Jack's Reef components, no distinct Middle Woodland cultures have been identified in New Jersey. Similarities in material culture with both earlier and later cultures have limited the recognition of discrete Middle Woodland expressions. This situation is changing, however, as careful dating places more archaeological assemblages in the period between 1,000 and 2,000 B.P. (Mounier 1997).

The Late Woodland period begins between A.D. 800 and 1000 and continues to the time of European intrusion in the seventeenth century. Some patterns of Late Woodland life developed as an outgrowth of earlier cultural adaptations, although Late Woodland populations differ from their ancestors in several ways. There is an apparent increase in the size and number of occupied settlements, and some sites contain pits for food storage. Ceramics tend to become recognizable as local products. These changes suggest a trend toward settlement in permanently occupied territories. Within these territories, the Late Woodland populations are thought to have comprised a number of relatively small bands made up of related families.

Although utilitarian ceramic wares persist to the end of aboriginal times, Late Woodland potters produced increasingly refined wares, often with intricate and exquisitely executed decorations. The rise of distinctive ceramic styles seems to reflect local or subregional traditions based on kinship. Concurrently, as the ceramic arts became more refined, stonework in general declined. The earlier knapping traditions based on carefully prepared quarry preforms and flake blanks of exotic materials were supplanted by a technology based on the expedient, almost haphazard, flaking of common pebbles.

A mixed foraging and farming economy has been postulated, especially in the north. Archaeological evidence for horticulture is generally lacking in southern and central New Jersey. Although some settlements may have been occupied for extended periods of time, others may have been used intermittently, following the rhythms of the seasons. Late Woodland settlements tend to cluster along the coast and along the trunks of major rivers. Although the stream basins above tidewater were occupied, sites in the headwaters are less numerous in the Late Woodland period than in former times.

Late Woodland components in New Jersey characteristically contain one or more related ceramic types, clay tobacco pipes in a range of styles, a preponderance of small triangular bifacial tools and weapons, and other chipped stone implements of locally available flinty materials. Celts (ungrooved axes) of ground stone occur with some frequency, along with polished stone ornaments that are generally classed as "pendants."

The ceramics of the Late Woodland in southern New Jersey show a conservative adherence to simple conoidal or baglike forms developed early in the Woodland sequence. These later ceramics are distinguished from the earlier ones by the qualities of the paste, decoration, and surface finish, which often emphasizes fabric impressions. Among the most common ceramic wares are variants of the Riggins Fabric-Impressed type, which generally date between A.D. 900 and 1500 (McCann 1950:315; Mounier 1991:VI:6–11; Morris et al. 1996:25–31; R. Stewart 1998:75–77, 98, 111–112). The earliest forms of Late Woodland fabric-impressed vessels were simple unadorned conoidal or bag-shaped pots, which resemble the pottery of the Point Peninsula or early Owasco series in New York State (Ritchie and MacNeish 1949). Decorations exhibit considerable differentiation both in motif and in technique, ranging from simple single-cord impressions or linear incising to elaborate zoned or filled geometric patterns that sometimes cover half to three-quarters of the body.

In the north, the ceramics evolved into a variety of globular vessels, often with accentuated and ornately decorated collars. Based largely on ceramic associations and radiocarbon dates, Herbert Kraft (1974c:33–46, 1975a:59–61) differentiated two Late Woodland cultures. The earlier, dating from A.D. 1000 to 1350, is the Pahaquarra culture, whose pottery resembled the pre-Iroquoian (Owasco) ceramics of New York State (Ritchie 1965:271–274). The pottery of this culture is typified by collarless, conoidal vessels, carefully marked on the exterior with cord markings or fabric impressions. The rims are straight or slightly constricted, and decoration is often limited to cord impressions applied to the lips or to the inside surfaces of the rims. The Sackett Corded type, initially described by William Ritchie and Richard MacNeish (1949), is typical of Pahaquarra ceramics (H. Kraft 1975a:124–129). Bowmans Brook and Overpeck Incised pottery types also occur with some frequency, suggesting cultural connections with groups to the south of the Water Gap (C. Smith 1950:192; Cross 1956:153–154; Staats 1974).

The later entity identified by Kraft is the Minisink culture, which he dated between A.D. 1350 and 1600. This culture shows distinct parallels with the late prehistoric and historic Iroquois of New York (Ritchie 1965:303, 308, 313). The predominate pottery consists of globular vessels with decorated collars that become increasingly accentuated through time. The decorations are incised, rather than impressed, in a variety of horizontal, diagonal, and vertical lines that frequently form ornamental fields around the rims. Some of the vessels are indistinguishable from Chance Incised pottery from New York State (Ritchie and MacNeish 1949). The Munsee Incised type, first described by John Witthoft (Witthoft and Kinsey 1959:51–56), is typical of the latest ceramics of the Minisink culture (H. Kraft 1975a:132–147). Increasingly pronounced peaks or castellations appeared through time as ornaments on the collars, which were taller than formerly. Often, effigies of human faces appeared upon the castellations. These countenances were generally created by oblong incisions or impressions that represent only the eyes and mouth.

Despite the similarities that are seen between the Pahaquarra and Minisink cultures and their counterparts to the north, Kraft (1975a:60) convincingly argued that the former cannot be viewed simply as adjuncts to the Owasco and Iroquois cultures. Apart from technological differences, he noted the lack of hilltop settlements and defensive works, as well as linguistic distinctions, which are well known from ethnographic studies.

Through years of concentrated excavation and analysis, Kraft was able to demonstrate that the people of the Pahaquarra and Minisink cultures lived fairly sedentary lives in settlements that were more or less permanently occupied. There is good evidence that they practiced horticulture and stored produce against future needs, all the while continuing to harvest fish and game. Similar evidence from the south is largely lacking. This situation arises partly from relatively poor preservation in the sandy soils on the coastal plains and the lack of protracted excavations on all but a very few sites. The cumulative evidence strongly suggests that the prehistoric peoples in southern New Jersey continued in a mobile lifestyle that relied heavily upon a traditional foraging economy.

Even though Europeans had explored much of New Jersey by the middle of the seventeenth century and occupied small outposts, settlement did not begin in earnest until the end of the century. Within a period of approximately 80 years, most of the native populations had been displaced from their ancestral homelands.

Environmental Context

Archaeological research has repeatedly demonstrated that evidence of human occupation is likely to occur unevenly across the landscape, varying with respect to cultural and ecological factors alike. Therefore, it is critical to have some understanding of the environmental conditions that prevailed when the sites under investigation were actively occupied.

Data about ancient environments in New Jersey can be abstracted from natural history research conducted in the state and in other parts of the Middle Atlantic region (Carbone 1976, 1982; J. Kraft 1977; Sirkin 1977; J. Kraft and John 1978; Hartzog 1982; Custer 1984a). Rising sea levels in post-Pleistocene times, climatic shifts, and the stabilization of shorelines and of estuaries are seen as critical factors affecting human settlement (Salwen 1962; Braun 1974; Custer 1978, 1984a, 1987; Catlin, Custer, and Stewart 1982; Thorbahn and Cox 1988). The following paragraphs present a summary of paleoenvironmental development in the region during the last 15,000 years.

The retreat of the Late Wisconsin ice sheet began in the vicinity of Kittatinny Mountain, in Sussex County, approximately 15,000 years ago (Crowl and Stuckenrath 1977). Studies of ancient pollen show that a cold period associated with this glaciation persisted in the Middle Atlantic region until 13,000 years ago. Even unglaciated terrain had a "periglacial" (or glacial-edge) environment, characterized by temperatures below freezing most of the year. The ground contained "permafrost," a zone that remained permanently frozen except for a shallow layer near the surface, where temporary thawing might occur during warm seasons. Pollen cores from various bogs in the region indicate the presence of jack pine and spruce, as well as shrubs and herbs ordinarily associated with tundra environments.

Within another 600 years or so the climate warmed, allowing spruce forests to displace the tundra. With continued warming, pine became dominant in pollen cores between 11,000 and 7,000 years ago, after which oak forests prevailed throughout the region (Sirkin 1977). The amelioration of the climate in postglacial times eventually permitted human occupation in the upper Delaware Valley by 10,600 B.P. (Crowl and Stuckenrath 1977).

At that time, the topography and hydrology of the region were much different than they are today. Interior landscapes, especially on the coastal plains, contained many small ponds or waterholes that resulted from the melting of ground ice and subterranean ice wedges in the permafrost (Wolfe 1977:292). Today, many of these features survive as relict wet depressions. Neither geologists nor archaeologists agree about the processes leading to the formation of these basins—or, for that matter, what to call them (Wolfe 1977:290–293; Bonfiglio and Cresson 1982; Marshall 1982:34; Custer 1986). Hugh French from the University of Ottawa has taken up the challenge of sorting out the geological origins of these features (Hugh French, pers. comm.). Independent research by Anthony J. Bonfiglio and Jack Cresson (1982) demonstrates that from Paleoindian to Late Archaic times, these basins were focal points for human occupation, presumably as hunting places.

The ancient valley of the Delaware River was narrower and much more deeply incised than at present, as demonstrated by a paleogeographic reconstruction of the lower Delaware River and Delaware Bay. This analysis is based upon geological cores, pollen examination, and radiocarbon dating (J. Kraft and John 1978). Of particular interest are the findings with respect to geological cores taken near Holly Oak, Delaware, just across the river from the mouth of Oldmans Creek in Salem County, New Jersey. About 6,000 years ago, the Delaware River had a maximum width of 1,640 feet, or about 500 meters (J. Kraft and John 1978: fig. 7). This is somewhat less than one-quarter of the river's width under present conditions. A narrow band of tidal marsh separated the river from the adjoining uplands.

This paleogeographic reconstruction reflects conditions during Middle Archaic times. Given the available information, one can reasonably infer that the river was even narrower in Paleoindian and Early Archaic times, with the

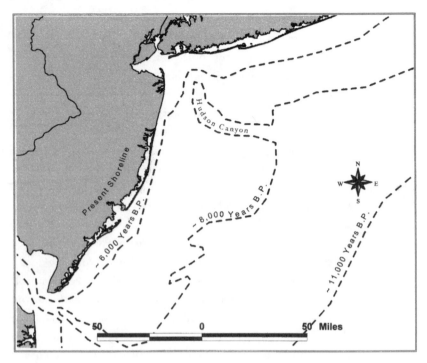

FIGURE 10. New Jersey's shorelines from approximately 11,000 B.P. to the present (after Edwards and Emery 1977). Courtesy of Joseph R. Arsenault Environmental Consulting.

left bank of the ancient Delaware standing in or near what is now the ship channel. Thus, most of the ancient shoreline—and ancient cultural evidence—has been lost to erosion and dredging in modern times.

The same holds true for the Atlantic shore. About 11,000 years ago the sea stood as much as 262 feet (80 m) below its present level, and the shoreline lay as much as 100 miles (160 km) to the east of its current position (Edwards and Emery 1977: fig. 3). Thus, sites that once occupied the continental shelf now lie far out to sea. Moreover, the sea level continues to rise, in places at a rate of nearly 15 feet (5 m) per millennium (Wolfe 1977:313–314).

As nearly as can be determined with the limited data available, the local climate and landforms, as well as flora and fauna, began to approximate their present configurations during Early Archaic times, about 7,000 years ago (Salwen 1975; J. Kraft 1977; Sirkin 1977), although new evidence suggests that vegetation very similar to modern communities may have been present as early as 10,000 years ago (McWeeney 1990b). From 6,000 to 8,000 years ago, there was a period of apparently dry conditions, known as the "Xerothermic Interval," which seems to have accelerated aeolian (wind-caused) erosion and redeposition. These geological events presumably resulted from reduced vegetative cover and radical swings in climate during this period (Carbone 1976, 1982; Custer 1978, 1984a; Curry 1980; R. Stewart 1994).

Some archaeologists have found unsettling inconsistencies in the inferred chronology of the Xerothermic, however, and in the data on which it is based (Joyce 1984, 1988; Cavallo and Joyce 1985). These scholars have argued that aeolian events could have resulted from human intervention in the form of land clearing, intentionally set fires, and so forth. They have also expressed concern over insecurely dated, or undated, pollen cores, which have been used to support a rather broad, inferred chronological range for the Xerothermic. There is also skepticism about reconstructions of floral and faunal communities related to this putative dry period. In addition, the very interpretation of pollen data as reflecting principally, or solely, upon past climatic conditions has been called into question (Joyce 1983; McWeeney 1984, 1990a, 1990b). In any case, climatic inferences based upon geomorphological and sedimentological data (Custer 1978; Curry 1980; Curry and Custer 1982; Curry and Ebright 1989; R. Stewart 1994) must be viewed with caution because erosional and depositional events can be very complex and difficult to interpret. Also, the events themselves may be very localized (Gladfelter 1985).

Early in Woodland times (ca. 2,800 B.P.) an essentially modern environment had emerged (Carbone 1976:192; Custer 1984a:91–93; Hummer 1994: 143). Variability in the composition and distribution of wildlife communities doubtless reflects changes in environmental conditions, including those induced by aboriginal populations. Some of the conjectured shifts in ecological relationships would have, in turn, resulted in changing adaptations by resident human populations.

THE LANDSCAPE

All cultures adapt to the landscapes in which they live. The present area of New Jersey encompasses a broad range of physiographic settings that differ in terms of the underlying geology, landforms, and climate. These differences are expressed in variations in the flora and fauna and in the nature of human settlement. Therefore, it is not surprising that variability is also expressed in the kinds of archaeological remains that occur around the state. In the north, for example, prehistoric settlement patterns necessarily followed the ridges and valleys, and numerous habitations occurred in natural enclosures formed by large rock formations. By contrast, aboriginal settlement on the flat ground of the coastal plains was not so severely limited by topography, but still tended to follow stream channels. In all regions, archaeological sites have been found primarily where well-drained, fertile soils could support economically valuable plant and animal communities. The distribution of such soils varies a good deal among physiographic regions as well as within them, and the archaeology shows similar variability.

New Jersey has five major physiographic provinces: the Ridge and Valley, the Highlands, the Piedmont, and the Inner and Outer Coastal Plains. Each of these provinces is part of a larger region with similar geological structures and histories. These regions extend well beyond the borders of New Jersey in a northeast to southwest trend along the eastern seaboard (Widmer 1964; Robichaud and Buell 1973; Wolfe 1977). The following introduction to the geographic provinces of New Jersey will aid in understanding the details of archaeological settings presented in later chapters.

Ridge and Valley

The Ridge and Valley physiographic province occupies about 635 square miles in northern Sussex and Warren Counties. The geology consists of folded and faulted rocks, primarily composed of limestones, shales, sandstones, and conglomerates of early to middle Paleozoic age (from 600 to 400 million years ago). Pleistocene glaciers not only deposited sediments but also left ponds. Valleys were formed by the erosion of the softer limestones and shales, leaving pronounced ridges composed of the more resistant sandstone and conglomerates. Kittatinny Mountain is the best known of the ridges. It rises to an elevation of 1,803 feet above sea level and is from 1 to 5 miles wide at the crest. To the east of the mountain is Kittatinny Valley, which is about 40 miles long and 12 miles wide. Here, the elevations range from about 400 to 1,000 feet above sea level. In contrast to the thin, barren soil on the ridges—or no soil at all—the soil in the valleys is often deep, fertile, and well drained.

Highlands

Covering about 900 square miles, the Highlands region lies to the southeast of Kittatinny Valley. It occupies southern Sussex and Warren Counties and

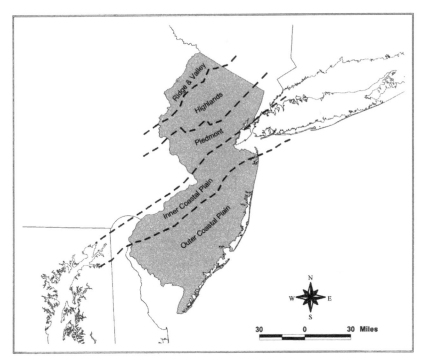

FIGURE 11. Physiographic provinces of New Jersey (after Widmer 1964). Courtesy of Joseph R. Arsenault Environmental Consulting.

the adjoining portions of Passaic, Morris, and Hunterdon Counties. The geology is dominated by metamorphic rocks of Precambrian age (more than 600 million years ago), but glaciers left drift or till deposits that contain many kinds of stones. Cobbles from glacial drift provided the natives with a ready source material for stone tools and weapons.

The Highlands consist of broad, flat-topped hills separated by parallel valleys. The ridges are generally more massive and broader than those in the Ridge and Valley region, while the valleys are narrower and have steeper walls. Lake Hopatcong is one of several glacially formed lakes. The elevations rise from 987 feet above sea level along the Delaware River to a maximum of 1,496 feet near Vernon, in Sussex County. The valley bottoms stand between 500 and 800 feet above sea level.

As with the Ridge and Valley region, the topography of the Highlands resulted from differential erosion of the underlying geological materials. The ridges are composed of hard gneisses, whereas the valleys are formed in softer limestones and shales. This region was also largely covered by the glaciers. In the lowlands, accumulated sediments and organic material combine to make some of the richest soils in the state.

Piedmont

The Piedmont region lies between the Highlands to the northwest and the coastal plains to the southeast. This region covers about 1,500 square miles in various counties. It includes the southeastern portions of Hunterdon, Morris, and Passaic Counties, as well as large parts of Mercer, Somerset, and Middlesex Counties. All of Union, Essex, Hudson, and Bergen Counties fall within the Piedmont.

Here the geological bedrock mostly consists of shales, argillites, siltstones, and sandstones of Triassic age (from 225 to 180 million years ago). There are also igneous formations of diabase and basalt, which are expressed as prominent elevations (the Watchung Mountains and the Palisades being two examples). Soil development is generally thin, and the soils are often stony. The best soils in the region are loamy with good drainage. The geology in this region was kind to aboriginal populations. The abundance of argillite and metamorphosed shale was very widely exploited for the production of stone tools.

The Coastal Plains

The coastal plains cover about three-fifths of the land area of New Jersey, including all of Cape May, Cumberland, Salem, Gloucester, Camden, Atlantic, Burlington, Ocean, and Monmouth Counties. This expansive region consists of geological formations that include large deposits of clay, silt, sand, and gravel. The region is commonly divided into two districts—the Inner and Outer Coastal Plains—because of differences in geological history, soil development, and biological communities.

Not more than 15 miles wide, the Inner Coastal Plain is a relatively narrow band that skirts the southeastern edge of the Piedmont from Raritan Bay to Trenton, thence along the Delaware River into Salem County. The Outer Coastal Plain is a much broader district. The geological boundary between the two is marked by a band of hills or cuestas, which are crowned with relatively hard, consolidated sandstones and gravels. North and west of this line of cuestas, the land drains respectively into Raritan Bay and the Delaware River. The Outer Coastal Plain, on the other hand, drains southward and eastward into Delaware Bay and the Atlantic Ocean.

The Inner Coastal Plain contains unconsolidated deposits of clay, sand, and gravel of Pleistocene age (up to 1 million years old) superimposed upon beds of Cretaceous marl and related strata (dating between 135 and 70 million years ago), whereas the Outer Coastal Plain is composed of deep deposits of quartz sand, gravel, and clay of Tertiary (from 70 to 1 million years ago) and Quaternary age (from 1 million to 100,000 years ago).

Compared with the soils on the Outer Coastal Plain, those on the Inner Coastal Plain possess generally finer textures and, with higher clay fractions, tend to retain moisture for longer periods of time following precipitation. Largely owing to the presence of marly deposits, the Inner Coastal Plain soils also have a greater natural fertility than those on the Outer Coastal Plain.

CLIMATE, VEGETATION, AND WILDLIFE

Although it is a small state, New Jersey experiences a wide range of climatic conditions, which are reflected in prevalent vegetative and animal communities (Widmer 1964:152–157; Robichaud and Buell 1973:54–64). The average winter temperature is about 30°F in the north, approximately 33°F in the south, and somewhat higher (34.5°F) along the coast, owing to the moderating effects of the ocean. In the summer, the average temperatures are about 74°F in the north, slightly above 75°F in the south, and fractionally less along the coast.

The average annual precipitation is almost 47 inches in the northern districts, approximately 45 inches in the south, and about 43 inches along the coast. Most of the precipitation falls as rain, and it is ordinarily distributed evenly throughout the year. Heavy downpours from thunderstorms and hurricanes in the summer and fall can skew the figures slightly upward for those seasons.

The data just presented are calculated averages and may not accurately reflect the extremes in the modern era. For example, temperatures as low as −32°F and as high as 108°F have been recorded in the historic period (Widmer 1964:154). Conditions in antiquity can only be conjectured. However, as we have seen previously, the climate in New Jersey began to approximate present conditions by 7,000 B.P., and modern data give at least some sense of what the climate might have been like in ancient times.

The vegetation in New Jersey varies with respect to soils, moisture, temperature, and the impact of human activities. Under mostly wild conditions, a mixed hardwood forest dominated by maples would succeed in the Piedmont and mountainous regions. The Inner Coastal Plain soils, if left undisturbed, generally succeed to hardwood forest types supportive of a wide range of wildlife of economic value to hunters and gatherers. The Outer Coastal Plain, including the immense region historically known as the Pine Barrens, has expansive stands of pitch pine forest. Hardwoods such as oak and hickory succeed on the more fertile ground there. To judge from modern biological data, the wildlife on the Inner Plain tends to be more robust, if not more vigorous, than that on the Outer Plain. These qualitative differences are reflected in the prehistoric settlements in these two zones (Mounier 1978b). Archaeological sites on the Inner Coastal Plain appear to be larger, more numerous, and more intensively occupied than those on the Outer Coastal Plain. Comparative studies of archaeological site distribution are lacking for most of the other physiographic provinces of New Jersey. (However, see R. Stewart, Hummer, and Custer 1986 for valuable data and interpretation concerning aboriginal settlements in the lower and middle Delaware Valley.)

New Jersey supports a fauna that is typical of most of the Carolinian biotic province, that is, the region from southern New England to Georgia and from the Atlantic Ocean to the 100th meridian (Robichaud and Buell 1973). Familiar mammals include whitetail deer, gray squirrel, red and gray fox, raccoon, skunk, beaver, muskrat, cottontail rabbit, and opossum, each occurring within a specific habitat or range of habitats. Formerly, bison, black bear, elk, wolf, and wildcat were present or thought to be present. Seals and whales are still occasionally spotted along the Atlantic coast and well up the Delaware River.

Native birds include wild turkey, grouse, quail, crows, eagles, and various hawks, as well as migratory waterfowl and songbirds, again distributed throughout a range of habitats.

Catfish, sunfish, bass, pickerel, perch, and other coarse fish are among the species that inhabit the lakes and ponds throughout the state. Sturgeon, shad, alewives, herring, and eels are (or were) common migratory fish. Most of these species still travel to the headwaters and tributaries of the Delaware River to spawn, but their distribution has been limited by pollution and by dams that block their passage. Freshwater mollusks were common and the saline waters of the bays and ocean yielded an abundance of oysters, hard-shell clams, and conchs.

Common reptiles include snapping turtles, box turtles, and mud turtles. The Northern diamondback terrapin is (and was) prevalent in coastal zones.

In addition to the species just mentioned, the area of the Pine Barrens supports numerous highly specialized animals and plants that are infrequently found elsewhere. These are species that have evolved selectively to the peculiar ecological conditions in that region (McCormick 1970).

THE HISTORY OF ARCHAEOLOGY IN NEW JERSEY

The history of archaeological inquiry in New Jersey is long, complex, and often troubled. What follows is a brief survey of archaeological researches in the state. (See Cross 1941:1–3, 1956:1–10, for more detail.)

The earliest archaeologists in New Jersey were men who simply took an interest in antiquities and tried to gather fundamental information about curious artifacts and the people who made them. Pierre Eugène Du Simitière (ca. 1736–1784) may have been the first person to regard the archaeological remains of New Jersey's native peoples in a more scientific fashion. He collected many artifacts, from New Jersey and elsewhere, and seems to have had ambitions to start the first museum in the United States. In 1782 he advertised the "American Museum" in his home in Philadelphia, where his collections—which included fossils, books, and coins, along with Indian relics—were on display (Veit 1993:72). The museum seems not to have survived his death in 1784.

In the last decades of the nineteenth century, interest in the antiquity of man—heightened in Europe by the discovery of some early human remains—spilled over into America. Many would-be archaeologists dug into native sites in this country; some sought nothing more than booty, but others were seeking parallels with ancient cultural developments in Europe. As early as the 1860s, and continuing for decades afterward, shell middens (dumps) along the New Jersey coast were opened in search of artifacts and food remains that would show how ancient people lived (Rau 1865; Abbott 1881; Fountain 1897; Jordan 1906). From at least 1865, native burials above the Water Gap were frequently pillaged for relics (Heye and Pepper 1915:12–14). Clearly, these private antiquarian inquiries did not focus on solving well-defined anthropological or historical questions. As often as not, the goal was simply to find archaeological curiosities.

As the discoveries accumulated, however, the quest gradually turned from curio-seeking to solving the mysteries of the past. The earliest "problem-oriented" archaeological studies in New Jersey concerned "paleolithic man" and the "argillite culture" at the Abbott Farm, near Trenton. These researches—and the bitter, long-lived controversy that followed—focused the attention of early archaeologists on New Jersey.

As early as 1872, Charles Conrad Abbott suggested the possibility of identifying "glacial man" in the New World on the basis of crude argillite artifacts found on his farm along the Delaware River (Abbott 1872). Abbott thought that these implements resembled the tools of early "Stone Age" cultures in Europe, then much in the forefront of scientific news. From time to time Abbott revised his thinking but all the while clung steadfast to his belief in the early origin of these crude implements (1876a). By 1883 he had developed a sequence of three distinct cultures at the Abbott Farm, namely, the "paleolithic" culture, the "argillite" culture, and the modern Indian culture (Abbott 1883). The paleolithic culture was characterized by crude chipped stone artifacts, which Abbott presumed to be of glacial age because of their discovery in the ancient Trenton outwash gravels. He also intimated that human skeletal remains—equivalent to paleolithic man in Europe—had been found in the glacial drift (Abbott 1885a). The argillite culture was deemed to be intermediate in content and age between paleolithic man and the historic Lenape. Roughly formed argillite spear points were the hallmark of this culture in Abbott's scheme, whereas finely chipped flint projectile points and pottery were the cultural indicators of the modern Indians. These cultures were attributed to distinct levels within the site, but were in fact later shown to represent parts of mixed assemblages.

Abbott's discoveries and theories were appealing and novel, and he had no difficulty in attracting a number of ardent supporters, among them the geologist and theologian George Frederick Wright (1892) and archaeologist Frederick Ward Putnam of Harvard University. W. J. McGee of the Smithsonian Institution presented a favorable, if somewhat cautious, synopsis of the various finds around the country relating to "glacial man": "However, the doubtful cases may be neglected, the testimony is cumulative, parts of it are unimpeachable, and the proof of the existence of glacial man seems conclusive" (McGee 1888:25). Later, McGee would repudiate glacial man and attack Wright, one of the theory's proponents.

As the concept of paleolithic man came under critical professional review, the question of human antiquity became the focal point of a heated and protracted debate concerning the finds at Trenton (Cross 1941:1–3, 1956:1–8; J. Mason 1956:153; Mounier 1972b; Joyce, Sandy, and Horan 1989; H. Kraft 1993). After an initial phase of acceptance, Abbott's theory fell into disrepute. Among his most persistent critics was William Henry Holmes, an archaeologist then with the Field Museum in Chicago (Macgowan 1953:95) and later with the Smithsonian Institution (Willey and Sabloff 1974:56). Holmes (1890, 1892) argued that the "paleoliths" were identical to the "shop-wasters" (unfinished specimens) of the modern Indians. He was joined in this assessment by Henry C. Mercer (1893, 1897), a friend of Abbott and one of his earlier supporters.

Holmes (1893) and others (McGee 1893; Powell 1893) also questioned the validity of the reported associations between the relics and ancient geological strata. They concluded that many objects from recent horizons near the surface had probably tumbled down valley walls or earth cuts onto talus slopes or the exposed faces of ancient, underlying sediments (Powell 1893). Still, Abbott and his supporters insisted that their antagonists simply had not looked long enough, hard enough, or in the right places (Wright 1897:xii–xiii).

Although Abbott recoiled, Putnam (1898) was neither fazed nor deterred by detractors. In 1889 he hired Ernest Volk to continue the search for early traces around Trenton. Volk's excavations—variously financed by the Peabody Museum of Harvard University, the World's Columbian Exposition in Chicago, and the American Museum of Natural History in New York— lasted more than 20 years, eventually outliving the glacial man debate that had sparked the work in the first place (Volk 1911; Cross 1956:8).

Because the age of the critical artifacts remained in doubt, it was thought that an analysis of skeletal remains might help settle the controversy. After all, a few human bones had been found under circumstances that suggested an early origin. Putnam enlisted the noted physical anthropologist Aleš Hrdlička to examine human bones from presumed early contexts. Hrdlička (1907) concluded that "in every instance where enough of the bones is preserved for comparison, the somatological evidence bears witness against the geological antiquity of the remains and for their close affinity to or identity with those of the modern Indians." Frank Russell (1899) also reached the same conclusion. Thus, skeletal materials that had been interpreted as being coeval with the "paleoliths" were similarly dismissed as being modern specimens found out of place.

By the end of the nineteenth century, the question of human presence in the glacial era at Trenton had been all but laid to rest—the lingering protestations of a few advocates notwithstanding (Wright 1897; Abbott 1889a, 1889b, 1907, 1908, 1909; Putnam 1898). Interestingly, no one had actually denied the *possibility* of early man at Trenton or, for that matter, elsewhere in America. Rather, the criticisms had been leveled against haphazard modes of data collection, careless analysis, and adherence to preconceived notions. In the absence of solid dating methods, the skeptics simply found no justification for the great antiquity adduced by Abbott and his supporters. Holmes reiterated this point in 1898: "The questions raised by me were not those of the age of man in America. I have always taken the view that the race must have occupied this continent for a very long period. . . . The only questions I have ventured to discuss and the only ones that now claim my attention are as to whether the evidence already brought forward to demonstrate the antiquity of man on the Atlantic slope will stand the test of scientific scrutiny" (364). In a similar vein, Hrdlička (1907:98) observed that only "one conclusion is justified, which is that thus far on this continent no human bones of undisputed geological antiquity are known. This must not be regarded as equivalent to a declaration that there was no early man in this country; it means only that if early man did exist in North America, convincing proof of the fact from the standpoint of physical anthropology still remains to be produced."

While neither Holmes nor Hrdlička denied the antiquity of humans, they held to the view, then quite common, that antiquity would be measured, at most, in terms of a few thousand years. In this belief they were mistaken, as the indisputable association of human artifacts with extinct animals and radiocarbon dating would later dramatically demonstrate.

As sometimes happens when strong wills collide and fervently held opinions are at stake, the debate turned ugly, and parties on both sides of the issue hurled invectives. Defending his position, Abbott (1889b:303) railed that the progress of archaeology was being "hindered by the obstacles that ignorance, prejudice, and hasty conclusions heaped about it. . . ." For this, he blamed "the interdictions of the baffled prophets." At one point, he even upbraided his detractors' publishers: "It is a blot upon American Letters that editors should solicit from incompetency, however prominent politically, articles that their authors know are misleading. Unfortunately, the public cannot always discriminate" (Abbott 1892:3).

In a particularly caustic attack, W. J. McGee (1893:95) skewered George Frederick Wright, one of Abbott's strongest supporters: "The imposing list of titles which the author appends to his name conveys the impression that he is a geologist rather than a theologian, which is misleading; that he is a professor of geology, which is not true; and that he is an 'assistant on the United States Geological Survey,' which is sheer mendacity and theft of reputation. . . . Wright is a betinseled charlatan whose potions are poison. Would that science might be well rid of such harpies." This repudiation is all the more pointed in light of McGee's earlier support for the theory of ancient humans at Trenton (1888:25).

Although both were willing to defend their positions zealously, neither Holmes nor Hrdlička issued personal rebukes or slanders, at least not during the height of the fray. Late in his career, Hrdlička remembered his opponents as men who indulged in "wishful thinking, imagination, opinionated amateurism, and desire for self-manifestation" (Hrdlička 1942:53).

As for Abbott, perhaps Mercer's rejection stung him most deeply, as the following bit of verse reveals. These lines were inscribed in Abbott's own hand in a copy of his *Primitive Industry* (1881), apparently presented to Mercer in 1893 (J. Mason 1956:162):

June 3 [1893] [1]

Dear Mercer

Why, O why, this studied silence?
What, O what, have I been doing?
You to friendship should do vi-lence?
Why your present course pursuing?
Moorehead [2] writes me you are ready
At Wisconsin, [3] to destroy
Paleolithics that I've steady
Stood for since I was a boy.
What's it mean; are you determined
To make modern all mankind?
If so, you should be be-sermoned
And brought back to healthy mind.
He who follows Holmes' mad school
Will live to see himself a f———l.
E'en Brinton, [4] now upon the fence,
Will very soon come down from thence
And the level-headed folk
Give Holmes a devil of a poke.
Write a letter; say you're sorry
Men could lead you so astray.
Dig into some new-found quarry
And get facts as clear as day,
That will prove me a true prophet

---

1 The date of composition is inferred from Abbott's mention in the postscript that he was about to celebrate his fiftieth birthday. He was born in 1843.
2 Warren King Moorehead, a prominent archaeologist and student of Midwestern burial mounds and sites in Maine. For many years he was director of the Department of American Archaeology at the Phillips Academy in Andover, Massachusetts.
3 Probably the venue of a scientific convention.
4 Daniel G. Brinton, archaeologist and linguist at the University of Pennsylvania.

Or historian as you choose;

(Or kick against me, harshly buffet:)

But remember, t'aint no use.

There's no need to more unravel,

I've found the old cuss, in the gravel!

C.C.A.

I'm fifty tomorrow. Think kind of the old man—

Mercer's response, if any, was never recorded.

Even if the question of glacial man had been dispensed with, though not entirely settled, the existence of the argillite culture was another matter entirely. For the most part, the continuing discussion centered around the investigations of Ernest Volk, who excavated sites near Trenton from 1889 to 1910. At issue was the age of the "yellow sand" that contained many of the argillite artifacts. Obviously, the artifacts could be no older than the sand in which they were found (but they could be much more recent). As we have seen, archaeological dating by reference to the age of geological deposits was an inexact method of placing cultures in a temporal context, but in the days before radiocarbon dating, there was not much else to go on.

In 1914 Alanson Skinner and Leslie Spier hoped to clarify the validity of the argillite culture by further excavations at the Abbott Farm (Spier 1918). About the same time, E. W. Hawkes and Ralph Linton (1916) undertook excavations at the Crispin Farm near Medford, Burlington County, with the same goal in mind. These investigators concurred that a pre-Lenape—but not necessarily pre-Indian—culture was present. Nevertheless, the question was not resolved to everyone's satisfaction, and the issue was revived in the Indian Site Survey research in the 1930s and 1940s.

In particular, the massive excavations conducted by the Works Progress Administration (WPA) at the Abbott Farm suggested that the argillite culture might not be as ancient as Abbott had believed (Richards 1939). Dorothy Cross (1956:191) concluded that "there was no 'argillite culture' as a separate entity which can be placed in a given period of time." We now know that both the so-called paleoliths and the "pre-Lenape" argillite artifacts reflect aboriginal activities during Archaic and Woodland times. With the advent of radiocarbon dating, it became obvious that some of these relics were of considerable age after all. Thus were Abbott's theories at least partially vindicated.

Apart from issues of paleolithic man and the argillite culture, early archaeological research in New Jersey was devoted to general site surveys aimed at creating artifact typologies and listing site distributions. Individual investigations also continued in some quarters. Charles Abbott, now and again working for the Peabody Museum at Harvard University and the University of Pennsylvania Museum, traveled about New Jersey, collecting artifacts. In 1890 he took part in excavations at various sites around southern New Jersey. Abbott's son Richard also conducted excavations in South Jersey, as did Henry Mercer and E. W. Hawkes (J. Mason 1956:158; Grossman-Bailey 2001:58–59).

New Jersey's first statewide archaeological survey was authorized by the legislature in April 1912, and fieldwork commenced later that year under the direction of Alanson B. Skinner, aided by Max Schrabisch. Skinner spent only two months in the field, and Schrabisch somewhat less, but the latter had the benefit of his previous independent research into the archaeology of the Passaic River basin. A couple of other men worked for a few days, and several volunteers, including the venerable Abbott, rendered valuable assistance. Although the appropriation for the work amounted to only $500, this expenditure yielded a record of 1,000 archaeological sites. In what now seems like a grand understatement, Henry Kümmel, the state geologist, reported that the progress made in the first year of the survey had been "very gratifying" (Kümmel 1913).

The survey continued during 1913 under the supervision of Schrabisch and Leslie Spier (Schrabisch 1915; Spier 1915). (Skinner had gone on to a promising career as an ethnologist [a student of native cultures], only to meet an untimely death beneath the twisted wreck of an automobile in 1925 [Harrington 1925].) Schrabisch concentrated his efforts in the northwestern corner of the state, while Spier visited sites along the Raritan River in Union County, the Maurice River in Cumberland County, and various tributaries of the Delaware River in Salem and Gloucester Counties.

At about the same time, investigations were carried out on behalf of out-of-state institutions. In 1909 the New York State Museum sent a field crew to excavate the so-called Munsee cemetery above the Water Gap in Sussex County, resulting in the examination of 30 graves, several hearths, and refuse pits. Edward S. Dalrymple, acting independently, also dug around in this site early in the twentieth century. In April 1914 the Museum of the American Indian, headquartered in New York City, began excavations here. This operation was halted just a few months later by the arrest of the workmen for grave robbing. George G. Heye, the leader of the expedition, was tried and convicted in Sussex County Court on charges of having "removed the remains of persons . . . unknown from their graves and places of sepulture . . . from mere wantonness." He was ordered to pay a fine of $100. Heye appealed his conviction to the New Jersey Supreme Court, which reversed the lower court in November 1914. It was a time of speedy justice. The high court ruled that "the plaintiff [may have] . . . violated the laws of decency and morality, but it does not seem to us that he brought himself within the purview of . . . the Crimes Act" (Heye and Pepper 1915:3—4). Heye and his associates immediately resumed their labors, eventually exhuming 68 skeletons. The resulting publication (Heye and Pepper 1915) has become a classic piece of early archaeological reporting in New Jersey.

Perhaps spurred on by the published investigations, artifact collecting became a very popular pastime in the 1920s, and many large collections were amassed. An old farmer once told me of relic collectors who arrived in South Jersey on barges from Philadelphia. While the barge crews unloaded their cargoes of manure and loaded the vessels with vegetables for the return trip, the collectors would search the fields for relics. Bushel baskets full of axes, arrowheads, bannerstones, and pottery made their way into private collections in this manner. Later, other collectors would travel by automobile for the same purpose.

In 1930 a number of collectors, archaeologists, and other enthusiasts teamed up to establish the New Jersey State Museum Advisory Committee for Indian Research (Boissevain 1956). This committee formed the nucleus of the Archaeological Society of New Jersey, which was incorporated in 1931. Charles A. Philhower, an avid collector of relics and Indian lore, became the advisory committee's first chairman. Later, he became the editor and publications chairman for the society. For a period of about three decades, Philhower showered New Jersey with articles about Indian artifacts and various aspects of native culture (see the bibliography). Today, his writings appear to be a curious mixture of fact, myth, and fantasy; but at the time, he was instrumental in keeping New Jersey archaeology in front of the public.

In 1931, Dorothy Cross excavated two rock shelters in Sussex County with financial backing from the New Jersey State Museum and the University of Pennsylvania. Cross had been working in New Jersey since 1929, "when she catalogued the permanent collections of the State Museum and arranged some of them for exhibit" (Cross 1956: dust jacket notes). Cross eventually earned a doctoral degree (her dissertation focused on ancient Turkish pottery) from the University of Pennsylvania in 1940, and she went on to a long career at Hunter College in New York City. She continued to serve as archaeological adviser to the New Jersey State Museum for many years.

FIGURE 12. Indian Site Survey excavation, May 1936. This is part of Excavation 2 at the Abbott Farm. Engineers use surveying equipment to mark the location of a cultural feature containing antlers. The WPA workmen have not been identified. Courtesy of the New Jersey State Museum.

Official interest in archaeology subsided during the Depression, until 1936. Then, in conjunction with the WPA's efforts to put unemployed men to work, the state government mobilized large workforces to conduct the Indian Site Survey (1936–1942). Old-timers used to joke that the initials WPA really stood for "We poke along!" Whether poking along or making great strides, the Indian Site Survey continued for six years under the supervision of Dorothy Cross, Allan H. Smith, and Nathaniel Knowles, serving in consecutive terms. To Cross eventually fell the task of summarizing the results of the research (Cross 1941, 1956).

The survey recorded hundreds of prehistoric sites in all parts of the state, and about 40 were at least partially excavated. Most of the work concentrated on the so-called Abbott Farm, which in reality was a cluster of sites on properties adjoining Abbott's tract. This locality became the focal point of the investigations because of its unusual archaeological productivity, its earlier notoriety, and its proximity to administrative headquarters in Trenton.

The object of the Indian Site Survey was, primarily, to provide work for the unemployed and, secondarily, to investigate problems of archaeological interest, although these priorities were never expressed in the ensuing reports. As with the survey of 1912, the Indian Site Survey sought to establish a firm typological schedule that would allow "comparative study of artifacts or a determination of the change and interrelation of cultures" (Cross 1941:3). The question of a pre-Lenape horizon was revived, but that such a horizon did not exist seemed almost a foregone conclusion. The vertical distribution of artifacts was presented using simple statistics (Knowles 1941b), which were employed to argue for an unbroken cultural continuum (Cross 1941:209).

The final report of the excavations beyond the Abbott Farm, *The Archaeology of New Jersey*, Volume 1, showed that, apart from creating a neater typology, the state of archaeology had advanced little over former times (Cross 1941). However, within 15 years *The Archaeology of New Jersey*, Volume 2, would present the results of the Abbott Farm excavations in a cleaner "cultural reconstruction" that foreshadowed our present cultural sequence (Cross 1956). Considering the limitations imposed on the survey by untrained WPA labor, skimpy funding, and a vacuous theoretical framework, Cross proved herself to be a highly skilled and very perceptive archaeologist.

During the war years New Jersey once again became fallow ground for archaeology. With the folding of the Indian Site Survey, the state government ended its support of field archaeology. It was not until the late 1940s that the Delaware Project, sponsored by the Indiana Historical Society, with financial backing from the pharmaceutical magnate Eli Lilly, breathed new life into New Jersey studies (Lilly et al. 1954). The Delaware Project, headed by the capable Dorothy Cross, was created for the purposes of identifying historic villages of the Delaware Indians and testing the validity of the *Walam Olum*, a purported pictographic history of the Lenape that had emerged mysteriously in the early nineteenth century (Rafinesque 1836). From 1947 to 1949 the Delaware Project employed an imposing list of prominent professional archaeologists, as well as linguists, ethnologists, and physical anthropologists.

As part of this undertaking, William A. Ritchie, for many years the state archaeologist for New York, excavated the famous Bell-Philhower site in Sussex County, adjacent to the site that had led George Heye into court in 1914 (Ritchie 1949). John Witthoft and Richard S. MacNeish labored at the Overpeck site in Bucks County, Pennsylvania, while Catherine McCann (1950, 1957) concentrated on sites in central and southern New Jersey. The project was valuable in airing new data but failed to locate unequivocal historic Lenape settlements. It also failed to substantiate the *Walam Olum*, which was finally demonstrated to be a hoax in the early 1990s. This work fell to David M.

Oestreicher, then an energetic doctoral student at Rutgers University (Oestreicher 1994).

The 1950s produced few professional studies, most of them single-site investigations (Gruber and Mason 1956; R. Mason 1957). At this time much of the burden of archaeological inquiry was borne by the Archaeological Society of New Jersey, and more particularly by a few dedicated nonprofessional archaeologists, of whom Charles F. Kier Jr. of Hammonton was perhaps the most emblematic. Aided by Fred Calverley, Kier's labors at the important Raccoon Point site in Gloucester County continued for three years until the site was finally destroyed by earthwork for a huge dredge spoil basin. The report that followed (Kier and Calverley 1957), while now dated in some respects, still ranks among the most comprehensive and discerning contributions to our present understanding of New Jersey prehistory. Kier also conducted excavations at the King's Bog site in Atlantic County and at other sites in Cumberland County. In addition, he helped organize surveys in Cape May County, along the Delaware Bay, and in the Pine Barrens region. Anyone who took a genuine interest in New Jersey archaeology could count on a generous commitment of his time and personal resources.

Beyond the state's boundaries, numerous noteworthy contributions continued to be made. Most outstanding are Ritchie's impressive publications, which span several decades of seminal research. Ritchie can be credited with providing the framework for ordering archaeological data in the whole of the Northeast. His work also serves as a counterpoise to the relative dearth of published material elsewhere during this period (see bibliography). Other noteworthy additions to the emerging literature of the Northeast and Middle Atlantic region are memorialized in the writings of Carlyle S. Smith (1950) and John Witthoft (1952, 1953).

In the late 1960s and early 1970s professional interest in the archaeology of New Jersey and adjacent states was reawakened, oftentimes by the need to salvage data from sites threatened by public works and the rapid acceleration of suburban sprawl. In New Jersey, a good deal of this work focused on the upper Delaware Valley in response to the abortive Tocks Island dam project. In some cases, however, the methodologies employed proved to be even more threatening than "progress" itself. One would-be archaeologist actually mined a site in this region with earthmoving equipment, conveyor belts, and mechanical sieves—and then boasted about the monetary savings, the loss of irreplaceable archaeological data notwithstanding (Sloshberg 1964)!

Most of the other work yielded valuable new insights about cultures in

New Jersey and elsewhere. The formative work of several archaeologists beyond our borders has had a profound influence on the development of modern archaeology in New Jersey (Kinsey 1959, 1972; Ritchie 1959, 1961, 1965, 1969; Coe 1964; Broyles 1966, 1971; Dincauze 1971; Ritchie and Funk 1971). Within the state, Herbert C. Kraft's tireless efforts to record the archaeology of the upper Delaware Valley are particularly noteworthy. Until his death in 2000, Kraft was the leading advocate for the scientific study of archaeology in New Jersey. His accomplishments are too numerous to cite here, but a glance at the bibliography will give a sense of his commitment to New Jersey archaeology.

As new data emerged, a clearer cultural-temporal framework evolved, and research interests expanded to consider more sophisticated aspects of ancient life. By the 1970s, the so-called New Archaeology aimed at placing the discipline firmly among the "hard sciences." One aspect of the new paradigm was the search for lawlike generalities of human behavior, analogous to the predictable behavior of atoms in chemical reactions. In my view, this particular effort has borne little fruit: archaeology has not added much to a general view of human nature beyond that anciently adduced in philosophy, literature, and scripture. Nor is this outcome surprising: unlike atoms, humans possess the capacity for memory and foresight. Through the medium of culture, they continually adapt, often opportunistically, to changes in their physical and social environments.

Another aspect of the new paradigm was an interest in expressing cultural and ecological relationships mathematically, especially in terms of statistical probabilities. The addition of statistics to the toolkit has offered some advantages, for it allows the archaeologist to evaluate the extent to which observed relationships may have occurred by chance alone. This tool also allows some measure of prediction, but statistics can be difficult to understand and difficult to apply correctly. The results are sometimes problematical, and much of the writing from this period is unintelligible to the uninitiated. So far, probabilistic studies have tended to confirm what was already fairly well known from decades of empirical research (for example, see H. Kraft 1978:49–50; Ranere and Hansell 1985; Walwer and Pagoulatos 1990).

A heightened awareness of the intricate relationships between human cultures and their environment was a major contribution of archaeology in the last half of the twentieth century. This emphasis emerged as part of the environmental movement, which gained political momentum in the 1960s and 1970s. Much of our understanding of aboriginal settlement patterns and social structures hinges on knowledge of ancient environments (Mounier 1978a;

Moeller 1982; R. Stewart, Hummer, and Custer 1986). This relationship goes both ways. Archaeology also contributes to an understanding of environmental conditions in the past (Mounier 1998c; Stewart 1994).

The era of the archaeocrat began in the mid-1970s as an outgrowth of the environmental movement. Federal laws and associated regulations have been expanded to incorporate the evaluation of archaeological and historical sites—"cultural resources" in the bureaucratic jargon. The principal laws are the National Historic Preservation Act of 1966 and the National Environmental Policy Act of 1970. Since the early and mid-1970s most of the archaeological studies in New Jersey have been conducted in the context of "cultural resource management," the bureaucratized oversight of archaeology in advance of public works and a good deal of private development. The Coastal Area Facility Review Act (better known as CAFRA) was implemented by 1973, and the Pinelands Comprehensive Management Plan became effective in 1981. The State Historic Preservation Office (SHPO), operating under a variety of names over the years, has prepared regulations to implement these laws and to manage mandated archaeological studies. Although many archaeological projects still advance solely by the efforts of volunteers, archaeology in New Jersey, to a very large extent, has been transformed from the labor of a few mendicant scholars into a multimillion-dollar enterprise.

Experimental Archaeology

Exactly how were arrowheads made? How effective was aboriginal hunting equipment? Why were some materials used for certain things and not for others? How would you make a pottery kettle or a length of cord? Sometimes the mysteries of the past can be unraveled by direct observation of archaeological remains; but some things can be learned only by attempting to replicate ancient artifacts, using nothing but native materials and primitive tools.

At one time or another, most archaeologists have dabbled in primitive technology. More than 30 years ago, I learned the rudiments of flint knapping by chipping away at glass bottle fragments, but a few cut fingers and glass chips in the eyes were enough to quench my thirst for this particular subject. Other investigators have been less easily discouraged. A small cadre of curious archaeologists understands the profound importance of experimentation in developing a more complete picture of ancient life in New Jersey (and elsewhere). These scholars have spent their own resources, have bloodied their

FIGURE 13. Fluted points replicated by Jack Cresson. Note the channel flake, derived from the specimen at left. Photograph by the author.

knuckles, and have scorched their fingers in their efforts to re-create the lost arts of flint knapping, pottery manufacture, fire making, and a host of other skills. They have fabricated their own equipment, using nothing but primitive tools and indigenous materials. They have tested that equipment to discover patterns of wear and fracture that cannot be learned directly in any other way. Their unstinting labors have immeasurably increased the breadth and depth of our grasp of ancient lifeways.

New Jersey's foremost experimental archaeologist is Jack Cresson, whose knowledge—hard-won by decades of independent research—is unrivaled. Cresson is a capable pot, axe, and bow maker. He has also experimented extensively with making twine, adhesives, and bindings. But it is in the realm of flaking stone that Cresson's virtuosity shines most brightly.

By dint of implacable persistence, Cresson has discovered techniques for manufacturing every class of flaked stone tool known from the entire span of prehistory in the region. Through his mastery of technique and his profound knowledge of materials, Cresson makes exact replicas of ancient artifacts in the very materials used by aboriginal knappers. Almost anyone can learn to fashion a serviceable arrowhead from obsidian, flint, or argillite, but few have attempted, much less mastered, the flawless production of stone tools and weapons from refractory materials such as quartz, quartzite, and other meta-sediments.

Further, Cresson has shown that the form of flakes precisely reflects the ancient processes of knapping (Cresson 1990, 1994). He has learned the "language of the flakes." It is a nearly mystical experience to be in his company as he correctly predicts, from nothing more than one or two small flakes, the age, cultural association, and form of finished bifaces ("arrowheads") that will be found on a site. He performs this magic on a daily basis when afield. In short, Cresson has transformed the humble flake—often regarded as essentially useless, if ancient, waste—into a tremendously revealing artifact.

Cresson and his comrades gather several times a year to swap rediscovered secrets and to put their replicated equipment to work. With their handmade bows and arrows, these experimental archaeologists will shoot at a variety of targets—tree stumps, rocks, and burlap sacks filled with butcher bones— and examine the patterns of fracture that result. In this way, they are able to interpret similarly broken specimens that appear in archaeological sites.

In their search for knappable materials, experimental flint knappers have rediscovered many ancient quarries. They work hand in hand with geologists and lithologists to identify the actual sources of archaeologically discovered specimens (Lavin and Prothero 1987; LaPorta 1989, 1994; Hatch 1994).

Almost every large archaeological site has produced hundreds, if not thousands, of pounds of thermally altered rocks. These fire-cracked rocks are generally thought of as hearthstones. However, experimental work by John Cavallo and Shari Kondrup demonstrates that many of these heat-shattered rocks were most likely used to boil water in perishable containers that could not be placed directly on a fire (Cavallo 1987:168–181). Their experiments show that the immersion of heated rocks can immediately bring water to a rolling boil. Their study further suggests that many "hearths" actually may have been dumps where boiling stones were emptied from hide bags or tightly woven containers (Cavallo 1987:181–195). Other concentrations may have been caches of rocks that were being saved for future use (Cavallo 1987:195–203).

Many archaeologists have turned their attention to discovering the techniques of prehistoric ceramic manufacture. In the Middle Atlantic region, the foremost ceramicist is Maria-Louise Sidoroff. For more than 30 years, she has sought out clay sources, prepared the paste, and then formed and fired the vessels in an effort to rediscover this lost art (Sidoroff 1991). Other experimenters have mastered the production of cordage, fabrics, and nets, as well as leather, footwear, and sundry other primitive articles. Still others have butchered dead animals using only stone knives so that the nicks and scratches on the bones could be compared with archaeological faunal remains. One group of archae-

ologists actually secured permission to experiment on the carcass of a dead
elephant to determine the effectiveness of replicated Paleoindian implements
(Callahan 1994). The various issues of the *Bulletin of Primitive Technology* (Rex-
burg, Ida.: Society of Primitive Technology) are the single best source of information on these experiments.

Based on archaeological and ethnographic data, John T. Kraft has reconstructed a Lenape village in Stanhope, Sussex County. The replicated settlement contains bark-covered houses, hearths, and a mock burial ground. It is
adorned with carvings and duplicated artifacts that give the place an uncommon air of authenticity. Visitors sense that they have wandered into an Indian
camp at the turn of the seventeenth century (H. Kraft 1989c). The site has been
opened on occasion to experimenters pursuing their studies (Sidoroff 1991).

It is important to understand that successful replications do not prove
that the actual processes employed in antiquity have been rediscovered, only
that creditable facsimiles can be produced using traditional materials, implements, or weapons. Even so, some of the experimental techniques must nearly
approximate ancient production methods. To the extent possible, the experimenters have fleshed out their routines based upon sketchy ethnographic
information. Their work has been invaluable in understanding the material
cultures of ancient societies.

———

THIS CHAPTER has defined archaeology, described the sequence of archaeological cultures, and placed those cultures in time. Ancient and modern environmental conditions have been noted, and the history of archaeological studies
in New Jersey has been summarized. We have also peeked into the world of
experimental archaeology, which continues to supplement our knowledge by
a direct, hands-on approach to rediscovering the lost secrets of ancient people.
Later chapters will describe the kinds of remains that comprise New Jersey's
rich archaeological heritage and present vignettes of archaeological excavations around the state.

CHAPTER

2

What in the World?

We cannot truly say that the Indian was
living in an age of stone alone.

ALANSON B. SKINNER
(SKINNER AND SCHRABISCH 1913)

A mysterious object appears dimly through a haze, shrouded as if by the mist of time. Gradually the light brightens, the mist fades, and the object comes into full view. Archaeologists and anthropologists surround the piece and ponder the question, "What in the world?" Eventually, the identity of the item is revealed amid commentary concerning the circumstances of its discovery, its age, and its cultural origin. This allegorical scene was revisited many times on an early television program, whose name provides the title for this chapter.

All human groups develop social and physical solutions to the problems of surviving in the world. Collectively these solutions are known to anthropologists as "culture." The social aspects of culture, such as language, kinship systems, and rules for personal behavior, are intangible. Such things generally do not survive in forms that are archaeologically detectable.

On the other hand, artifacts constitute the material culture or technology whereby people gather sustenance, secure shelter, commune with the supernatural world, and so forth. Examples include weapons for hunting, equipment for grinding grain, implements for making clothing, tools for building houses, and the houses themselves, not to mention religious paraphernalia and items of personal adornment. Such things have physical substance as well as cultural meaning. To the extent that they survive in the earth, artifacts are the essential elements of archaeological research.

Usually, archaeological traces are far from complete. Consider what might remain of an arrow that was lost a thousand years ago. All of the organic components—the bindings, feathers, and shaft (along with whatever ornamentation they might have carried)—have decayed without a trace, leaving only the stone point. And if the point had been fashioned of wood, bone, or antler, nothing at all might remain. Thus, most archaeological specimens are items of stone or pottery, which can survive in the ground.

Where conditions mitigate exposure to the elements, items of bone and antler occasionally persist along with shell ornaments or tools. Many of these items were skillfully crafted and remain objects of surpassing beauty despite the ravages of time (Heye and Pepper 1915; Ritchie 1944, 1965; Tuck 1976a). Rarely, scraps of cordage, fabric, or wood are preserved by charring or by exposure to verdigris (copper salts), which are released by the decomposition of copper or brass artifacts (H. Kraft 1976a:56, 1992c; Mounier 1981b:59–60). Textiles and cordage are more commonly represented by impressions on ceramic vessel fragments than as actual remnants.

Lucky accidents of preservation give faint testimony to the richness of the material culture that existed in antiquity. Alanson Skinner, who was well acquainted with the traditional artifacts of the Lenape and other eastern Indian groups, noted that "wood, clay, bone, antler, fabrics and a dozen other things were used . . . simultaneously with stone, the latter indeed, only . . . furnished such tools for which we employ metal today" (Skinner and Schrabisch 1913: 21). Wood was the basic material for baskets, bowls, mortars and pestles, utensils, and masks, as well as bows, arrow shafts, and canoes (which were fashioned by hollowing out tree trunks). Cordage, nets, bags, and baskets were made from leaves, plant stems, and fibers as well as bark. Pigments were obtained from the juices of plants and by grinding minerals. Garments and moccasins were carefully tailored from animal skins and woven from turkey feathers. Porcupine quills provided delicate embroidery. Native artisans worked mollusk shells into utensils and also into beads and other ornaments. Bone and antler were used for weapon tips, skewers, awls, and needles, while turtle shells were made into rattles, bowls, and cups. Therefore, despite the prevalence of lithic artifacts in archaeological assemblages, native populations did not live a Stone Age existence.

The following sections present a general discussion of the kinds of artifacts that have been found on aboriginal sites in New Jersey. Space does not permit a detailed accounting of all formally recognized artifact types, but references to artifact typologies will be offered for readers who wish to pursue classifications in more detail. In keeping with traditional classificatory schemes, I shall categorize the relics according to material composition, modes of production, form, and function (Abbott 1876b, 1881; Skinner and Schrabisch 1913: 21–30; Cross 1941:23–28). Articles made of stone, pottery, and perishable materials will be listed along with metallic artifacts and European trade goods. In addition, I shall touch briefly upon the evaluation of artifact function and the important role of experimental archaeology in artifact analysis.

STONE ARTIFACTS

Nature provides many kinds of stone. Some are very hard but brittle. Others are not especially hard but are very tough. Still others are quite soft and easily worked. Native peoples exploited these varied properties of stone for the manufacture of a wide range of useful and decorative objects. Very hard, brittle stones—such as jasper, chert, and argillite—were flaked into sharp-edged implements and weapons. Hard but resilient materials, such as diabase and sandstone, were often used without modification for rough-service work or were shaped for specific tasks by flaking, pecking, and grinding. Softer substances, such as steatite (soapstone or talc) and serpentine, were carved, ground, and polished. Some of these materials do not occur naturally in New Jersey and were imported, often over long distances, either as raw materials or as artifacts.

Flaked Stone Artifacts

Stones that are hard, fine grained, and brittle can be formed into tools and weapons by the process of knapping, which is the sequential removal of flakes by controlled percussion with a hammer or by the application of pressure with a pointed instrument.

Alanson Skinner described the knapping process in simplified terms as follows:

> The flint, jasper, quartz, or argillite was quarried from the bed rock, or drift pebbles were broken up into rough blocks with a stone maul. The blocks were further dressed roughly into shape by means of a stone hammer . . . and the finishing touches were made by flaking with a piece of bone or antler. The last

tool was about the size and shape of a lead pencil, and was manipulated by placing one end against the edge of the flint and pressing firmly. The pressure caused
long delicate flakes or chips to fly off, and so the work was done. (Skinner and
Schrabisch 1913:25)

The flakes removed by knapping resemble clam or mussel shells and are
said to have a conchoidal (shell-shaped) form. These flakes are often very sharp
and can be used immediately as cutting tools. In fact, experimental knappers
quickly learn that a certain amount of bleeding is an inescapable part of the
flaking process. Large flakes can be reduced by further knapping into a variety of tools and weapons that have culturally prescribed forms.

Many lithic materials are well suited to knapping. As noted by Skinner,
commonly used materials include very fine-grained stones, such as flint, jasper,
chalcedony, chert, and quartz. Like glass, these stones are composed principally of silica and have an amorphous or "hidden" crystal structure. For this
reason, these are sometimes called cryptocrystalline materials. Certain metamorphosed sediments—such as quartzite, argillite, and argillaceous shale—
also display conchoidal fracture and were widely used in aboriginal times for
the manufacture of flaked stone tools. The implements popularly known as
"arrowheads" were shaped by knapping. Other flaked stone implements include scrapers, drills, and knives.

BIFACES. Bifaces are implements that have been reduced from quarry cores,
pebbles, or flakes by two-sided knapping to provide working edges suitable
for cutting, sawing, piercing, drilling, reaming, and chopping. The generic
term *biface* does not imply a particular function for the object in question. By
contrast, the traditional terms *arrowhead* and *projectile point* clearly denote use as
weapons. This terminology poses potential interpretative problems because
many pointed stone implements were used not as projectiles but as knives or
other tools. In particular, the term *arrowhead* is something of a misnomer, because most of the objects so called never saw service at the end of an arrow.
The bow and arrow were introduced about 1,300 years ago; all of the weapon
tips used earlier would more properly be called javelin or spear points. To
avoid unwarranted functional implications, many archaeologists now simply
refer to all bifacially worked implements as bifaces, and specific functional
identifications are limited to those items that show evidence of particular
kinds of use. Nevertheless, the terms *arrowheads* and *points* remain embedded in
the literature as well as in popular usage. So long as the functional distinctions

FIGURE 14. Early-stage bifaces. Sometimes called preforms, these implements could be shaped by stages into a variety of useful tools and weapons. The specimen at left is similar to the so-called paleoliths central to the "paleolithic man" controversy at the end of the nineteenth century. Photograph by the author.

are clearly understood, the continued use of traditional nomenclature poses no particular problem.

Biface manufacture requires thinning the parent material to appropriate proportions by the systematic removal of flakes. The process of thinning is intended to reduce the thickness of the mass while maintaining as much length and breadth as possible. This is especially true when the raw material is a block of stone or a large cobble. Bifaces made directly from flakes or small, flat pebbles require relatively little additional thinning.

Incompletely formed bifaces—lacking refinements in edge finish, hafting elements, or other details—are called *early-stage bifaces*. Formerly, these objects were sometimes called *preforms*, but now this term has taken on a different meaning, as explained below. Some of these crude, thick forms resemble paleolithic hand axes from the Old World; indeed, this resemblance was at the heart of the "paleolithic man" controversy during the late nineteenth and early twentieth centuries (see chapter 1).

As the term is now defined, biface preforms are artifacts that have been reduced to ideal dimensions by knapping. The broad faces show a very regular lanceolate (leaf-shaped) configuration. Preforms were useful as cutting and scraping tools. Final trimming and the creation of a stem or notches for hafting was all that was needed to alter the preforms into formal bifaces.

Formal bifaces followed culturally prescribed designs and thus are recognizable as examples of discrete types, such as stemmed points or knives. Various formal biface types are associated with particular archaeological cultures or time periods. For example, fluted bifaces are characteristic of Paleoindian cultures (8,000–12,000 B.P.). These bifaces have narrow channels, or flutes, formed by longitudinal flaking from one or both sides of the base. The most common style of Paleoindian biface in the East is known as the Clovis Point. Typical bifaces of the Archaic period (3,000–8,000 B.P.) have stemmed or notched bases, but other forms—such as triangles and convex-base points— are also well known. In addition, the use of notching to create a hafting element extends into the Woodland period (500–3,000 B.P.), as, for example, in the Jack's Reef corner-notched type. True arrowheads of the Late Woodland and historic periods are most commonly triangular in outline. Space does not permit the description of the many biface types recognized within the region. Readers with an interest in biface typology should consult the works of Dorothy Cross (1941:23–27, 1956:72–81), William A. Ritchie (1961, 1965), and others (Chesler 1982).

Experimental work with replicated equipment has allowed investigators to ascertain artifact functions, because different types of use create distinctive patterns of wear and fracture. Thus, we have reason to believe that bifaces frequently progressed through a series of applications during their useful lives. The implements often show evidence of early use as hand-held tools, such as knives or perforators. Later on they may have served as weapon tips, though continuing to function when necessary as knives or multipurpose tools. Frequently, the last use was as a projectile point. With repeated resharpening —known among archaeologists as "retouching"—the blades became progressively shorter and narrower, eventually reaching a state beyond which further sharpening was impracticable. At this stage, the exhausted bifaces were converted once more into hand tools or simply discarded. Often, drills and scrapers fashioned from broken or nearly spent bifaces retain a distinctive stem or hafting element that reflects the original form.

FLAKES OR DEBITAGE. Flakes—collectively known as *debitage*—are the by-products of stone knapping. Because it is a learned cultural behavior, knapping commonly follows certain formalized procedures, each of which yields

FIGURE 15. Unifacial tools. The curved and denticulate edges have been prepared for various cutting, planing, and scraping jobs. The spokeshave (second from left, upper row) has concave as well as convex cutting edges. The small specimen at far right in the second row was notched to facilitate hafting. Photograph by the author.

particular kinds of flakes. For example, the production of tools from pebbles requires removing the cortex or "rind" from the stone. The discovery of flakes that contain vestiges of cortex is a sure indication of pebble reduction. When bifaces are produced by progressive thinning of quarried stone, relatively long, flat, thinning flakes give testimony to the fact.

Careful analysis of flaking debris provides invaluable clues to the technology of stoneworking. Experimental flint knappers and lithic analysts, who are commonly one in the same, can identify archaeological cultures from nothing more than the flakes that occur on a site (Cresson 1994).

UNIFACES. As the name implies, unifaces generally exhibit shaping on a single face; however, minor trimming along the working edges may involve both faces. Unifaces include scrapers, flake tools, and flake blanks. Unifacial scrapers are flakes that have been intentionally modified to produce an isolated cutting edge for working hides, shaping wood, and similar tasks. These tools are usually oval, triangular, or elliptical in plan and thin in cross section.

Any flake that exhibits evidence of edge modification resulting from use

FIGURE 16. Tools for abrading and grinding. At left are two shaft-smoothers, both broken through the groove. The matching half of the lower specimen was not recovered. At center is a whetstone. An anvil or shallow mortar is at right. Photograph by the author.

or design is termed a *flake tool*. Such items commonly show evidence of expedient use as cutting or scraping tools, but edge damage can be incidental to function. Therefore, it is necessary to distinguish edges worn by use from those damaged by inadvertent trampling, collision with agricultural implements, and other noncultural agencies.

Flake tools that exhibit intentional edge preparation and episodic rejuvenation are recognized as "curated" forms, which have been intentionally maintained and possibly transported from site to site in anticipation of use. In this respect they differ from expedient tools, which are discarded soon after use.

Flake blanks are flakes that are are potentially useful as tools but usually show only minimal formalization or evidence of use. Flake blanks also may serve as the parent material for bifaces. Indeed, some cultures appear to have used standardized flake blanks in a formalized process of biface manufacture. For example, bifaces of the late prehistoric Jack's Reef type appear to be made on carefully crafted and "curated" flake blanks.

FIGURE 17. A pitted cobble. The indentation in this piece is the result of pecking. Such implements may have been used for cracking nuts. Photograph by the author.

MICROTOOLS. Microtools are very small, splinterlike flakes that have been sharpened for service as perforators or graving tools. Most are under ½ inch (1.3 cm) in length and are rendered in cryptocrystalline materials (Kier and Calverley 1957:82–83; Mounier 1997:8).

CORES. Cores are masses of stone—whether from quarries or pebble beds—that show flake removals in the process of tool manufacture or flake production. Some cores show haphazard flaking, intended solely for the procurement of a few useful flakes; others exhibit systematic reduction aimed at the manufacture of formalized artifacts, such as bifaces. Core fragments and remnants frequently bear signs of modification for use as wedges, gravers, or scrapers. Some were evidently employed without intentional modification for expedient service as hammers or abraders. Aboriginal knappers frequently chipped the edges of pebbles while prospecting for good workable stone.

Expedient Rough Stone Tools

Many metamorphic and igneous rocks—such as diabase, gneiss, porphyry, and sandstone—are capable of prolonged rough service without breaking. Suitably shaped cobbles of these materials were commonly used without purposeful modification as hammers, anvils, or cutting tables. These simple tools also were employed for knapping, food preparation, and processing raw materials. They bear the scars of service in the form of pitting, battering, or abrasion on use-worn surfaces.

HAMMERS. It is not uncommon to find cobbles that were used with little or no modification for generalized hammering, that is, for cracking nuts, driving wedges, and so forth. Certain faceted hammerstones—principally employed for biface percussion—show evidence of purposeful design and prolonged use. Experiments in stoneworking suggest that these hammerstones were probably first shaped to a generally rounded form by trimming cobbles or quarry blanks of quartzite or sandstone. The rounded form was progressively supplanted by a multifaceted spheroid by prolonged use in flaking. Faceted hammerstones are associated with Archaic cultures that specialized in the use of argillite for chipped implements. There are also baton-shaped flaking hammers, whose ends usually exhibit paired facets that form chisel-like edges.

MORTARS. Dished or deeply cupped stones are classed as mortars, which were used in conjunction with a hand-held pestle for grinding nuts and seeds for food and minerals for use in pottery manufacture. Stone mortars from New Jersey are analogous to the milling stones known as querns in the Old World and as metates in the American Southwest, Mexico, and Central America. Some mortars were simply formed by prolonged use. Occasionally, natives took advantage of rocks with natural potholes, that is, concavities created by abrasion in stream eddies (Abbott 1881:150–151). Some mortars are small enough to be portable; others must have been difficult or impossible to move because of their bulk and weight. Wooden examples, made from sections of tree trunks, are known from ethnographic studies.

ABRADING STONES. Abrading stones were made on pieces of gritty metamorphosed sediments. Tabular pieces often show flattened surfaces, grooves, or striations from extended wear. Other abraders were typically made on oval or round cobbles of quartzite or sandstone. The abrading surfaces are generally located on the broader faces of the cobble and often exhibit extensive wear from grinding upon a stone mortar or other rough surface. Abrading stones with worn surfaces that are both broad and flat, are usually interpreted as food-processing implements, especially when they occur in association with mortars. Some doubtless served as whetstones, and other industrial uses cannot be ruled out.

SHAFT-SMOOTHERS. Some grooved sandstone tablets were clearly used to fabricate shafts or pointed implements of wood, bone, or antler. It is likely that these tools were employed in conjunction with an abrasive medium, such as wet sand. When the grooves are semicircular in cross section, the smoothing of round shafts can be inferred; in fact, such objects are commonly called *shaft-smoothers*. Grooves with V-shaped sections were probably used for grinding points on awls, skewers, or weapon tips (Mounier 1990a:IV-7–10).

Related to shaft-smoothers are the so-called sinewstones, which have been interpreted as implements for dressing sinews, gut, or plant fibers (Abbott 1881:145–148; Cross 1941:27, 1956:105; Bello 1988b; Martin 1995; Jack Cresson, pers. comm.). Grooves on sinewstones are typically narrow and U-shaped in section. Because the grooves wrap around the edges of the stone, they must have been formed by the passage of pliable materials. Sinewstones are usually small, smoothly rounded pebbles of fine-grained sedimentary or metamorphic materials.

HOES. Hoes are identified by peripheral flaking on flat pebbles or large flakes. Sometimes the tools were notched, or a stem was created to facilitate hafting. These tools were probably used for rough digging, grubbing, or chopping. Some may have been used for gardening, but there is very little direct archaeological evidence of horticulture on sites in New Jersey, particularly in the south.

Hoes have been reported from the complex of sites around Tocks and Minisink Islands in the upper Delaware Valley (Heye and Pepper 1915:71 [pl. 32a]; Ritchie 1949:175 [pl. 8, figs. 13, 19]; H. Kraft 1975a:106 [fig. 68q], 1978:74–75). Dorothy Cross (1941) reported 23 hoes or choppers from nine sites around the state. Seventy-eight objects of this sort were unearthed at the Abbott Farm (Cross 1956:86–87).

NETSINKERS. Small, flat, oblong pebbles of variable size were often notched for use as netsinkers. Some consist of tabular sandstone or siltstone, split and trimmed to rectangular or oval form. Less often, rounded pebbles were grooved around the short axis for suspension (Ritchie 1949:175; Cross 1956:104; H. Kraft 1975a:112, 1992a:13–18; Staats 1990). Simple notched sinkers date from Late Archaic through Late Woodland times; the trimmed and grooved varieties appear to occur predominately on very late sites (Ritchie 1949:175; Cross 1956:189; H. Kraft 1992a:13–18).

Herbert Kraft (1975a:112–113, 1992a:16) and others (Wren 1914:84; Ritchie 1965:309; Mounier n.d.a) have properly observed that some notched stones may not have been used for fishing. In most cases, however, the abundance of these items at ideal fishing places leaves little question as to their function. At sites beyond New Jersey, the evidence for the use of notched

FIGURE 18. Notched netsinkers. Flat river pebbles with a pair of notches are common elements on fishing sites. The scale is in inches. Collection of F. Dayton Staats. Photograph by the author.

FIGURE 19. A perforated cobble. No one really knows how objects of this sort, sometimes called netsinkers or canoe anchors, were used. The scale is in inches. Photograph by the author.

weights in net fishing is indisputable. For example, at the Lamoka Lake site in New York State, 8,000 notched netsinkers were found in assemblages that also contained bone fishhooks and gorges, as well as the remains of four species of fish. At the Morrow site, also in New York, sinkers of this form were found attached to remnants of a carbonized net (Ritchie 1965:48−50, 55−56, 185).

Less common in New Jersey are larger stones that bear a single, centrally located perforation formed by drilling or pecking. Charles Abbott (1881:243−245) and Paul Sargent (1953) cite several examples. The discovery of these items along watercourses reinforces their inferred use in fishing. Some very large notched, grooved, or perforated specimens may have been anchors for watercraft, as suggested by Abbott (1881:243), but the actual functions remain unknown (Morris 1986). A site along Raccoon Creek in Gloucester County has yielded several large notched stones in association with an incinerated scute (bony scale or plate), apparently of sturgeon (Mounier 2001). Smaller pebbles, modified for attachment to a line or thong, might have been used as bolas stones (Cross 1941:26; Staats 1986).

Pecked and Ground Stone Tools

Rough-service implements were often fashioned by pecking and grinding. Refractory materials, such as basalt, diorite, gabbro, gneiss, porphyry, and sandstone, were worked this way. As the name implies, the pecking process —sometimes called *crumbling*—involved selectively striking the work piece with a stone hammer or pick. Each impact pulverized a small spot on the surface of the intended tool, until gradually the implement took form (Holmes 1919:330−335; Payne 1990:12; R. Stewart 1990:6−7). Pestles, axes, adzes, and celts were fashioned by this process.

The work was made less tedious by selecting a cobble whose natural contours approximated the shape of the finished tool. Preliminary flaking also hastened the work. Usually, cutting edges were sharpened by grinding and polishing after the rough work was done. Some finely crafted tools were entirely polished. By contrast, some adzes and celts were formed primarily by knapping, and on these items grinding, if present, was restricted to the cutting edge (Hawkes and Linton 1916:73 [fig. 16]; Mounier 1974b:36; Staats 1991a, 1991b).

PESTLES. Pestles were used in conjunction with mortars for milling seeds, nuts, and minerals. In Southwestern archaeology, such items are known as manos. Common stone pestles occur in two forms: roller pestles and pounders. Roller pestles are cylindrical in cross section and taper to bluntly pointed or rounded

FIGURE 20. Hammers and pestles. At upper left is a hammerstone that doubled as an expedient anvil. Beneath it is a grooved hammer or maul. Two pestles are at right. Photograph by the author.

ends. These pestles were apparently rolled upon a flattened stone slab or other hard surface, much in the manner of a modern rolling pin. Pounders are roughly cylindrical stones with squared ends, perhaps initially formed by pecking, but maintained by use. Pounders would have been used in conjunction with deeply dished mortars.

Rarely, pestles have effigies pecked, carved, or ground onto one end. A variety of reptilian, mammalian, and phallic effigies have been reported from the region (Ritchie 1965: pl. 47; H. Kraft 1978:68 [figs. 34, 35], 1986b:65 [fig. 17]; Bello 1987b).

GROOVED AXES, ADZES, AND MAULS. Aboriginal stone axes occur in two general forms, grooved or plain. The latter are generally called *celts.* Axes have a sharpened bit on one end; the opposite end, known as the poll, is left blunt, just like a modern, single-edged steel axe. Grooved axes have a channel or groove that lies parallel to the cutting edge (Abbott 1876b:253–261, 1881:5–34; Holmes 1897:98–99; Cross 1941:26; Witthoft and Miller 1952; Bello 1989). This groove permitted attachment to a wooden handle, technically known as a *helve.* The helve, worked to an appropriate size, was wrapped around the groove and lashed tightly with sinew or cord.

On some specimens the groove entirely encircles the axe head. These are known as *full-grooved axes*, which are ordinarily regarded as originating among Middle or Late Archaic cultures. This style persisted at least into Early Woodland times (MacNeish 1952:54; Witthoft and Miller 1952:83). Another variety, which occurs later in time (MacNeish 1952:55; Witthoft and Miller 1952:83; Schmitt 1952:60), has a flat spot or a transverse furrow along one edge adjacent to the groove, apparently to permit tightening of the head by means of a wedge, eliminating the need to adjust the bindings when the handle worked loose. Because the groove does not entirely circumscribe the head, these implements are known as *¾-grooved axes*. Staats (1992c:92) discovered an unusual axe in northern New Jersey whose hafting element was formed entirely by notching. Axes of this style were fairly common in adjacent parts of Pennsylvania (Witthoft and Miller 1952:85–87).

The bit of an axe is symmetrical when viewed on end. By contrast, the cutting edge of an adze is arranged off-center, rather like a chisel. Axes were used for felling trees and chopping wood, while adzes were used to hew a smooth, flat surface. In short, these tools are believed to have functioned in the same manner as their historic counterparts.

When the bit of an axe or adze fractured, the tool could be resharpened

FIGURE 21. Tools for chopping. At upper left is a limonite tablet with a flaked cutting edge (at left). Beneath it is a roughly flaked chopper or knife. At right are two full-grooved axes. Photograph by the author.

FIGURE 22. A ³/₄-grooved axe. Leaving a flat spot beneath the groove allowed for inserting a wedge to keep the binding tight. Note peck marks left from the manufacturing process. The scale is in inches. Photograph by the author.

FIGURE 23. A celt. This finely made celt is an ungrooved axe. The scale is in inches. Photograph by the author.

but was frequently put to service as a hammer or maul. Some grooved mauls, simply made on rounded cobbles, never saw service as chopping tools.

CELTS. Celts are stone axes or adzes that are not grooved. They have been recovered from sites dating from the Archaic and Woodland periods. Very small celts were probably used as chisels; indeed, the word derives from the Latin *celtis*, meaning "chisel." Ordinarily, celts taper from bit to poll in a trapezoidal configuration. Some celts have rounded appendages about midway along the length of the tool, apparently to facilitate hafting (Hawkes and Linton 1916:73 [fig. 16]; Philhower 1935:4 [pl. 5]; Cross 1941:87, 124 [pls. 38a, 56b]). These items, peculiar to certain Late Archaic cultures, are known as *knobbed celts*.

When used for chopping, trapezoidal celts were wedged into a hole in a club-shaped helve, with the bit oriented parallel to the long axis of the handle. Because a number of celts have been preserved with the handle intact, this manner of mounting the head is not a matter of speculation (Skinner and Schrabisch 1913:24; Skinner 1932:28). When used as an adze, the head was set with the blade perpendicular to the long axis of the handle. In this configuration the head was lashed to the short leg of an L-shaped wooden helve or set into an antler socket (Willoughby 1935: figs. 18–20; Ritchie 1944:50, 66 [pl. 29, figs. 23, 24]).

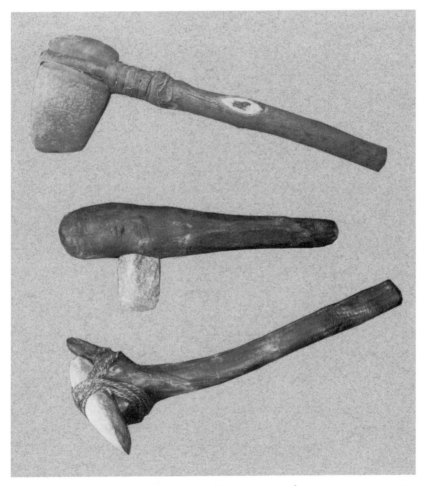

FIGURE 24. Simulated hafts. The upper specimen shows a ³⁄₄-grooved axe mounted in a bent-sapling helve (replication by the author). In the middle is a celt mounted in a club-style handle (replication by Jack Cresson). At bottom is an adze mounted in an L-shaped helve (replication by the author).

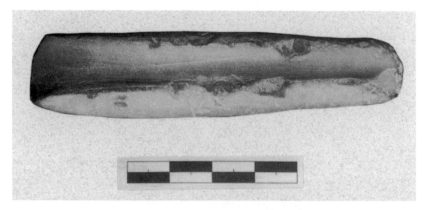

FIGURE 25. A gouge. This polished gouge was marred by agricultural equipment. The scale is in inches. Collection of Joseph R. Arsenault. Photograph by the author.

GOUGES. Stone gouges, very similar in form to modern examples in steel, rarely occur on sites in New Jersey (Philhower 1935; Cross 1941:124, 209, 211; Mounier 1999d). They are more common in toolkits of the Archaic period in New York State (Ritchie 1965:79ff.), New England (Moorehead 1922:104– 107; Willoughby 1935:31–41; B. Smith 1948:27; Dincauze 1968:34; Robbins 1968:63–65; Snow 1980:211–216), and into the Canadian Maritime provinces (Tuck 1976a:43, 1976b:32 [pls. 1, 9]). Some were well finished by grinding and polishing.

PLUMMETS. Plummets are cylindrical or conical objects, usually with one rounded or pointed end; a short stem or knob, formed by pecking, is at the opposite pole. The name derives from a resemblance to the builders' plumb bob, but the functions served by these objects in antiquity have not been as-certained. Their occurrence along the seacoast in New England and at inland sites near rivers and lakes suggests their use as sinkers or lures for fishing (Ab-bott 1881:227; Willoughby 1935:41–50; Ritchie 1965:79, 95). However, several well-made examples have been found near Medford, Burlington County, under circumstances that suggest ceremonial rather than practical uses (Jack Cresson, pers. comm.). Other specimens from Burlington County are held by the Uni-versity of Pennsylvania Museum in Philadelphia (Richard Veit, pers. comm.).

Plummets, which are common in Archaic sites of the Laurentian tradition in New England and parts of New York (Ritchie 1965:79), are quite rare in New Jersey. A few were found at the Abbott Farm during excavations by the Indian Site Survey (Cross 1956:96), and others have been reported from various parts of the state (Middleton 1932:49–50, 55; F. Stewart 1932:41 [pl. B]; Cross 1941:112; Staats 1978; H. Kraft 1986b:75 [fig. 21f]; Bello 1998).

Petroglyphs

Petroglyphs are rocks that bear "carved" images or glyphs. These objects are quite rare in New Jersey, limited to a few specimens that have pecked or incised figures, often depicting apparent human or animal forms or shapes for which no conclusive interpretation can be offered. Two examples were reported by Herbert Kraft (1969:13–16) from sites in the upper Delaware Valley. One is a large sandstone tablet that contains nearly three dozen figures, each of which was executed by a process of pecking and rubbing. Twenty-one of the images are stick figures that can be plausibly interpreted to represent human or animal forms, the human face, and so forth. Another 12 glyphs defy conventional interpretation. The largest figures measure about $7\frac{1}{4} \times 8\frac{1}{2}$ inches (18.3 × 21.6 cm). This stone, now housed at the Seton Hall University Museum, measures about 4 × 5 feet (1.2 × 1.5 m) and is estimated to weigh about 1,500 pounds.

The second petroglyph is a slab of red sandstone measuring about 12 inches (30 cm) square and about 2 inches (5.1 cm) thick. It contains two stylized human hands, executed by pecking and polishing. These impressions are almost life-size, but lack proper anatomical proportions.

Another petroglyph, also reported by Herbert Kraft (1996b), is a sandstone cobble that bears two effigies. On the broad face of the stone, which measures about $4\frac{1}{2} \times 7\frac{1}{2}$ inches (11.4 × 19 cm), is a pecked lizardlike form. One end of the cobble has two closely spaced indentations over a long, straight groove, possibly representing the visage of the lizardlike form.

Edward Lenik (1973) has described a petroglyph that was retrieved from a stone wall near Newton, Sussex County. This piece, now in the collections of the Sussex County Historical Society in Newton, contains nine images carved into the face of a flat shale cobble. Among the images are a rayed circle or "sun symbol," a stylized quadruped (perhaps symbolizing a dog or a deer), and what appears to be an arrow. The others do not lend themselves to immediate interpretation.

Still other petroglyphs, mostly bearing single images in the form of human faces, have been reported from various parts of the state, primarily from northerly districts (Philhower 1933; H. Kraft and Wershing 1974; Lenik 1974; H. Kraft 1977, 1991, 1996a). These stone "masks" may to be related to the miniature effigy faces that appear on pendants and ceramic vessels with some frequency in late prehistoric times.

Generally, petroglyphs are enigmatic. We do not know whether they represent ritualistic behavior or were intended to convey information. They may simply be idiosyncratic artistic expressions. Many of the depictions seem bizarre from the perspective of Western civilization, and none can be interpreted with absolute clarity.

The carving of glyphs is an ancient art that has inspired a certain amount of modern fakery, and this ever-present possibility casts suspicion on reported finds. Differing interpretations as to the authenticity of petroglyphs has occasionally inspired heated debate (cf. Lenik 1992, 1995a, 1995b; H. Kraft 1995a, 1995b).

Fire-Cracked Rock or Thermally Altered Rock

Aboriginal populations frequently lined their hearths with rocks, which would retain heat long after the fires had been reduced to ashes. Usually the rocks selected for this use were composed of refractory materials, such as sandstone and other metamorphosed sediments that could withstand thermal stresses without exploding. Nevertheless, rocks that have been exposed to fire show reddening, cracking, and rough angular fractures. Cobble tools and axes sometimes ended their careers in aboriginal hearths.

Heat-modified rocks appear to be related to industrial and therapeutic activities as well as to cooking. Kier and Calverley (1957:87–88) identified a pottery kiln at the Raccoon Point site in Gloucester County. Alan E. Carman (1998:126) has discovered many thermally altered stone clusters that appear to be the remains of sweat lodges, the use of which was recorded among the historic Lenape (Heckewelder 1819:218–220; Cross 1941:98n.22; Myers 1970:49–51; Tantaquidgeon 1972:20–24; H. Kraft 1986b:180). Early white settlers were said to have observed similar features near the town of Delaware in Warren County (Schrabisch 1917:51).

Some hearth rocks were employed in "stone boiling." In this process heated stones—especially small pebbles—were introduced into a liquid for purposes of raising its temperature (H. Kraft 1986b:66; Cavallo 1987:168–181). Generally, stone boiling implies cooking in perishable containers.

Polished Stone Artifacts

Soft stones, such as steatite, slate, and serpentine, were carved, etched, engraved, and sometimes polished. This artifact class includes pendants, gorgets,

FIGURE 26. Pendants. The largest specimen might be called a gorget. The scale is in inches. Collection of Alan E. Carman. Photograph by the author.

bannerstones, boatstones, and birdstones, as well as carved stone knives and smoking pipes. Many polished stone artifacts have no direct analogues in contemporary material culture, and their forms frequently offer few clues as to their manner of use. Indeed, their functions are not much better understood now than a century ago (Abbott 1881:377; Fowke 1896:115–118).

Polished stone objects are among the rarest and most beautifully crafted artifacts from archaeological sites in New Jersey. Many are quite small and have enigmatic designs suggesting use as personal charms or amulets. Some polished stone artifacts were perforated for suspension or for attachment to other objects. Holes were made by drilling into the opposing faces of the piece with a rotating stone bit. A small perforation formed where the bottoms of these holes meet. In cross section these bi-conical holes resemble an hourglass.

Similarly, the repair of broken articles was accomplished by drilling holes adjacent to the fractures and lacing the pieces back together. This ancient technique—probably originating in the manufacture or repair of wooden, antler, and bone artifacts—was also applied to stone kettles and pottery (Skinner and Schrabisch 1913:26, 57).

PENDANTS. Pendants are small stone pieces that have been drilled for suspension, usually with one hole, but sometimes with two or more. When only one hole is present, it is usually found near an edge. Pendants were commonly fashioned from smooth, flat, oblong pebbles, from pieces of soapstone or

FIGURE 27. An edge-perforated stone. This sandstone pebble has a biconical hole near one edge. The scale is in inches. Photograph by the author.

other soft minerals, or from shell, bone, or pottery. Many are plain, but others carry incised geometric designs or stylized human effigy faces (Abbott 1876b:329–330 [fig. 167], 1881:398 [fig. 375], 390–391 [figs. 368–370]; H. Kraft 1975c; Bello 1995). Some effigy-face pendants were perforated at the bottom of the image so that the wearer would see the face in proper perspective. Other observers would see the inverted countenance. From this evidence, Herbert Kraft (1975c) plausibly suggested that these pendants had personal spiritual meaning that transcended ornamentation. Some pendants appear in bizarre forms that resemble fish or reptiles (Thomas 1987; Bello and Eisenberg 1988:48). Pendants are assumed to be ornaments but probably had spiritual, religious, or totemic significance for their owners.

EDGE-PERFORATED STONES. Some rather large, edge-perforated stones may be classed as pendants for want of a better term, although their true function remains problematical. Some exceed 4 inches (>10 cm) in length, 2 inches or more (>5 cm) in width, and 1 inch (>2.5 cm) or more in thickness (Bello 1987a, 1988a, 1988b). These objects are generally flat stones with a single bi-conically drilled perforation near one edge. The hole is often offset from the end so that, when suspended, the object would not hang symmetrically along either its length or breadth. Often weighing the better part of a pound (>300 g), such objects seem too large to have been worn comfortably. Some are highly polished, whereas others have an unmodified rough texture. Still others have grooves, apparently from use as tools, such as sinew dressers. Such items are not numerous, but have a fairly broad distribution along the Atlantic seaboard, at least from southern New Jersey into New England (Willoughby 1935:111–112; Lavin 1994). Within this range, Lucianne Lavin (1994) has noted a remarkable standardization in size, shape, and placement of the perforation.

FIGURE 28. A fancy trapezoidal gorget. Made of banded slate, this gorget is typical of burial assemblages of the Meadowood and Middlesex complexes. Courtesy of Charles A. Bello, Archaeological Society of New Jersey.

GORGETS. Gorgets are thin stone bars or tablets that were perforated by one or more holes centered in the broad face. Ordinarily, perforation was accomplished by bi-conical drilling. Gorgets are usually well made—frequently of exotic materials—often polished, and sometimes ornamented with notches or incisions. Rectangular, trapezoidal, pentagonal, oval, and reel-shaped forms were fairly common among Early and Middle Woodland cultures, sometimes appearing as grave furniture (H. Kraft 1976b:15, 23, 38 [figs. 2a–f, fig. 9c, figs. 15h, i], 1989a). Similar objects occur rarely in shell and copper. Gorgets may have been employed as ornaments or status symbols, as spear-thrower weights or bracers (arm guards used in conjunction with archery equipment), and as tools for scraping or smoothing pottery.

BANNERSTONES. Winged, shield-shaped, and pick-shaped bannerstones (spear-thrower or atlatl weights) are known from sites around the state. Many were roughly worked, although some were exquisitely manufactured with a

keen sense of symmetry and careful attention to the finish. Finely crafted bannerstones are among the loveliest artifacts produced by ancient artisans. Common among Archaic cultures, bannerstones reached their zenith of popularity
in New Jersey on burial sites of the Koens-Crispin culture. On these sites,
well-made bannerstones were placed in graves as offerings (Hawkes and Linton 1916; Cross 1941:81–90, 117–127; Regensburg 1971; Burrow 1997:36).

Originally, these objects were called bannerstones because they were assumed to have been symbols of high station, owing to their aesthetic qualities
and the care expended in their manufacture (Knoblock 1939:31). We now know
from sites in the American South and Southwest (Webb 1946:319–333) that
these items were probably parts of dart- or spear-throwing devices, known by
their Aztec name as atlatls.

The spear-thrower consisted of a short stick or board, 18 to 30 inches
(46–76 cm) in length, fitted with a hook or pin that mated with a dimple in
the base of the projectile. The atlatl was held about shoulder height, with the
base of the spear united with the hooked end. Then the thrusting arm was
brought forward in a quick arcing motion toward the target. The increased
leverage afforded by the spear-thrower imparted greater velocity and accuracy
to the projectile than could be attained by the human arm alone.

Archaeologists theorize that the addition of weights helped to offset the
mass of the projectile or to match the length and flexibility of the atlatl to
the projectile (Perkins 2000:70–71). This is akin to an archer matching the
weight and flexibility of his arrows to the strength of his bow. However, some
very small bannerstones (and analogues in other materials) were unlikely to
have been effectual as counterweights. Apart from any technological advantages, bannerstones may have had symbolic purposes, conferring magical
power to ensure success in the hunt. From an anthropological perspective, ritual and symbolism cannot be divorced from utility.

Some bannerstones were perforated; others were grooved or notched
for attachment to a shaft; still others were left flat. The bores of perforated
bannerstones almost always measure about ½ inch (1.3 cm) in diameter (Abbott 1876b:333–334; Hawkes and Linton 1916:64, 71–72; Cross 1941:88, 125,
1956:100; Webb 1946:322; Petrosky 1983; Bello 1992; Staats 1992b; Mounier
1999b). This fidelity to size strongly suggests a cultural or a technological im-
perative, or both. Perkins (2000:70–71) has theorized that a springy throwing stick—presumably one of small diameter—would enhance the efficiency
of projectile delivery. This effect might account for the small bore diameters
observed in most bannerstones.

FIGURE 29. A bannerstone from the Koens-Crispin site. The scale is in inches. Courtesy of the New Jersey State Museum.

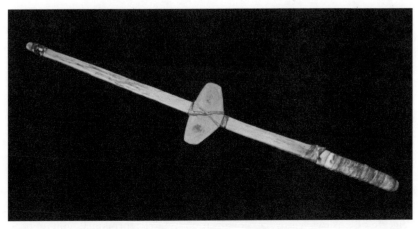

FIGURE 30. A replicated atlatl, or spear-thrower. The shaft is of hickory, terminating in a rawhide-bound handle at right and a bone hook at left. This hook fits a cavity in the end of the spear to be thrown. A counterweight (sometimes known as a bannerstone) is fixed to the middle of the device. The length is $30\frac{1}{2}$ inches (77.5 cm). Replication by Jack Cresson. Photograph by the author.

FIGURE 31. A broken bannerstone. Weakened by drilling, this piece broke through the drill hole. The hole reveals drilling with a blunt rod loaded with abrasive. The scale is in inches. Photograph by the author.

Evidence from several sites indicates that the bores were drilled by means of a stick, bone rod, or reed loaded with abrasive materials, probably fine wet sand (Hawkes and Linton 1916:76). Abbott (1876a:333–334) reported the probable use of river cane (*Arundinaria macrosperma*) as well as bluntly pointed sticks as drill rods. The occasional discovery of waste cores substantiates the use of hollow reeds for drilling (Mounier 1999b:55). Incompletely drilled specimens demonstrate boring with either hollow or solid rods.

BOATSTONES AND BIRDSTONES. Carved, ground, and polished stone pieces that resemble boats (H. Kraft 1976a:32 [figs. 13a, 15a, b]), canoes (H. Kraft 1972:25 [fig. 7ss, tt], 1974a:11–12, 1976a:71–72 [fig. 23]), and birds (Abbott 1876b:331 [fig. 170]; Blenk 1977a) are occasionally found. Rarely, forms analogous to boatstones occur in copper (Cross 1956:60, 123 [fig. 3]; H. Kraft 1976a:21 [fig. 8a]) and in bone (H. Kraft 1974b). These items are almost always perforated or notched for attachment to other objects. Although ceremonial and ornamental uses have been suggested, boatstones and birdstones probably served as components of spear-throwers (Webb 1959).

SEMILUNAR KNIVES. Semilunar knives, usually made of ground and sometimes polished slate, have a semicircular or half-moon shape from which their name derives (Abbott 1876b:303–304 [fig. 114], 1881:63–74; Willoughby 1935:70–75; Philhower 1936). The cutting edge follows the convex side in the manner of the old-time saddler's knife or the modern mincing knife. The blade tapers from the sharp edge, thickening upward to a blunt handle on the straight side. The junction of the blade and handle often forms a distinct line. Specimens that lack an integral handle may have been fitted with a grip of wood, bone, or antler. These handles would have been attached by pitch and lashings through holes that were incised (rather than drilled) from both sides of the blade. Perforation by incision rather than drilling is generally considered to be a characteristic of northern cultures.

The semilunar knife is a trait of the Archaic Laurentian tradition (Ritchie 1965:80, 84) and, like related elements, is far more common in New England and New York State than in New Jersey. The persistence into modern times of traditional semilunar knives, or *ulus,* among the Eskimos attests to the northern origin of the form. Philhower (1936) and Cross (1941:26, 1956:94–96) reported semilunar knives from various sites around the state. Analogous forms also occur in chipped stone in Archaic components.

FIGURE 32. A semilunar knife. This piece is monolithic. A handle has been worked into the stone. Some semilunar knives have holes for mounting a handle of bone, antler, or wood. Courtesy of Charles A. Bello, Archaeological Society of New Jersey.

FIGURE 33. Blocked-end tubular pipes. These cylindrical pipes have a constriction in the mouthpiece, sometimes partially closed off with a pebble or a clay plug. Pipes of this form are elements of the Middlesex complex. Courtesy of Charles A. Bello, Archaeological Society of New Jersey.

PIPES. Smoking pipes of carved and, sometimes, polished stone are occasionally found (Abbott 1876b:341–344; Philhower 1934; H. Kraft 1992b; R. Stewart 1992; Bello and Veit 1997). These are all products of Woodland cultures, dating from ca. 3,000 to 500 B.P. A variety of forms are known. Rarely seen are blocked-end tubes, which are cylindrical pipes with a constricted opening in one end, often partially blocked with a small pebble or clay plug. The plug apparently prevented inhalation of the tobacco or herbs that were being smoked (Ritchie 1944:199; H. Kraft 1976a:21, 24, 28, 32, 35).

Another rare form is the platform or monitor pipe, so called because the bowl surmounts a flattened stem in a manner resembling the famous Civil War ironclad (Philhower 1934:12, 14 [fig. 9]; H. Kraft 1992b; R. Stewart 1992; Bello and Veit 1997). Blocked-end tubes and platform pipes are elements of the Adena and Hopewell cultures that find somewhat diminished expression on burial sites of the Middlesex and Meadowood complexes in the East during Early and Middle Woodland times (Ritchie and Dragoo 1960; Dragoo 1963).

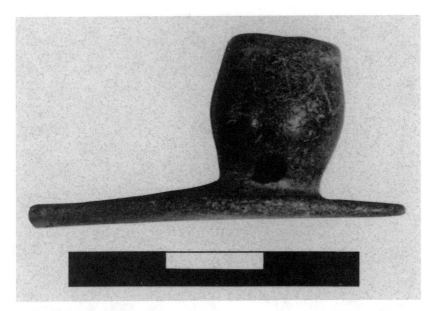

FIGURE 34. A platform pipe of soapstone. This pipe has a perforation at the base of the bowl, suggesting ritual "killing." The intentional destruction of valuable objects is a hallmark of certain burial cults. Courtesy of Charles A. Bello, Archaeological Society of New Jersey.

Finally, there are various types of elbow pipes, whose stems and bowls join at obtuse angles. These forms are mostly of late prehistoric origin. Pipes made from clay are much more common than their counterparts in stone.

Minerals and Fossils

Aboriginal peoples sometimes used minerals and fossils. For example, small pebbles of hematite and graphite have been found under circumstances that indicate the preparation of pigments (Volk 1911:197; Hawkes and Linton 1916: 76; Cross 1956:162; Mounier 1972a:24, 1974b:34, 1975:7). Indeed, red ochre (pulverized hematite) found in caches and grave sites attests to this activity (Hawkes and Linton 1916:76; Cross 1956:162–163; Regensburg 1971:23; H. Kraft 1976a:18, 21, 32; Mounier 1981b:54, 56). Fossils occur here and there in burials and, occasionally, with no apparent association to interments (Mounier and Martin 1992:IV-125). At the Crispin Farm, E. W. Hawkes and Ralph Linton (1916:76) found red-painted fossil brachiopods in what are almost certainly cremation burials, and Richard Regensburg (1971:21) reported other

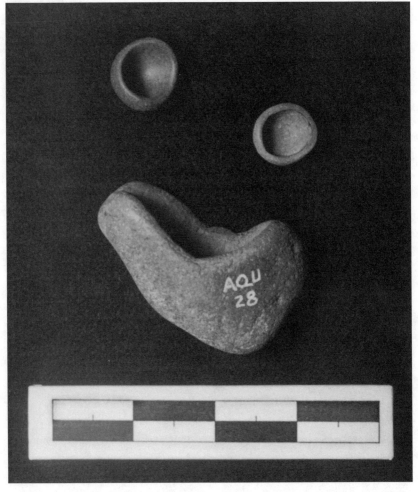

FIGURE 35. Hematite paint cups. Hematite, limonite, and graphite were sometimes ground for use as pigment. Scale is in inches. Photograph by the author.

fossils from the Savich Farm. At a site near Port Elizabeth, in Cumberland County, Alan E. Carman found a fossilized trilobite nestled inside a miniature ceramic container. The suspected ritual use of petrified wood has been noted on a number of sites in southern New Jersey (Mounier 1974a, 1975:7). Mica was exploited for tempering pottery, and at the Abbott Farm large sheets of it—up to 12 inches in length and ¾ inch in thickness (30 × 1.9 cm) —were used ornamentally or in rituals (Volk 1911:78, 83; Cross 1956:10, 16, 161–162). Although mica occurs as particles in local rocks, the larger pieces must have been imported (Parris and Williams 1986). Quartz crystals, in natural or modified condition, and oddly shaped limonite concretions have also been reported (Hawkes and Linton 1916:76; Mounier, Cresson, and Martin 1993:6, 16; Mounier 2000b:48).

CERAMIC ARTIFACTS

The introduction of pottery, about 3,000 years ago, marked a great technological advance. Aboriginal potters found that a mixture of water-softened clay and various other ingredients could be formed into useful shapes while still plastic and then hardened by fire. Constituents other than clay—collectively known as *temper*—included vegetable fibers, sand, crushed rock, and shell. These materials were added to the paste to prevent cracking during the firing process.

This new technology allowed for the construction of durable containers that could be used for storage and for cooking directly over fire. In addition, smoking pipes, balls, beads, and other ornaments were produced. Pottery also provided a versatile medium for artistic expression, not only in the variety of forms that could be produced, but also in their decoration.

Precursors in Stone

Most archaeological cultures in New Jersey, spanning at least the first 8,000 years of prehistory, lacked pottery of any kind. These pre-ceramic peoples must have fashioned containers from wood, bark, or plant fibers, almost none of which survives directly in archaeological situations. By Late Archaic times, perhaps as early as 4,000 B.P., pots were carved from steatite, which is also known as soapstone or talc (Abbott 1881:185–190; Holmes 1897:106–133; Willoughby 1935:157–161; Cross 1941:35; Kier and Calverley 1957:84–86; Ritchie 1959:63–64). A number of complete soapstone bowls have been found in New Jersey (Cross 1941:35 [pl. 5a]; Morris 1974), and fragments are fairly common. Herbert Kraft (1987) reported the rare discovery of a sandstone bowl. Stone vessels have been found in association with elaborate burials on Long Island. Many show evidence of repair by drilling and lacing. When interred with the dead, these vessels were almost always intentionally broken or "killed" (Ritchie 1944:227–235, 1959:62–66, 74, 1965:170–173).

The earliest of the stone vessels—generally rectangular or oblong in plan

FIGURE 36. A complete soapstone bowl. Courtesy of the New Jersey State Museum.

—had flat bottoms, vertical or sloping sides, and, often, lug handles. The handles and pot lips were often ornamented by notching. These pots probably resembled earlier containers fashioned from wood or bark (Holmes 1897: 110; R. Stewart 1998:237). Frequently, the exterior surfaces show tool marks, demonstrating that the stone had been shaped with chisels or picks. Another, apparently later, style of soapstone kettle has a more rounded, bowl-like form and smoothed exterior surfaces, again decorated with notches on the rim or handles (Cross 1941: pl. 5a; Kier and Calverley 1957:86; Ritchie 1959:62, 74; Morris 1974). Exposure to fire as cooking vessels is often evidenced by fire smudging or by thermal deterioration on the exterior surfaces (Kier and Calverley 1957:86; Ritchie 1959:65).

Some soapstone utensils were quite shallow and might be called dishes or trays rather than pots (Abbott 1881:185; Kier and Calverley 1957:86; Ritchie 1959:65). John Cavallo (1987:238–242) has suggested that these containers functioned as oil lamps. The physical evidence is weak, however, and there are no ethnographic examples from our area to support this contention.

Fragments of stone vessels were carved into pendants, gorgets, doughnut-shaped beads, ladles, and grooved or notched pieces that might have been ornaments, fishing weights, or bolas stones (Witthoft 1953:12; Ritchie 1965:150, 158, 161).

Soapstone quarries that contain obvious evidence of pot making have been identified around Washington, D.C. (Holmes 1897:106–133, 1919:228–240), and at various locations in Pennsylvania and New England (Holmes

FIGURE 37. A portion of a soapstone bowl. This bowl was partially reconstructed from fragments. Note the mending holes, the lug handle (at right), and the notches around the rim. The scale is in inches. Collection of Alan E. Carman. Photograph by the author.

FIGURE 38. Grooved soapstone weights. The scale is in inches. Collection of Alan E. Carman. Photograph by the author.

1897:106–133; Willoughby 1935: 157–159 [fig. 86]; Crozier 1938; Cross 1941:35, 56; Witthoft 1953:13; Ritchie 1959:62, 1965:150, 161). Soapstone was probably imported to New Jersey from quarries at these distant places. Although steatite occurs in bedrock near Phillipsburg in Warren County (Richards 1941:22; Cross 1956:194), no aboriginal quarry is known at this location or elsewhere in New Jersey.

Pottery

Two distinct ceramic traditions appeared simultaneously in New Jersey about 3,000 years ago, or slightly earlier. The first is represented by tub-shaped, flat-bottomed ware, the second by simple conoidal, ovate, or baglike forms. Why two distinctly different forms of ceramics should appear at the same time is puzzling, but they may simply reflect the flexibility of the medium to reproduce various forms—tubs and baskets—already in existence in other materials.

FLAT-BOTTOMED POTTERY. The flat-bottomed ware—produced by modeling or kneading—mimics the form of soapstone kettles common in the region during Late Archaic times (Holmes 1903:157; Manson 1948:225). Indeed, vessels of this form are often tempered with fragments of broken soapstone kettles. The Marcey Creek Plain type characterizes this sort of pottery, but many variations in shape, temper, and surface treatment have been recorded (Hoerler 1939:6; Cross 1941:60, 65, 88; Manson 1948:225; McCann 1950:316; Kier and Calverley 1957:86–88; H. Kraft 1972:37–38; Mounier 1974b:44–46; Morris et al. 1996:18–20; R. Stewart 1998:124–125, 136–137). The surfaces may be plain or finished with impressions of cordage or textiles, and the flat bottoms often bear the impressions of woven mats, twined textiles, cordage, or basketry. In addition to steatite as a tempering agent, crushed shell, rock, and fibers also occur in the paste. This style appears to have arisen in the Chesapeake Bay region and diffused northward into Pennsylvania, New Jersey, and New York State.

CONOIDAL POTTERY. The second ceramic tradition is typified by simple conoidal or parabolic vessels. Skinner aptly described the form as resembling "an egg with the top cut off" (Skinner and Schrabisch 1913:25). These kettles were built from spiraling coils of clay, tempered with grit, crushed rock, shell, or other substances (Skinner and Schrabisch 1913:26; Cross 1941:181). While still wet, the coils were welded together by smoothing with the hands and by

FIGURE 39. Fragments of flat-bottomed pottery. At left is a basal sherd showing the heel at the junction of the base and side wall. At right is a rim sherd. The clay is tempered with crushed soapstone. These sherds resemble the Marcey Creek Plain type. Photograph by the author.

FIGURE 40. Fragments of flat-bottomed pottery. At left are basal sherds. The upper specimen shows the exterior; the bottom, the interior. Note the junction of the base and side wall. At right are exterior (top) and interior (bottom) views of rim sherds. This vessel was cord-marked on all surfaces. The temper is crushed oyster shell. Photograph by the author.

paddling the surface with cordage, netting, or fabric. Failures along the coil junctions clearly betray the manner of manufacture. This type of pottery appears to have originated to the north or northwest of New Jersey. The ancestral ware is known as the Vinette 1 type, which is rock-tempered and cord-marked on both interior and exterior surfaces (Ritchie and MacNeish 1949:100).

The modeled, flat-bottomed ware was both heavy and prone to structural failure, especially at the junction of the base and sides. Therefore, it was eventually abandoned in favor of the conoidal form, which was relatively strong in relation to its weight. The strength derives from the ovate form, perhaps inspired by the shape of bird eggs. The inherent durability of the design, which permitted the construction of light, thin-walled vessels, also economized on raw materials. Naturally, the bluntly pointed bottoms made these vessels wobbly, but this problem was easily overcome by surrounding the base with rocks or by partial burial in the earth.

The basic coil-constructed, ovate form persisted in numerous variations on the coastal plains and in the piedmont of New Jersey up to historic times. Elaborations were mostly limited to minor variations in the form of the neck and rim, the surface treatment, and the decorative motifs. Following the Vinette 1 style, many kettles had a wide orifice and declined in diameter progressively toward the base. In some cases, the pot bodies were constricted slightly below the mouth to form a neck, and the vessel rims were gently turned outward or everted. Other vessels had moderately in-turned rims and were somewhat smaller at the mouth than at mid-body. In all cases, the bottom was more or less pointed.

The various vessel forms were probably related to function. Wide-mouthed pots would be best suited to storing or dispensing foodstuffs or other materials, while constricted necks and rims would serve to contain liquids, especially if stirred during cooking.

Trends in surface finishes changed over time. As already noted, the inner and outer walls of the earliest conoidal pots were marked with cord impressions. About 2,600 years ago net impressing became common, and fabric marking predominates after ca. A.D. 700 (R. Stewart 1998:257, 265). Corded and plain surfaces persisted throughout the period of aboriginal ceramic manufacture.

The size varied considerably, from small cups with a capacity of a few fluid ounces to large storage vessels capable of holding many gallons. The proportions of conoidal pots are quite similar throughout their size range, and this adherence to form clearly suggests a culturally prescribed ideal. As a rule,

FIGURE 41. A conoidal pot. This form of ceramic construction persisted in southern New Jersey up to the time of European intrusion. This specimen was restored from fragments by Alan E. Carman. The scale is in inches. Photograph by the author.

FIGURE 42. Coil-based pottery construction. Sketch by the author.

these vessels were slightly taller than wide, although the reverse is true in some specimens.

Several reconstructed vessels from the Abbott Farm near Trenton averaged a little less than a foot (29.9 cm) in height and slightly more than 10 inches (25.5 cm) in maximum diameter (Cross 1956:133, 136). The smallest vessel was less than 3½ inches (8.9 cm) tall and about 2½ inches (6.4 cm) in diameter. This cup has a capacity of less than ¼ pint (approximately 140 cc) as determined

FIGURE 43. A large subterranean storage pot. Drs. Dorothy Cross and Eugene Golom-shtok are shown excavating this large net-impressed vessel at the Abbott Farm, September 1936. The restored vessel has a capacity of nearly 50 gallons. Courtesy of the New Jersey State Museum.

by mathematical estimation (cf. Mounier 1987). R. Michael Stewart (1998:180 [fig. 72]) illustrates another, slightly smaller cup from the same locale. The largest vessel from the Abbott Farm stood 26 inches high (66 cm) and 27½ inches (70 cm) in diameter (Cross 1956:140). This large container, which has an estimated capacity of nearly 50 gallons (181.75 liters), was set into the ground as a storage bin or silo (Cross 1956:140 [pl. 19b]).

The average dimensions noted above are typical of reconstructed pots seen in collections from around the state. Several miniature pots have been found, usually in late prehistoric contexts, but these items are rare enough to be considered exceptional (Cross 1956: figs. 4, 6; Staats 1992a; de Vries 1994:109; R. Stewart 1998:175 [figs. 70, 72]). Most share the basic conoidal form of larger vessels, but a small pedestaled cup was found at the Ware site in Salem County (Morris and Reed 1990). This item resembles a small, squat wine glass or an eye cup. A similar specimen was found in a historic Susquehannock Indian grave in Pennsylvania (Kent 1984:377 [fig. 105]). While sometimes regarded as toy pots, these vessels may have been small jars for keeping herbs, condiments, or ointments. Some may have been kept as part of medicine bundles. So far as is known, the huge storage vessels from the Abbott Farm have no analogues anywhere else in the region.

The size of ceramic kettles diminished through time, at least on sites in the interior of the coastal plains (Mounier 1987; Morris et al. 1996:32). In a study of pottery from Site 28-GL-123, in Deptford Township, Gloucester County (Mounier 1987), I found that the average estimated capacity of Early Woodland vessels was 13.20 gallons (49.98 liters). Middle Woodland kettles averaged 7.91 gallons (29.95 liters), and Late Woodland pots, 1.41 gallons (5.33 liters). This trend suggests that later populations may have been more mobile than earlier ones. The larger vessels were too large to allow easy transportation (except possibly by watercraft) and presumably were used near the place of manufacture for storage or for cooking. At the Abbott Farm the largest vessels occur during Middle Woodland times (Cross 1956:140; R. Stewart 1998:253), but gigantic pots of the sort noted above are not typical.

In the northern part of the state, vessel forms evolved over time toward a

FIGURE 44. Miniature clay pots. These little pots are sometimes called toys but probably held ointments or other special substances. The cup at right contained a fossilized trilobite. The scale is in inches. Collection of Alan E. Carman. Photograph by the author.

FIGURE 45. A conoidal pot from Cumberland County. Note the fabric-impressed surface finish and corded decoration. This vessel falls within the typological range of the Riggins Fabric-Impressed type. The scale is in inches. Collection of Alan E. Carman. Photograph by the author.

globular shape with a somewhat constricted neck. However, simple parabolic kettles constituted a minor element of the ceramic production well into late prehistoric times (H. Kraft 1975a:119, 1975b:103). As time progressed, the globular vessels developed well-defined collars between the neck and rim. Eventually, the collars became higher and more ornately decorated, sometimes terminating in pronounced points or castellations. Cord-marked, check-stamped, and smoothed surface finishes have been noted. The largest vessels appear to have a capacity of about 5 gallons (19 liters) (H. Kraft 1975a:119–149, 1975b).

Both in general form and in decorative motifs, the late prehistoric globular vessels from northern New Jersey strongly resemble the pottery of the Owasco and Iroquois cultures in adjacent portions of New York State (Ritchie and MacNeish 1949; MacNeish 1952). A fairly precise evolution of styles and decorative themes in late prehistoric times gives the pottery from this region particular value in estimating the ages of the related sites. The earlier wares relate to the Pahaquarra culture (A.D. 1000–1350) and the later to the Minisink culture (A.D. 1350–1600). These cultures, defined by Herbert Kraft (1974c:33–46, 1975a:59–61), are roughly equivalent in age and technological development to the Owasco (pre-Iroquois) and Iroquois cultures of New York State (Ritchie 1965:271–274, 303, 308, 313).

FIGURE 46. A globular pot of the Chance Incised type, from Warren County. The constricted neck and collar are typical of northern New Jersey pottery. The scale is in inches. Collection of F. Dayton Staats. Photograph by the author.

FIGURE 47. A collared pot of the Munsee Incised type, from Warren County. The high collar and the intricate incised decoration and castellations mark this vessel as the work of a late prehistoric potter. The specimen is typical of northern districts. Note the human face effigy in the corner of the castellation at right. The scale is in inches. Collection of F. Dayton Staats. Photograph by the author.

The evolution of two distinct ceramic traditions in late prehistoric times reflects the cultural divergence of the ancestral Lenape into a southern group, known as the Unami, and a northern group, known as the Munsee. This distinction is supported by linguistic as well as archaeological evidence. The boundary between these two groups ran westward along the southern edge of

FIGURE 48. A fragment of a collar. Note the complex design in the general style of the Munsee Incised vessels. The scale is in inches. Collection of F. Dayton Staats. Photograph by the author.

Raritan Bay and up the Raritan and Lamington Rivers to the Delaware River at the Water Gap (Goddard 1974:103, 1978a:213–216 [fig. 2], 1978b:72–73).

In both the north and the south, the pottery was decorated with designs that were impressed, incised, or gouged into the clay before firing. The use of decorative painting is unknown, but occasionally a thin wash of ochre was applied. Impressed decorations were implemented with cord-wound sticks or single lengths of string. Other embellishments show incisions with sharpened instruments, punctations with hollow reeds or quills, and even fingernail impressions. Dentate stamping was done by means of a toothed stylus or roulette.

The design motifs may reflect traditional decorative elements on textiles or tatoos marks (Holmes 1903:79–80, 151; R. Stewart 1998:265). Most of the decorations take the form of geometric figures, which evolved over time. Because ceramic production passed from one generation to the next, the evolving forms probably describe social groupings in ways that are not now well understood. Curvilinear designs and depictions of life forms are rare, especially in the southern part of the state. (However, see Blenk 1986, 1990 for descriptions of animal effigies on ceramic kettles from Cumberland County.)

Simple human face effigies—usually created by three punctations, representing the eyes and mouth—become fairly common on pottery and pipes by late prehistoric times, particularly at sites around Trenton and in northern New Jersey (Cross 1956:129 [pl. 31b, c]; H. Kraft 1975a: fig. 83h, 1982:157; Bello 1993; Staats 1995; R. Stewart 1998:229 [fig. 108]). Animal effigies also occasionally adorn pottery on late sites in the north (H. Kraft 1989b).

It should be noted that plain conoidal vessels sometimes occur in the north, and ornate, globular, collared pots in the south. Highly decorated open-mouthed pots, with designs restricted to broad bands or zones, occur at

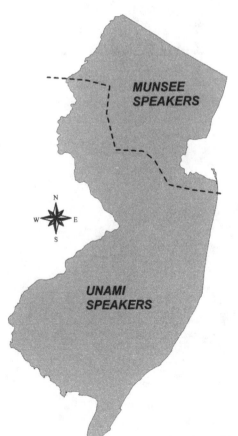

FIGURE 49. Boundary between northern and southern Lenape (after Goddard 1978b). Not surprisingly, differences in the distribution of late prehistoric pottery types generally follow the linguistic boundary between the Munsee and Unami. Courtesy of Joseph R. Arsenault Environmental Consulting.

FIGURE 50. A human face effigy on pottery. This fragment of a castellated clay vessel bears a typical human face effigy, formed by three strokes of a stylus. Notches at the base of the collar appear to define a chin, while incised decoration gives the impression of a headdress. The scale is in inches. Collection of F. Dayton Staats. Photograph by the author.

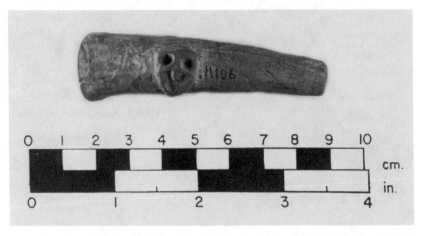

FIGURE 51. A human face effigy pipe. The heel on the underside of this small smoking pipe contains the image of a human face. Collection of George Woodruff. Courtesy of Charles A. Bello, Archaeological Society of New Jersey.

FIGURE 52. A zoömorphic effigy on pottery. The castellation of this collared vessel contains a striking effigy, which appears to depict the snout of a turtle. The scale is in inches. Collection of F. Dayton Staats. Photograph by the author.

sites around Trenton (Cross 1953:8–9, 1956:144–149; R. Stewart 1998:190–213), in Old Bridge in eastern Middlesex County (Richard Veit, pers. comm.), and occasionally elsewhere (Morris et al. 1996:31).

Over the years, archaeologists have devised several typological schemes to classify the ceramics of the region (Cross 1941:27–28, 1953, 1956:131–160; Ritchie and MacNeish 1949; McCann 1950:315–317, 1957; H. Kraft 1975a:119–150, 1975b; Morris et al. 1996; R. Stewart 1998). These schemes are not without problems. They frequently tend to coalesce elements that are distinct but, at the same time, offer a confusing multiplicity of local names for wares that are essentially equivalent in their physical and associative attributes (R. Stewart 1998:5–14). As Herbert Kraft (1975a:121) has noted with appropriate irony, "it is all too obvious that the Indian potters were not making their vessels to suit our typologies." The named ceramic types are too numerous to describe here, and no attempt will be made to unravel the intricacies of the existing

FIGURE 53. A small, high-collared vessel. Found in southern Cumberland County, this Late Woodland vessel shows a form more typical of the Susquehanna Valley of Pennsylvania. The scale is in inches. Collection of Alan E. Carman. Photograph by the author.

FIGURE 54. A zoned-incised vessel. This exquisite Middle Woodland vessel of the Abbott Zoned-Incised type was found at the Abbott Farm during the WPA excavations. The scale is in inches. Collection of the New Jersey State Museum. Photograph by the author.

classifications. However, references to specific, well-established types that have regional importance will be used here in the text and illustration captions.

Pipes and Other Clay Artifacts

Clay pipes were manufactured in a variety of styles. Usually the paste was similar to that used in pottery, but coarse-textured temper was avoided. Although most pottery was fashioned by coiling, virtually all ceramic pipes were formed by modeling. Most of the clay pipes were decorated, some exquisitely, in motifs that mirrored the designs on related containers. Some of the earliest pipes were straight or cigar-shaped tubes. Monitor or platform pipes are quite rare. Later forms, sometimes known as elbow pipes, had bowls set at obtuse angles to the stem (as measured from the top of the stem to the near side of the bowl). A sample of elbow pipes from the Abbott Farm showed a range of stem-to-bowl angles between 122° and 174.5° (Cross 1956:126). The bulbous bowls generally expand from the stem to an in-turned rim. Some trumpet-shaped bowls terminate in an everted rim. Depictions of life forms are rare, but human effigy faces sometimes occur (Cross 1956:129 [pl. 31b, c]; Bello 1993; R. Stewart 1998:229 [fig. 108]).

Small perforated clay disks have been reported from the Abbott Farm (Cross 1956:124). These and another from the Ware site in Salem County (Hummer 1981) are somewhat greater than an inch (2.7–3.7 cm) in diameter and about ¼ inch (5–9 mm) in thickness. The examples from the Abbott Farm were cut from the walls of pottery vessels and were smoothed around the circumference. The Ware site specimen, apparently modeled individually, bears notches around the edge and decorative inscribing on the flat surfaces. These disks may have been gaming pieces or ornaments.

Large ceramic disks—the largest more than 6 inches (16.7 cm) in diameter—have been reported from sites in Cumberland County (Morris 1988). These may have been serving dishes, or possibly lids for small containers. At the Abbott Farm, Dorothy Cross (1956:124) also noted an oblong clay tablet that she interpreted as a "pottery smoother." It measures a little over 3 × 4 inches (8.5 × 11.2 cm) in plan view and somewhat less than ⅜ inch (0.9 mm) in thickness. Jack Cresson has a fragmentary pottery plate with an estimated diameter of 6⅞ inches (17.5 cm) and a thickness of ½ inch (1.3 cm). This specimen, from the bank of Woodbury Creek in Gloucester County, was recycled from the circular base of a flat-bottomed kettle. The broken edges were smoothed over by intentional grinding.

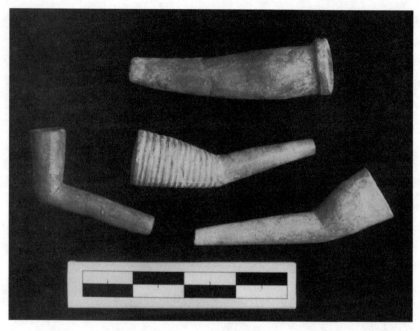

FIGURE 55. Late prehistoric pipes. This assortment of smoking pipes is from the collection of Alan E. Carman. The scale is in inches. Photograph by the author.

FIGURE 56. A decorated elbow pipe. Collection of George Morris. Courtesy of Charles A. Bello, Archaeological Society of New Jersey.

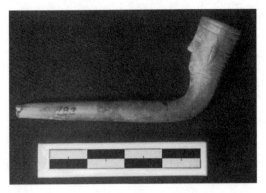

FIGURE 57. A human face effigy pipe. This unusual pipe has the modeled and carved image of a human face. Typical of pipes of very late prehistoric cultures, the image faces the smoker. The scale is in inches. (The detail is enlarged 22 percent.) Collection of F. Dayton Staats. Photograph by the author.

FIGURE 58. A ceramic plate. The scale is in inches. Collection of Alan E. Carman. Photograph by the author.

Spherical ceramic beads have been found on the Minisink and Dark Moon sites in Sussex County (H. Kraft 1978:75; Hartzell and Staats 1983) and on a site near Leesburg in Cumberland County (Alan E. Carman, pers. comm.). Charles Rau (1865:373) reported clay beads from Keyport, in Monmouth County, but he gave no particulars as to their size or shape. Skinner suggested that some of these beads may have been trimmed from the stems of smoking pipes (Skinner and Schrabisch 1913:46).

I discovered a small ceramic sphere—about the size of a large marble—

on the Fralinger site in Cumberland County (Mounier 1974b:37). R. Michael Stewart (1998:230–231) described a fired clay frustrum, or "ceramic cork," from the Lister site near Trenton. This piece measures slightly less than ½ inch (1.1 cm) in length and tapers from a maximum width of ¹⁹/₆₄ to ⁷/₃₂ inches (7.5 mm to 5.4 mm). Stewart has suggested that this piece may have been used to constrict the end of a tubular pipe.

ITEMS OF PERISHABLE MATERIALS

We know from archaeological evidence and ethnographic observations that aboriginal material culture was not limited to items of stone and pottery. Perishable materials were undoubtedly used for a broad array of tools, weapons, utensils, and ornaments.

Bone and Antler

Artifacts of bone and antler are relatively rare on archaeological sites in New Jersey. Of the 58,000 artifacts recovered during the Indian Site Survey excavations (1936–1942), only 66 were made of bone or antler (Curbishley 1954:13). Cross (1941:211) concluded that "bone work in New Jersey is not only 'weakly developed' but almost non-existent." Although it is true that not all aboriginal cultures had highly evolved bone and antler industries (Ritchie 1949:177), the scarcity of organic artifacts results at least in part from poor preservation.

Bone and antler implements can be classified according to imputed functions. For example, awls, needles, projectile points, and flaking tools have been identified, along with scrapers, chisels, ornaments, cups, and rattles. There are also miscellaneous bone fragments that might have served as spatulas or spoons (Mounier 1974b:47 [pl. 5, fig. 3]). The following sections will summarize the kinds of bone and antler artifacts that have been found on New Jersey sites.

AWLS. The most common bone implements are the so-called awls, made from sharpened bones or bone splinters (Heye and Pepper 1915:46, 74 [pl. 10b]; Cross 1941:146 [pl. 70a, figs. 5, 6, 8], 1956:119–120 [pl. 29a, figs. 3, 4, 6, 12]; Marchiando 1972:142 [fig. 42u–w]; H. Kraft 1978:70, 72 [fig. 41]). Because of its availability, light weight, and strength, bone has been a favorite material for awls throughout most of human history. The long bones of deer and other large mammals were used for large, stout implements, which sometimes retain

FIGURE 59. Bone and antler objects. At top are three sharpened bone splinters, which may have served as awls or skewers. At bottom are two deer antler tines, both cut by circumcision and snapping. The scale is in inches. Photograph by the author.

the joint (comprising the articular surfaces or condyles) at the end of the bone. When the condyles are present, the animal species often can be identified. Smaller awls are simply tapered bone fragments. The most finely pointed awls were made from the hollow bones of turkeys and other birds.

Like modern screwdrivers, awls were versatile tools that doubtless served many purposes beyond those that are immediately apparent (Hodge 1920:79–97). Certainly, some bone awls were used as perforators, as suggested by analogy to historical counterparts in steel, but the larger implements would have been impractical as sewing aids. The context of discovery often suggests the pertinent application. For example, Skinner, observing the association of awls with food refuse, concluded that "they sometimes saw service as forks for pulling scalding morsels from the kettle" (Skinner and Schrabisch 1913:28; also see Abbott 1893; Volk 1911:70; Kraft 1976a:52, 54; Cantwell 1980).

The awl is also an essential tool in basket making and in working with cordage. In textile work, the awl serves to spread woven or twisted elements to allow the insertion of materials for splices or bindings (O. Mason 1904:87). Heavy mammalian leg bones, such as the metatarsus and ulna, were favored for basket work. Tools of this sort have a wide distribution in space and time; indeed, the metatarsal awl has endured into modern times among basket makers in Europe, especially for the manufacture of straw skeps or beehives (Crane 1975).

Although direct archaeological evidence is lacking, finely pointed awls would have served admirably for applying incised designs on aboriginal ceramics. In addition, some may have been used as pins to secure clothing in the absence of buttons or to bundle hides together. Long, slender examples, especially those with ornamented ends, might have functioned as hairpins.

NEEDLES. Small sewing needles are unknown from sites in New Jersey, but aboriginal sewing technology was well developed in the Northeast at least by Late Archaic times (Ritchie 1965:112 [pl. 38, fig. 10]; Tuck 1976a:41–43 [pl. 32, figs. 1, 2]). Among the very few needles reported from New Jersey are long, flat, and bluntly pointed ones—made from the ribs of large mammals—retrieved from late prehistoric sites in Sussex County (Ritchie 1949:177 [pl. 7]; H. Kraft 1978:72 [fig. 46]). Perforated near mid-length, these needles were probably used for weaving nets or mats, as was the custom among ethnographically known Indian groups (Skinner and Schrabisch 1913:28).

A deer antler needle was found in an Early Woodland shell deposit near East Point on the Delaware Bay (Mounier 1974b:47 [pl. 5, fig. 5]). This specimen measures $3\frac{3}{8}$ inches in length, $\frac{3}{8}$ inches in width, and about $\frac{1}{4}$ inch in thickness (8.6 × 0.95 × 0.6 cm). Sharply pointed on one end, this needle is round in cross section near the point and flattens toward the notched base, which also bears a small bi-conical eye. The notch in the base is semicircular in outline, suggesting failure through an earlier perforation. Polish around the notch indicates that the needle may have been forced through fabric or knots in netting with a small stick or push-rod.

A small round-eyed needle from the Abbott Farm (Cross 1956:119 [pl. 29a, fig. 5]) may have been used to close fabric or net bags by stitching or, possibly, to run a loop of cord through meat for suspension while curing. Among Plains Indians, similar devices have been used for holding feathers or plumes for personal adornment (Ritchie 1965:118 [pl. 39, figs. 9–10]).

PROJECTILE POINTS. Antler tines were well suited to arming projectiles. The tines were cut into sections by grooving the circumference with a sharp instrument and snapping off the tip. Unfinished specimens from East Point at the mouth of the Maurice River in Cumberland County reveal this age-old technique (Mounier 1974b:47 [pl. 5, fig. 4]). M. R. Harrington (1909a) and Alanson Skinner (1932:44) reported that incomplete points and cut antlers

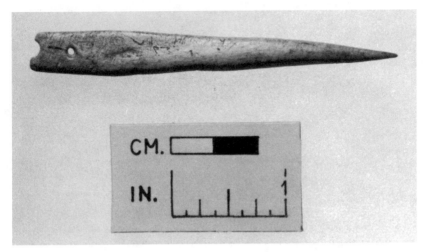

FIGURE 60. Deer antler needle. Photograph by the author.

were common in the shell heaps around New York City. The tips were sharpened and the points made symmetrical by grinding. Often the base was ground
perpendicular to the axis of the point, creating a flat-based cone. Sometimes
the base was cut on an angle or was notched to create barbs. Then the base
was hollowed to receive the arrow shaft, which, we suppose, was fixed with
pitch or hide glue.

Conical antler arrowheads have been found at a number of sites in New
Jersey and adjoining states (Harrington 1909a,b; Skinner 1909, 1932:17–19;
Skinner and Schrabisch 1913:29; Heye and Pepper 1915:74 [pl. 10a]; Cross
1956:118–119; Omwake 1963:11; Mounier 1974b:47; H. Kraft 1976b:24). Typical examples are 1–2 inches (2.5–5.0 cm) long and about ½ to ⅝ inch (1.3–
1.6 cm) in diameter. Similar points were made from tubular sections of bone,
cut on a long taper and honed to a sharp point. Apparently, triangular points
were also fashioned from flat plates of bone (Skinner and Schrabisch 1913:29;
Ritchie 1944:391 [pl. 160, fig. 11]; Curbishley 1954:16). The pointed tails of the
horseshoe crab (*Limulus polyphemus*) and the barbed dorsal spines of sting rays
(*Dasyatis spp.*) might have made effective arrowheads, but no weapons of this
sort are known from archaeology.

Although common elsewhere (Ritchie 1965:243–245; Tuck 1976a:36–
37), barbed bone or antler points for small game hunting and fishing are virtually nonexistent in archaeological situations in New Jersey. Cross (1956:119
[pl. 29a, fig. 2]) described one small irregularly notched bone point from the

FIGURE 61. Deer antler harpoon. Found at the Abbott Farm near the falls of the Delaware River, this harpoon was probably used for taking sturgeon during their seasonal runs. Courtesy of the New Jersey State Museum.

Abbott Farm. Although this object was listed as a "doubtful artifact," it may have been used as a weapon tip; the notches would have held fast in the traumatized flesh of the prey (cf. Ritchie 1965:245).

Two spectacular harpoons, both of antler, were found at the Abbott Farm (Cross 1956:119–120 [pl. 29a, fig. 11, and pl. 29b]). These are the only examples so far reported from New Jersey. One of the harpoons has two barbs, the other only one. The larger specimen measures 6¾ × 1 ½ inches (17 × 3.8 cm), the smaller 5¹⁄₁₆ × 1⅛ inches (12.9 × 2.9 cm). Both harpoons taper in thickness from the midsection toward each end, and both have a perforation or line hole near the base. Cross (1956:120), in a rare misstatement, reported that the perforations allowed the head to be secured to the shaft. By definition, however, harpoons are "barbed . . . weapons with a line hole and . . . a base designed *not* to be permanently fixed to a shaft" (Tuck 1976a:36, emphasis in original). Once embedded in the prey, the head would detach from the shaft, allowing the hunter to restrain the quarry by means of the line until it could be captured and killed. Such weapons were used for hunting fish or aquatic mammals that were too large and powerful to be taken directly. As Cross (1956:120) has correctly noted, these harpoons "undoubtedly were used in spearing large fish, presumably sturgeon, which were abundant in the vicinity of the Abbott Farm." This method of fishing has been described among the historic Indians of New England (Willoughby 1935:218). No fishhooks—save for possible double-pointed bone gorges—have been reported from sites in New Jersey.

FLAKING TOOLS. Antler was used for two kinds of stone-flaking tools: bluntly pointed pressure flakers and cylindrical batons. As described above, pressure flakers were used to drive off flakes by the application of pressure to the edge of a stone tool or weapon. Batons were used as hammers for knocking off flakes by percussion. Generally, antler tines were used for pressure work, whereas the beams were used as batons. Experimental archaeology demonstrates that bone could be used for either task, but antler, being at once more dense and less brittle, is better suited to the work. Carefully selected wooden batons also produce good results in the hands of an expert knapper. Of course, wooden batons do not survive archaeologically, and their use must be inferred from the characteristics of the flakes thereby produced (Jack Cresson, pers. comm.). Antler flaking tools have been found at various sites around the state (Cross 1941:141 [pl. 65b], 1956:119; Ritchie 1949:177 [pl. 7, fig. 7]; H. Kraft 1972:29, 1978:73 [fig. 40]; Marchiando 1972:142 [fig. 42x–z]; Mounier 1974b:52; Chrisbacher 1990:75 [fig. 9]).

CUTTING TOOLS. Scrapers, gouges, and chisels were sometimes made from sturdy pieces of bone or antler. At the Rosenkrans Ferry site in Sussex County, Cross (1941:141) found a small scraper that had been made by sharpening the edge of a bone fragment. She also noted chisel-pointed antler prongs from the Abbott Farm.

Hide-dressing tools have been reported from sites in Sussex County (Ritchie 1949:177; H. Kraft 1978:72–73), from the vicinity of Trenton (Skinner 1932:43), and from Cumberland County (Curbishley 1954:19). These tools were fashioned from the lower leg bones—usually the metatarsus or tibia—of deer and bears by removing a long, shallow slab from one surface. This process exposed the hollow core of the bone and left two sharp ridges, which were effective in defleshing animal hides. The joints served as handles. Among traditional tanners, these implements are known as "beaming tools" or "beamers," because the hide is draped over a beam (usually an inclined log or plank) while being worked.

The large front teeth (incisors) of beavers and woodchucks were employed as carving tools. This practice was widespread in the Northeast during Archaic and Woodland times. Numerous rodent incisors have been found, either loose or hafted in bone or antler grips. Many were ground to special forms for working wood and bone (Skinner 1932:44; Ritchie 1944, 1965; Omwake 1963:12; Tuck 1976a:47–48). Beaver incisors have been found on sites near Trenton (Volk 1911:78, 83) and in Gloucester County (Mounier 1974a).

BEADS AND TUBES. Beads and tubes, cut from bird bone, have been reported from sites around Trenton (Volk 1911:19; Curbishley 1954:19; Cross 1956: 119) and in the Delaware Valley above the Water Gap (Marchiando 1972:142 [fig. 42ee]; H. Kraft 1978:75). At the Minisink site, Herbert Kraft (1978:75 [fig. 47]) found a necklace consisting of five cut sections of bird bone, each about 5/16 inch in diameter and up to 2¼ inches in length (0.8 × 5.7 cm), along with a perforated shark's tooth. Several other short bird bone beads were recovered from the same site and from the nearby Bell-Browning site (Marchiando 1972:142 [fig. 42ee]). A triply perforated bird bone tube from the Pahaquarra site may have been a whistle or flute (H. Kraft 1976a:53 [fig. 18k]). At more distant sites, long bird bone tubes have been interpreted as musical instruments, game calls, drinking straws, and sucking tubes for shamanistic curing rituals (Ritchie 1944:84, 279, 298, 1965:69, 119, 138; Omwake 1963:12; Tuck 1976:72–74).

HAIR PINS AND COMBS. Artifacts that can be identified unequivocally as examples of decorative bone pins have not been reported from New Jersey. One knobbed bone rod from the Abbott Farm is a possible exception (Curbishley 1954:20; Cross 1956:119). Skinner reported a round-headed antler pin from Staten Island (Skinner and Schrabisch 1913:29; Skinner 1932:44). Slender pins that terminate in effigies or ornamented capitals are known from Kentucky (Webb 1945:291–294), New York State (Ritchie 1944:66 [pl. 30], 1965:298), and Canada (Tuck 1976a:58). Some of these have been found in circumstances that suggest probable service as hair pins or garment fasteners.

Decorative combs carved in antler or bone also appear in the assemblages just mentioned but are rare in New Jersey, where examples are limited to the vicinity of Minisink Island in Sussex County. These combs typically have several elongated teeth carved on one end and a decorative device on the other. Herbert Kraft (1978:75 [fig. 43]) found a fragmentary bone comb with three widely spaced teeth that take up about half the length of the piece; the other end bears an elongated V-shaped notch that terminates in an oval perforation. This specimen is about 4¼ inches long and about 1 inch wide (10.7 × 2.5 cm). Another bone comb from the same locale has ten teeth surmounted by a seated canine figure (Heye and Pepper 1915:18 [fig. 2]). It measures 3½ × 1⅜ inches (8.9 × 3.5 cm). Finally, Ritchie (1949:177) briefly reported on three bone and antler comb fragments that lacked the toothed section. The decorative fields consisted of geometric designs executed with small drilled pits (Ritchie 1949:250–255 [pl. 7, fig. 1, pl. 9, fig. 8, pl. 9, fig. 7]).

The use of perforated sharks' teeth for ornamentation has already been noted (also see Abbott 1881:405). The teeth of bears, wolves, large dogs, and other mammals were probably employed in this way, as in New York State (Ritchie 1965:62, 116 [pl. 20, fig. 8, pl. 39, figs. 13–15]) and New England (Willoughby 1935: fig. 1210), but the references to actual archaeological examples from New Jersey are very vague (Abbott 1881:406; Stanzeski 1996:43).

CUPS AND RATTLES. Native peoples used the natural cavity of the turtle carapace (upper shell) for cups, bowls, and rattles. The vertebral elements of the carapace were scraped away when the shell was used as a bowl or cup, and the edges were sometimes notched for decoration or identification. A perforation near the rim allowed for suspension. Objects of this sort have been recovered from various parts of the state, usually as furniture in late prehistoric graves (Volk 1911:22, 54 [pl. 37]; Heye and Pepper 1915:74; Skinner 1932:44; H. Kraft 1976a:52 [fig. 18l], 1978:79 [fig. 45]; Blenk 1977a) and always involving the common box turtle (*Terrapene carolina*). Similar finds have been reported from coastal areas of New York State (Harrington 1924:272; Ritchie 1965:266) and Delaware (Omwake 1963).

Rattles were made by sealing a few small pebbles within the turtle shells. A nice example was excavated from a grave at the Munsee cemetery (Heye and Pepper 1915:46 [pl. 11, fig. 18]). In this piece, the lower part of the shell, or plastron, had multiple perforations, perhaps for attachment of a handle or ornamental trinkets. The occasional discovery of small accumulations of quartz pebbles suggests the former presence of rattles whose organic components have been lost to decay (Hawkes and Linton 1916:76). Examples of turtle shell rattles are well known beyond New Jersey (Ritchie 1944:46, 1965:119, 252, 293, 299 [pl. 41, figs. 1, 3, 4]).

RECREATIONAL PIECES. Recreational pieces are rare. Small cups or cones made by hollowing out and perforating the toe bones of deer are thought to be elements of the traditional cup-and-pin game, in which the player attempts to catch a tossed cup on the end of a bone pin (Willoughby 1935:226–227 [fig. 121k–n, q]; Ritchie 1944:50 [pl. 29, figs. 27–31], 1949:177 [pl. 7, fig. 5], 1965:268, 288, 293 [pl. 92, fig. 16]; Webb 1946:291; H. Kraft 1978:81 [fig. 46]). William Ritchie (1944:50, 1965:268) suggested the possibility that these phalangeal cups also served as fringe ornaments on skin clothing.

At the Minisink site, Herbert Kraft (1978:73 [fig. 44]) found two polished rectangles cut from the plastrons of box turtles and measuring ½ ×

1½ inches (1.3 × 3.8 cm). He suggested a use in sewing or mat making; alternatively, they may have been gaming pieces.

REFUSE BONE. On sites where organic preservation is good, quantities of faunal remains have been found, including some calcined bone fragments. Refuse bones often show evidence of butchering, particularly cracking for marrow extraction. To the extent that they reflect human behavior, refuse bones can be considered as artifacts.

The widely varying species represented give an idea of the kinds of animals that were present at the time of occupation. The most common mammalian species found in faunal assemblages from archaeological sites in New Jersey (Volk 1911; Mounier 1974b:47; H. Kraft 1978:28–36; Parris n.d.) include the following: deer (*Odocoileus virginianus*), elk (*Cervus canadensis*), dog or wolf (*Canis familiaris* or *C. lupus*), gray fox (*Urocyon cinereoargenteus*), black bear (*Ursus americanus*), raccoon (*Procyon lotor*), beaver (*Castor fiber* or *C. canadensis*), porcupine (*Erethizon dorsatum*), lynx (*Lynx rufus*), gray squirrel (*Sciurus carolinensis*), and striped skunk (*Mephitis mephitis*). Wild turkey (*Meleagris gallopavo*), Canada goose (*Branta canadensis*), and ducks (various species) are among the large birds. Turtles include the common box turtle (*Terrapene carolina*), the common mud turtle (*Kinosternon subrubrum*), and, in coastal areas, the diamondback terrapin (*Malaclemys terrapin*). Fish bones, bony plates (or scutes), and scales are sometimes present. Excavations at the Abbott Farm (Volk 1911:67; Cross 1956: 120; Cavallo 1987:25, 231) revealed evidence for the taking of Atlantic sturgeon (*Acipenser oxyrhynchus*) and shad (*Alosa sappidissima*). Assorted mice, snakes, and toads make up a minority of the faunal assemblages. Although these species may have been captured and eaten or exploited in other ways, they also may have found their way into archaeological deposits simply by burrowing.

Wooden Artifacts

Because of their perishable nature, wooden artifacts are rarely seen on archaeological sites. Wood will survive only under special conditions that restrict decay or insect infestation. Inadvertent contamination with verdigris (copper salts) is one means of preservation, charring is another, and continuous immersion in water or saturated sediments is yet a third. At Minisink Island, Sussex County, a small wooden bowl found inside a brass kettle had been preserved by verdigris contact (H. Kraft 1992c). Charring can preserve organic materials (cf. Ritchie 1965:185); but so far as is known, no artifacts of carbonized wood—other than charcoal—have ever come to light in New Jersey. The most common wooden items to survive in archaeological situations are dugout canoes, several of which have been retrieved in waterlogged condition from anaerobic sediments in the banks of streams and ponds.

Canoes were hollowed out by selective burning, hewing, and scraping. The material weakened by charring was removed with axes, adzes, and gouges. The bow and stern were pointed to facilitate movement through the water. Cross (1986) mentioned lengths ranging from 12 to 40 feet. Complete examples in museums are from 12 to 16 feet long and not more than 3 feet in width, owing to the size of available trees. According to Lenape tradition, the tulip poplar (*Liriodendron tulipifera*) was the favored species for canoe making (Rementer 1987), but Atlantic white cedar (*Chamaecyparis thyoides*) and other trees were apparently used (Philhower 1931:17; Kier 1960; Cross 1986:25). Naturally, these vessels must have been quite ponderous, and portage would have been difficult or impossible. But once afloat, the canoes would have eased the transportation of heavy or bulky goods. Push poles or paddles would have provided propulsion. While such implements are unknown from New Jersey, Harrington (1924:258) reported the discovery in 1880 of a deteriorated oak paddle from Canoe Place on eastern Long Island.

Aboriginal watercraft were sometimes made from the bark of elm, oak, or hickory trees (Newcomb 1956:29), but none survive archaeologically, so far as is known. Contrary to popular opinion, there is no evidence for the manufacture of birch bark canoes, so common among more northerly peoples.

More than a dozen dugout canoes have been found around the state, mostly along the tidal meadows of the Delaware Bay and its tributaries. Philhower (1931:17) reported the discovery of dugouts near Seaville, Tuckahoe, and Dennisville in Cape May County, and at Dividing Creek and Newport Neck in Cumberland County. Another apparently came from the bay shore at Gandy's Beach, also in Cumberland County (Jean Jones, pers. comm.). Skinner mentioned a canoe from West Creek near Little Egg Harbor in Ocean County (Skinner and Schrabisch 1913:50), and Cross (1986) noted another from the Hackensack Meadows, probably in Bergen County.

Additional specimens have been retrieved near Port Republic and Da Costa in Atlantic County, at Vineland in Cumberland County, and at Hurffville in Gloucester County (Philhower 1931:17; F. Stewart 1932:22; Kier 1960; Cross 1986). The last three locations are in the headwaters of coastal streams, and these discoveries indicate that aboriginal navigation followed the watercourses well into the interior of the coastal plain.

A dugout canoe fragment was found many years ago in the bottom of Sand Pond, near Vernon in Sussex County. Radiocarbon dating demonstrates that this canoe probably was made about 450 years ago (*Advertiser-News*, North Edition, 11 July 1996).

About 25 years ago, two canoe fragments came to light in Cumberland County. One abandoned canoe had been morticed into the timbers of an old mill at Laurel Lake (Everett Turner, pers. comm.). The other, if the prevailing rumor is true, came from the vicinity of Dividing Creek, but the finder would not divulge the exact location of discovery. The specimen from Laurel Lake had a surviving length of 27 inches (68.6 cm), a width of 16 inches (40.6 cm), and a height of 11¼ inches (28.6 cm). The hollowed hull was 8–10 inches (20.3–25.4 cm) deep. The bottom was somewhat flattened and met the sidewalls at an obtuse angle (approximately 120°). Because the bottom had been hewn to fit into a historic timber structure, the original configuration could not be ascertained. The walls tapered to narrow, rounded edges at the gunwales.

The other canoe fragment had a length of 39 inches (99.1 cm), a width of 18½ inches (46.9 cm), and a height in the range of 10 to 11¼ inches (25.4–28.6 cm). The hollow in the hull was quite shallow, on the order of 6–8 inches (15.2 to 20.3 cm). The sides were tangent to the rounded bottom. The gunwales were squared off and had a width of approximately 2¼ inches (5.7 cm).

Because of deterioration, the parent wood of these two specimens could not be identified by direct observation. So far as is known, neither of these fragments received the treatment necessary to ensure conservation, and both have now almost certainly crumbled to dust.

Although most of the dugout canoes that have been recovered probably date to aboriginal times, the use of log canoes continued into the historic period. One log canoe, apparently of historic origin, is on display at the New Jersey Historical Society in Newark.

Shell Artifacts

Aboriginal shell artifacts, which are quite scarce, generally take the form of simple ornaments and utensils. After contact with European cultures, trade in elaborately worked shell beads and other trinkets increased appreciably. Animal effigies, disks, and elongated beads are more common on Iroquois sites in New York State (Skinner 1921:113–116 [figs. 28–30]) and Susquehannock sites around Lancaster, Pennsylvania (Kent 1984:171–174), than on any sites in New Jersey.

SIMPLE SHELL OBJECTS. A few simple shell beads have been found on prehistoric sites dating to Early Woodland times, mostly in mortuary contexts (H. Kraft 1976a:18, 23 [figs. 3k, 9e]). These beads were manufactured from the central column of conchs or whelks (*Busycon canaliculatum* or *B. carica*). Several small conch column cylinders—apparently intended for beadwork but never drilled—were found in a late prehistoric site near Avalon in Cape May County (Mounier 1998c:14). Herbert Kraft (1978:77 [fig. 50c]) found another worked conch whorl at the Minisink site.

Pendants and utensils fashioned from oyster shells (*Crassostrea virginica*) have turned up occasionally in native graves of the late prehistoric and historic eras (Cross 1941:112; Blenk 1977b; H. Kraft 1978:77 [fig. 50a]). Each of four triangular shell pendants from the Munsee cemetery takes the form of an isosceles triangle, broken through a perforation in the most acute corner. These simple pendants may have been the work of native craftsmen, but their association with items of European manufacture clouds the identity of their makers. At the nearby Minisink site, Herbert Kraft (1978:75 [fig. 50b]) also found a lozenge-shaped bead or pendant worked from a marine clam shell.

ANIMAL EFFIGY PENDANTS AND BEADS. The so-called Munsee cemetery yielded several ornaments in the form of birds, fish, and furbearers (Heye and Pepper 1915:30–44 [figs. 3–17, pls. 8–9]). These items were almost certainly produced by Europeans for trade with the natives. The bird effigies mostly represent geese and owls, generally with the wings folded. At first glance they resemble the form of bowling pins. The largest of these specimens stands about 1¼ inches (3.2 cm) high and ¾ inch (1.9 cm) in diameter. Similar animal effigy beads or pendants were also found in graves at Trenton (Skinner and Schrabisch 1913:29, 65; Veit and Bello 2001) and at West Long Branch in Monmouth County (Pietak 1995:194–195).

Some of the owl effigies from the Munsee cemetery appear with wings outspread (Heye and Pepper 1915:37 [figs. 10–13, pl. 9a, b]). One forked-tailed specimen, again with outspread wings, probably represents a swallow or kite. This object, the largest of the avian effigies, measures approximately 2⅛ inches (5.4 cm) high, with a wingspan of 3³⁄₁₆ inches (8.1 cm).

Found at the same site were piscine (fishlike) effigies in jumping postures, up to 3 inches (7.6 cm) in length, and a figure that represents a lamprey eel (also about 3 inches in length). Finally, there is a small beaver effigy that is about 2¼ inches (5.7 cm) in length.

Most of these objects have ornamentation in the form of shallow linear incisions and drill-pit punctations arranged in lines or geometric patterns. The

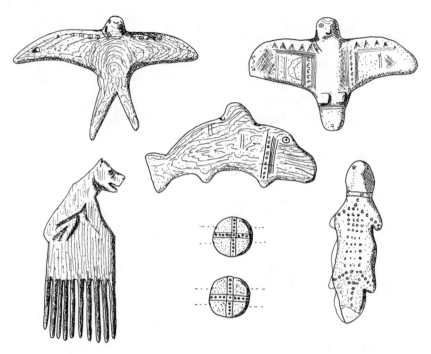

FIGURE 62. Zoömorphic effigies and runtees (after Heye and Pepper 1915). Shell ornaments depicting a kite (upper left), an owl (upper right), a fish (center), and a beaver (lower right) were found in Indian graves along the Delaware River in Sussex County. The decorative bone comb, with a canine effigy (lower left) and shell disks, or runtees, are from the same site. These items may have been made by Europeans for the Indian trade. Sketch by the author.

eyes and mouths are represented by dots and lines, respectively. The designs were generally filled in with black pigment to contrast with the white bodies.

SHELL DISKS. The Munsee cemetery contained several unusual shell disks, known as *runtees*. These items, apparently made from large conch shells, range from ¾ inch to 1³/₁₆ inches in diameter (1.9–3.0 cm) and are scarcely ¼ inch (0.6 cm) in thickness. These disks usually have two parallel, edgewise (or diametral) perforations. One or both faces carried simple cruciform designs executed by pairs of parallel incisions and shallow drill pits. In one grave, the arrangement of several runtees, alternating in a repeating series with glass and shell beads, indicates that these objects formed part of a close-fitting necklace or collar of the sort popularly known as a "choker" (Heye and Pepper 1915:32 [pl. 8b]; H. Kraft 1976a:62 [fig. 32i], 1986b:204 [fig. 39j]).

Larger disks of the same general style were up to 3 inches (7.6 cm) in diameter and sometimes bore intricate floral designs or patterns of intersecting arcs, which must have been laid out with the aid of dividers. Some of these large runtees were perforated diametrally; others were drilled through the center in the manner of buttons or through one edge as pendants (Heye and Pepper 1915:33–34 [figs. 4–5]; H. Kraft 1986b:204 [fig. 38t]).

HAIRPIPES. Also occasionally found in Indian graves of the historic period are long, slender beads known as *hairpipes* (Heye and Pepper 1915:43 [pl. 9c]; H. Kraft 1976a:59 [fig. 21d], 1986b:204 [fig. 39i]). These longitudinally drilled beads were as much as 6½ inches (16.5 cm) in length but scarcely ⅜ inch (0.95 cm) in diameter. A historic Indian burial from the Pahaquarra site shows that these ornaments were worn as choker necklaces or collars (H. Kraft 1976a:59 [fig. 21d]).

WAMPUM BEADS. The widespread ornamental use of shell, particularly for wampum beads, correlates with the period of European contact (H. Kraft 1986b:202). The manufacture of wampum apparently began in New England in the early years of the seventeenth century, if not before (Becker 1980:1–4). Wampum beads were small perforated cylinders made from the valves of hard-shell clam or quahog (*Mercenaria mercenaria*). The colors varied depending on the part of the shell from which the beads were cut. White beads came from the main body of the shell, while the colored varieties—purple, blue, black, and brown—derived from the tinted portion near the hinge. Ancient wampum beads generally measured about ¼ inch long and ⅛ inch thick (6.3 × 3.2 mm), with a small longitudinal perforation (Skinner and Schrabisch 1913: 12), but the overall size varied considerably. Later examples were markedly longer than the earlier ones (Becker 1980:8 [table 2]).

Wampum beads figured prominently in Indian trade around the time of European contact, partly because of the native practice of exchanging gifts when agreements were made between trading partners. A modest aboriginal industry assumed greater proportions as Europeans vied for furs and land. Wampum quickly became a medium of exchange, with values fixed in relation to various European currencies (Becker 1980:8 [table 1]). In fact, the use of wampum as "Indian money" gave rise to the species name, *mercenaria*, for the hard-shell clam: literally, the mollusk from which money was made. The colored beads, being less common, generally had twice the value of the white beads.

Skinner reported aboriginal wampum factories at Cape May, but no such sites have ever been investigated (Skinner and Schrabisch 1913:12). Realizing the importance of wampum in the native economy and in aboriginal social relations, Europeans quickly took to producing shell beads for the Indian trade in England (Becker 1980:6) and in Holland (H. Kraft 1986b:203). Wampum factories were also established by Europeans in New Jersey at Pascack, now Park Ridge (H. Kraft 1986b:207), and at Hawthorne (Haggerty 1980), both in Bergen County. The Campbell factory at Pascack continued to produce wampum for trade to Indians in the West as late as 1890 (Becker 1980:10; H. Kraft 1986b:207).

COMPOSITE ARTIFACTS. I reported the discovery of a composite earring, made of shell and brass beads, in an Indian burial (Mounier 1974c). This item may have been made by Europeans or fabricated by natives from a bit of shell and scraps of a brass trade kettle. The composite nature of many other complex artifacts—such as arrows, which were constructed of diverse materials—has been concealed by the decay of their organic components.

SHELL TOOLS. On some coastal sites, fragmentary valves of the hard-shell clam reveal notched and striated edges, suggestive of their use as scraping tools (Mounier 1974b:52). A number of acutely pointed specimens show worn edges that might have resulted from use as knives or scrapers (Brett 1974). Stanzeski (1981) has concluded that whole clams were used as hammers to open other clams. Stanzeski (1996:42) also mentioned, but did not describe, whelk shell tools. One supposes that the bulbous cavity of the whelk could have been used as a primitive scoop. At the Blue Hole site in Camden County, I found a unique shell object having a notched, semicircular edge, superficially resembling the string bridge on a violin (Mounier 1972a:24 [fig. 51]). Although its function has not been determined, it may have been a dentate stamp or roulette for decorating pottery.

Because the analysis of "shell tools" has never proceeded beyond an anecdotal level of reporting, any conclusions regarding their actual functions must be viewed with skepticism.

SHELL REFUSE. Shell refuse appears on many coastal sites in the form of cast-off oyster (*Crassostrea virginica*) and clam shells (both *Mercenaria mercenaria* and *Mya aranaria*), and, with less frequency, the shells of whelks or conchs (*Busycon spp.*), mussels (*Mytilus edulis*), and scallops (*Pecten irradians*). References to marine shellfish in archaeological deposits are common (Cook 1868:362, 501; Abbott 1881:447; Jordan 1906:11–18; Cross 1941:36, 39, 41–43, 1956:55, 161; Mounier 1974b:42, 51–52, 1998c:4–6). Some sites along nontidal streams have yielded shells of freshwater mussels (*Unio spp.* and *Elliptio complanatus*). Unio shells have been observed here and there, especially around Trenton (Abbott 1907:60; Volk 1911:19, 70), in the upper Delaware Valley, and in rock shelters in the mountainous parts of the state (Schrabisch 1915:19, 1917:31). Along the Delaware River, at Trenton and above the Water Gap, the exploitation of mussels, particularly *Elliptio complanatus*, was pronounced (Cross 1941:135, 138, 142, 149; H. Kraft 1972:42, 1975a:72–73, 155, 156–157, 1976a:43–46, 52).

TEXTILES

The direct survival of aboriginal textiles is extremely unusual, although in a few cases small scraps of woven material and cordage have been found. Graves of the Middlesex complex have yielded patches of textiles and short lengths of yarn, which were preserved by charring or by contact with copper artifacts (Kraft 1976b:24–25 [fig. 11f, g]; Mounier 1981b:59–60). Impressions left on pottery attest to a wide range of twined, twilled, and plaited fabrics or mats, as well as two- and three-ply cordage and nets (Hoerler 1939; Cross 1941, 1956; McCann 1950:315–317, 1957; Kier and Calverley 1957:86–90; Morris et al. 1996; R. Stewart 1998; Mounier n.d.a). The abundance of stone weights at good fishing spots clearly implies the use of cords and nets for taking fish. Positive casts of cordage and fabric impressions can be obtained by the use of plaster, modeling clay, wax, or latex.

ARTICLES OF SYNTHETIC MATERIALS

Ancient artisans devised a number of synthetic materials, that is, substances that do not occur in nature. The most obvious, by reason of preservation, is pottery, which has already been described in some detail. Occasionally, traces of pitch are found on the hafting elements of stone tools, and one supposes that a variety of adhesives were manufactured by heating naturally occurring gums and resins and by boiling skins, hides, and hooves. In addition, if only rarely, paints made by mixing powdered pigments with a vehicle of animal fat appear as faint coatings on artifacts and fossils, as previously noted.

FIGURE 63. Cord impressions in clay. This piece of modeling clay reveals the cast of cordage used to decorate a late prehistoric vessel. Although perishable artifacts seldom survive, their impressions are often preserved in pottery. Photograph by the author.

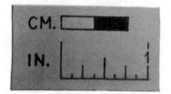

METALLIC ARTIFACTS

Aboriginal craftsmen possessed no metallurgical skills beyond shaping nuggets of copper; hence, we see no alloys, castings, or ironwork until the period of European intrusion, beginning in the seventeenth century. Copper spears or knives and a celt of the same material have been found at Trenton (Abbott 1885b; Skinner and Schrabisch 1913:30). Beads of beaten copper have been reported from the Abbott Farm, Rosenkrans Ferry, and a few other locations (Skinner 1915:8; Carpenter 1950; Cross 1956:60, 63, 121–123; H. Kraft 1976b, 1986b:99–104, 1998; Mounier 1981b). Both the Abbott Farm (Cross 1956:123) and the Rosenkrans Ferry sites (H. Kraft 1976b:21) yielded copper boatstones. Herbert Kraft (1976b:23, 31) also reported the discovery of a copper celt and a rare copper awl from the Rosenkrans Ferry site. Most of these finds represent elements of Middlesex complex burials. At the Abbott Farm, a splendid copper pin was found in the midst of a large cache of Fox Creek bifaces. This specimen measures nearly 14 inches (35.2 cm) in length and somewhat more than ¼ inch (8 mm) in diameter. The pin tapers to a point on one end, and an eye was formed in the opposite end by bending the shaft into a loop, which was bound with several turns of copper wire. Richard Veit reported an unusual copper axe in a private collection from Old Bridge in Middlesex County (Veit, pers. comm.).

Natives also made or used ornaments, trinkets, and arrowheads that had been fabricated from portions of brass kettles or iron implements obtained in trade with Europeans (Skinner 1932:44–45; Marchiando 1972:143; Mounier 1974c; H. Kraft 1978:77 [fig. 51]; Veit 1994; Stanzeski 1996:44).

TRADE GOODS

Abstracts of Indian deeds indicate a vigorous trade with Europeans for tools, weapons, ornaments, and other goods (F. Stewart 1932:60–87). Typical listings include axes, adzes, hoes, awls, fishhooks, guns, gunpowder, lead, knives, beads, needles, scissors, mirrors, jew's harps, clothing, kettles, and alcoholic drinks. However, relatively few objects of this sort have ever come to light on archaeological sites in New Jersey. Notable exceptions have been reported by Heye and Pepper (1915:49–58) and by Herbert Kraft (1976a:56–63, 1978:77) from sites along the Delaware River above the Water Gap, where Indian graves of the historic period contained an abundance of trade items. Cross (1941:111) found beads, trade pipes, and other commodities at the Lenhardt site in Monmouth County and at the Abbott Farm (1956:111). Volk (1911:191, 194, 197) reported the discovery of European trinkets in Indian graves near Trenton. Veit and Bello (2001) were able to locate some of the trade items—shell effigy beads, a brass snuff box, and the like—previously exhumed from historic Indian burials from the same locale (see Skinner and Schrabisch 1913:65). Native burials from West Long Branch, Monmouth County, contained necklaces and bracelets composed of shell effigies, wampum, and glass beads, as well as metal bracelets, bangles or jinglers, and pewter spoons (Pietak 1995:194–195). Stanzeski (1996:44) reported a small suite of trade goods from the West Creek site in Ocean County, and Lenik (1989) did the same for several sites in northeastern New Jersey.

The relative paucity of trade goods found in New Jersey stands in stark contrast to the wealth of such items discovered in the Susquehanna Valley of Pennsylvania (Kent 1984:203–294 [figs. 51–87]) and at the historic Iroquois sites of New York State (Ritchie 1965:323 [pls. 112, 113]). This disparity has baffled archaeologists in New Jersey for nearly a century. As early as 1912, Skinner lamented, "How rarely do we find an iron trade ax, a brass arrow point, or a glass bead" (Skinner and Schrabisch 1913:30). Perhaps one explanation is that the Susquehanna, Hudson, and Mohawk Rivers—which penetrate the interior far more deeply than the Delaware—were the major trade corridors in early historic times. Consequently, the inhabitants of the Delaware Valley would have received fewer trade goods than their neighbors to the west and north.

In addition, data from radiocarbon assays suggest a serious decline in New Jersey's native population by the time of the European incursion. Although there are numerous carbon-dated assemblages for the period from A.D. 1000 to 1300, only a few occur in the following centuries (Mounier 1991: VI-11; R. Stewart 1998:213–221). European—indeed, global—diseases had been imported to the Atlantic coast prior to colonization in the seventeenth century. Peter Lindeström (1925:127–128), a Swedish military engineer who visited the Delaware Valley in the middle of the seventeenth century, was aware of epidemics among natives probably before 1640, and in 1677 New Jersey's natives claimed that smallpox had afflicted them for three generations (S. Smith 1765:101–102). Arbitrarily assuming 25-year generations, this information would indicate epidemics at about 1625, 1650, and 1675. Witthoft (1963:64) pointed out that, through the agency of disease, "for most coastal areas, the archaeological record disappears at the very threshold of contact times. Stable Indian communities of prehistory had ceased to exist."

Furthermore, the fur trade rapidly declined in New Jersey under pressure from hunting. In 1644 Johan Printz, the governor of New Sweden, reported, "We have no beaver trade with them, but only the maize trade. They are a lot of poor rascals" (Printz 1912; also quoted in H. Kraft 1986b:200). Items received in trade rapidly found their way into Indian burials, and grave robbers—whose foul work was reported with disgust by Lindeström (1925:251) as early as the mid-1650s—undoubtedly dispersed quantities of trade goods back into European hands.

Still, the lack of trade goods may be more apparent than real. We have skimpy information about Contact Period cemeteries and even less concerning habitations. It may well be that many early trade articles reside unknown in private collections.

————

THE ANCIENT INHABITANTS of New Jersey possessed a varied material culture—or, more properly, a series of material cultures—that vastly exceeded the range of items known from archaeology. They developed all of the fundamental technologies necessary for long-term survival. They had a keen knowledge of the raw materials provided by nature and knew how to work them to their advantage, often in ingenious ways. Surviving artifacts frequently show a high level of technical sophistication accompanied by a well-developed regard for aesthetics. The ethereal and material aspects of culture were intimately intertwined, each permeating and influencing the other. Taken as a whole, the archaeological record demonstrates an integration of the social and natural environments in ways that were at once subtle and profound. Archaeology provides a slanted view of ancient life, largely because preservation favors artifacts of pottery and stone. Nevertheless, a close look—especially at those items least likely to survive in the ground—reveals that natives did not endure an impoverished Stone Age existence.

3

A Good Place to Live and Work

Settlement is man's first step towards adapting himself to his environment . . . and [is] the projection on the ground of the community's social structure.

———

AIMÉ VINCENT PERPILLOU (1966)

Just as we do today, our aboriginal forebears needed good places to live and work. Evidence in the form of artifacts, structural remains, and refuse deposits defines the primeval settlements of New Jersey. The geographic distribution of archaeological sites identifies the places that ancient people regarded as favorable for dwellings, work stations, and cemeteries. The material contents of those sites tell us how ancient folks lived and worked. This chapter describes the known types of sites and how they are arrayed on the landscape.

Literally thousands of prehistoric sites have been found in New Jersey, mostly on well-drained ground near streams or other bodies of water, where nature afforded opportunities for habitation, hunting, fishing, or foraging. Loose, sandy or loamy soils were preferred to hard, stony ground; the sandier ground provided both a modicum of personal comfort and freedom from flooding. Shelter from the elements was also a factor in site selection, especially for winter quarters. In addition, accessibility was important. Max Schrabisch (1917:13–14) noted that, as a rule, native settlements were situated "near the primitive thoroughfares, in the valleys or in less rugged regions. . . . Camping grounds are rarely met in the mountains or high upon their slopes."

Prehistoric sites vary in size from large, artifact-rich settlements that cover several acres to isolated findspots that have yielded nothing more than a stray arrowhead or a meager assortment of stone flakes. Most of the sites appear to represent small, intermittent occupations of short duration, perhaps devoted to specific tasks in a seasonal economic round—fishing in the springtime, harvesting clams and oysters in the warm months, nut harvesting in the fall, and hunting or trapping in the fall and winter. Gardening, to the extent that it was practiced, naturally occurred during the spring, summer, and fall. Some sites are found where knappable stone or useful fibers could be procured and processed. Others may have been trading places, where folks from different groups could gather to exchange goods and useful information, or to cement social relations by arranging marriages. Some of the larger sites doubtless combined many of these functions, whereas others apparently focused on a single economic task. Some small sites occupy hilltops that afforded a good view of the surrounding countryside (H. Kraft 1982:63; Lenik 1990). Such sites may have had some value as lookout stations for observing herds of game animals or, perhaps, as signal posts, although there is no evidence to indicate remote communications in antiquity.

From Cape May to High Point, from Salem to the Palisades, native peoples settled into virtually all parts of New Jersey. Alanson Skinner summarized the geographic distribution of the archaeological sites:

> The great mass of villages and cemeteries, with their countless varieties of artifacts, are along the Delaware River and its tributaries. In the sandy interior of the southern part of the State there are comparatively few traces; it was a hunting preserve. In the northern part, there are more, and there seem to have been extensive settlements about New York and Raritan Bays, especially on Staten Island. The lands adjacent to Newark Bay and the valleys of the Passaic and Hackensack are also filled with Indian traces; the ledges of the mountains furnish rock and cave shelters, and there were extensive settlements on the upper Delaware. (Skinner and Schrabisch 1913:16)

Thus, most recorded sites occur within the Inner Coastal Plain, upon the Piedmont, and along the upper Delaware River. However, prehistoric camps in the Highlands and in the Ridge and Valley section are fairly numerous, and even the Pine Barrens, traditionally believed to be devoid of aboriginal sites, have yielded numerous traces of prehistoric occupation (Cavallo and Mounier 1980).

The arrangement of sites on the landscape varies from one physiographic region to another. On the coastal plains, where the topography is essentially flat, the sites are mostly strung out beadlike along the streams. Likewise, along the coast, the sites follow the uplands behind the back bays and dot the innumerable islands that rise, sometimes almost imperceptibly, above the tidal meadows. Most of the well-known sites in the upper Delaware Valley occur directly upon the river terraces, with smaller encampments scattered along the edges of mountain streams to the east. In the Highlands, both open-air sites and rock shelters parallel the brooks, and some small sites occupy the hilltops. Wherever they occur, naturally wet depressions, springs, and swamps are surrounded by signs of ancient occupation.

Although almost all aboriginal habitations were situated near fresh water, present surface hydrology is not always an accurate indicator of site location. Environmental changes, brought about by natural processes or human agency, have destroyed many sites and have obscured others. For instance, countless coastal sites have been drowned by rising sea levels, a process that has persisted at varying rates since the retreat of the last glacier between 15,000 and 18,000 years ago (Crowl and Stuckenrath 1977; Wolfe 1977:129, 142). The relics tossed up on our sinking shorelines by winter storms give fleeting testimony to aboriginal life on sites that anciently stood on fast ground.

The filling of streams and marshes in historic times has obscured once favorable campsites, but remnants still survive. For example, aboriginal artifacts and even skeletons have been found in the shadow of the State House in Trenton, where the banks of Petty's Run, a tributary of the Delaware, once afforded opportunities for settlement. Well in advance of modern times, the stream had disappeared into a conduit beneath several feet of urban fill, but telltale vestiges of aboriginal occupation awaited the archaeologist's spade and trowel late in the twentieth century (Martin 1991; Mounier 1996b).

Citing evidence from earlier surveys, Lenik (1992:1) has counted no fewer than 90 prehistoric sites in the city of Paterson. The disturbed remains of once large aboriginal settlements have been found in New Brunswick and the surrounding urbanized areas (Philhower 1927; Sandy 1981). In addition, traces of prehistoric life have been observed in Newark and Bayonne (Skinner 1915), Camden (Mounier 1976b), and Gloucester City (Thomas 1987, 1990). Although archaeological deposits associated with our prehistoric forebears still survive in urban areas, frequently they are deeply buried and largely inaccessible. Research at Dundee along the Passaic River near Paterson is a case in point. Here archaeologists found evidence of a 3,000-year-old encampment entombed beneath deep deposits of fill (Tull and Slaughter 2001). Although New Jersey's major cities generally reveal a sparse archaeological record, aboriginal sites remain surprisingly numerous and widespread, especially in farm-lands and forests. Ilene Grossman-Bailey (2001) has estimated that prehistoric peoples on the Outer Coastal Plain alone occupied more than 100,000 distinct locations.

The largest and most complex settlements are found at locations that of-fered both an abundance and a diversity of natural resources. Thus, it is scarcely surprising that the most intensively occupied aboriginal settlements tended to occur along the trunks of the Delaware and other principal rivers. The juxta-position of riverine and terrestrial resources made many locations very attrac-tive to aboriginal peoples. Estuaries, tidal rivers, and marshes were particularly rich in valuable biological resources, especially fish, shellfish, fowl, and turtles, not to mention economically important plants. Hardwood forests yielded ample acorns, nuts, deer, and wood, while the freshwater streams and swamps in the interior contained fish, furbearers, and edible plants. The smallest and simplest sites occupy spots where resources were limited in variety, if not in abundance.

Knowledge of ancient settlement systems is proportional to the number of reported sites of particular ages or cultural associations. Thus Paleoindian and Early/Middle Archaic settlement patterns are not well understood be-cause their sites are less common than those of Late Archaic and Woodland cultures (see chapter 1 for the relative chronology of these cultural periods). As previously noted, many of the earliest sites may no longer exist because of rising sea levels and attendant topographic changes. Although traces still ex-ist, the character of ancient settlements in cities and suburbia is also poorly understood for want of adequate research opportunities.

SITE TYPES

Traditionally, archaeologists have categorized prehistoric settlements accord-ing to loosely defined types: villages and camps, rock shelters, work stations, and cemeteries. Rock carvings (petroglyphs) constitute another kind of site, although these are probably not really settlements in the ordinary sense of the word. The same is true of trails. Generally, villages and camps comprise habi-tations, which usually contain related features, such as hearths, storage and re-fuse pits, and, sometimes, evidence of shelters. Work stations include a variety of sites related to food gathering or production, as well as those connected with the procurement and processing of noncomestible (inedible) resources, such as stone, wood, and fibers. Traditionally, cemeteries have been treated as independent of habitations; however, burials frequently occur within or near residential locations (see chapter 4). Some sites contain caches (neatly clustered artifacts), which were set aside for storage or buried as ritual offerings.

Modern anthropological archaeologists understand that the various sites of a given culture formed integral parts of a subsistence-settlement system, which exploited natural resources within a given period of time and within a more or less confined geographic area. The occupants of each site performed tasks that were necessary for the continued survival of the group, and each site was situated so as to allow the collection and processing of required resources —food and building materials, raw materials for tools and utensils, items that might be valuable for trade, and so forth. In addition to their importance in economic terms, the sites also described geographic junctions in social networks; that is, they were places where people exchanged information and ideas, held ceremonies, and solidified or dissolved relationships, whether between individuals or groups.

Most anthropological settlement models involve some concept of group mobility; that is, people moved about, presumably in seasonal cycles. They might gather together in large villages for part of the year and disburse along rivers and trails to several hunting or foraging camps according to the seasonal availability of resources. Each group operated within a territory that it recognized as its own. Wallace (1947:4) has noted that, among the historic Lenape, there probably were individual territories of relatively small size, perhaps covering up to 200 square miles (518 km^2), which formed subdivisions of larger communal territories, ranging up to 1,500 square miles (3,885 km^2) in size. Similar arrangements might be supposed for more ancient societies as well.

The traditional characterizations of archaeological sites in New Jersey are described in the following pages.

Village and Camp Sites

The largest and most heavily occupied settlements are loosely classed as villages. Charles C. Abbott, writing in the early twentieth century, was probably the first to define large aboriginal sites in New Jersey by this term (Abbott 1907:53ff.). This usage has persisted to the present, although such sites are now often called "residential bases" or "macro-band camps" (R. Stewart, Hummer, and Custer 1986:71; Perazio 1988:60).

Village sites may cover from a few to several acres, usually along major waterways. For example, large prehistoric villages have been found at various locations along the Delaware River (Cross 1941:52–66, 1956; Kier and Calverley 1957; H. Kraft 1975a) and around Swartswood Lake in Sussex County (Schrabisch 1915:44). These sites, like many others, occupy environmentally rich settings, where multiple economic tasks—such as hunting, fishing, and nut harvesting—could have been performed simultaneously or in seasonal succession. The resident population at any given time must have been fairly large, perhaps consisting of several extended families and possibly a number of visitors.

Village sites present both an abundance and a large variety of artifacts and features. Typical artifacts might include bifaces ("arrowheads"), stone flakes, pottery, axes, hammers, and mortars and pestles, as well as ornaments. Fire-broken rocks from hearths and "stone boiling" (heating fluids by the immersion of heated stones) are especially plentiful.

Villages also contain numerous features, such as hearths, storage and refuse pits, burials, and, occasionally, evidence of housing. Cast-off food remains—mollusk shells and broken animal bones—also sometimes survive in deposits of discolored and charcoal-laden earth. In the early days of archaeology, such deposits were simply known as "black dirt" or "Indian dirt."

Similar kinds of remains are found in camps, but usually with less frequency and variety than in villages. In modern parlance, such sites are now often called "transient camps" (R. Stewart, Hummer, and Custer 1986:72; Perazio 1988:60). Camps generally cover less terrain than villages and may be found in more marginal settings, for example, along the banks of small streams. In addition, camps were likely to focus on a limited range of economic tasks. Except for these differences, "there are no certain criteria for telling a camp from a village" (Skinner and Schrabisch 1913:10). The distinction is largely a matter of scale.

The smallest camps—sometimes called "stations" or "specialized camps" (R. Stewart, Hummer, and Custer 1986:72; Perazio 1988:60)—are quite small, often covering less than a quarter acre. These locations reflect brief visits by an individual traveler or a small family group. The finds are characteristically limited to a few potsherds, an arrowhead or two, possibly an axe, some flakes, and a handful of charcoal. Not a few sites of this sort have been identified upon the banks of small streams or swamps, where one can visualize a mobile band hauling out a canoe at twilight to seek shelter before renewing their travels at daybreak.

Numerous village and camp sites were continually occupied for hundreds, if not thousands, of years, in many cases extending well back into Archaic times. In the end, Europeans simply supplanted the longtime tenants; indeed, the sites of most of New Jersey's oldest cities were initially settled by aboriginal populations. The qualities that define favorable settlements transcend cultural differences and chronological periods.

Houses

We have very little direct evidence of aboriginal housing in New Jersey, no doubt owing in large part to flimsy construction techniques, coupled with poor organic preservation and disturbances from activities during the historic period. Nevertheless, through careful research, a number of houses and shelters have been recorded, mostly at sites that would be classified as villages or camps. Although shelters dating back to the Archaic period have been excavated in New York (Ritchie 1965:74—75) and Massachusetts (Robbins 1972), no early examples are known from New Jersey. Rather, all relate to settlements of the Middle and Late Woodland periods.

Some of these structures have been identified by patterns of post molds, which mark the locations of poles or posts in the ground. Others survive as floors of packed or discolored earth, which contain concentrations of artifacts or features. Usually, northern sites, situated on heavy loamy soils, contain the best evidence of post molds, whereas earthen floors survive more often on loose, sandy ground on the coastal plains.

Archaeological research in the upper Delaware Valley has identified a total of 18 aboriginal houses on eight different sites (H. Kraft 1970, 1972:3, 1975a:73—86, 1976a:64—65, 1978:22, 1986b:122—127). The largest of these structures was found at the Miller Field site, in Warren County, where an arrangement of some 220 post molds described a round-ended longhouse that measured about 20 feet (6.1 m) in width and 60 feet (18.3 m) in length. The form and size of the other shelters varied; some were apparently circular, dome-shaped affairs, but all were similarly constructed.

Saplings, 2 or 3 inches (5—7.6 cm) in diameter, were driven a foot (30 cm) or so into the earth around the perimeter of the house. These poles were spaced at intervals of 6 to 12 inches (15—30 cm). The upper ends were bent inward toward the center and bound. Then, one supposes, a horizontal framework of smaller sticks was lashed to the uprights to form a rigid structure, which was finally covered with bark, mats, or skins. An opening in one wall

FIGURE 64. Cross section of a post mold. Posts or saplings set into the earth often leave a lasting impression. When enough post molds survive, the form of a structure can be defined. Filled with dark organic material, this post mold stands in stark contrast to the surrounding subsoil. The original post was a bluntly pointed sapling a little more than one inch in diameter. Photograph by the author.

served as a doorway, which could be closed off with a mat or drape as needed. Holes were left in the roof to allow smoke to escape from interior hearths. Rows of poles supported internal partitions or built-in furniture. This form of construction is broadly consistent with early historical accounts of Indian dwellings (S. Smith 1765:130–142; Lindeström 1925:211; Myers 1970:27; Dankers and Sluyter in Kraft 1986b:126–127; Becker 1993:66).

In the Ridge and Valley section of southern Sussex County, the Dark Moon site has yielded evidence of five houses (R. Stewart, Hummer, and Custer 1986:83). These structures have been identified from round to oval

FIGURE 65. Bent-sapling house construction. Arbor-roof structures were made by setting saplings in the ground and bending them to form an arch. A lattice of similar material provided the framework, which was covered with bark, skins, or reeds. Sketch by the
author.

patterns of post molds. The circular shelters measured about 15 feet (4.6 m)
in diameter. The others were as large as 22 × 35 feet (6.7 × 10.7 m).

In no instance has an orderly arrangement of houses been identified. This
situation suggests that houses were erected by individual families according to
their own preference or convenience. The association of hearths and storage
and refuse pits, as well as numerous artifacts of all sorts, implies lengthy periods of habitation. The possibility of year-round occupancy has been suggested (Kraft 1975a:85; R. Stewart, Hummer, and Custer 1986:83). There
appears to have been no need to seek defense within the confines of stockaded
villages (Kraft 1986b:122), a frequent necessity among the belligerent late prehistoric peoples of New York State (Ritchie 1965).

On the coastal plains, post molds are almost entirely lacking, owing to the
loose, sandy character of the soil (Cross 1941:210; Gruber and Mason 1956:11;
but see Kier and Calverley 1957:90, 95). Here, shelters are sometimes defined
by debris accumulated within apparently enclosed spaces. A typical "living
floor" consists of a deposit of reddish brown or gray-brown earth, interspersed with discarded or lost implements, potsherds, flakes, refuse bone, and

charcoal. These deposits are broad, thin, and horizontal and cannot be confused with refuse that was discarded in pits or over hillsides.

Several of these features have been identified in Cumberland, Gloucester, and Burlington Counties (Mounier 1981a:6–9, 1991:IV-15, IV-44, IV-138; Cresson n.d.a). Two cultural features at Site 28-GL-123 in Deptford Township, Gloucester County, consist of stained soil deposits in which were embedded dense accumulations of ceramics, stone tools and weapons, and organic refuse. These features appear to represent parts of a single living floor, perhaps originally contained within a structure. An unexcavated block containing a large tree separated the two features so that their continuity could not be established. Nevertheless, their proximity and orientation, and the identical nature of their contents, demonstrate contemporaneity and strongly suggest that both features were part of a single unit. If continuous, this living unit would have measured approximately 12 × 22 feet (3.7 × 6.7 m) in plan, dimensions that would adequately describe the proportions of a small oblong house.

At Site 28-GL-139, in the same vicinity, a similar patch of stained soil, covering 4.8 × 10.3 feet (1.5 × 3.2 m), has been interpreted as another living floor. The discolored soil of this feature contained numerous potsherds, flakes, and incinerated bone fragments, along with a few unidentified seeds. Charcoal collected from this deposit dates to ca. A.D. 1400 (Mounier 1991:IV-138). Cresson's (n.d.a) unpublished research at the Gruno Farm site in Mount Laurel Township, Burlington County, revealed an elongated, artifact-rich soil stain that measured about 25 feet (7.6 m) in width and more than 55 feet (16.8+ m) in length.

In a few places, floors of packed clay have been found. At the Fralinger site, along the Maurice River in Cumberland County, I found such a floor, again with late prehistoric cultural associations (Mounier 1974b:32–33). This feature covered an area of approximately 55 square feet (5.1 m²).

Although post molds are lacking, all of the living floors noted above seem to be the remains of aboriginal dwellings. The soil stains are horizontal, quite thin, but broad and sharply demarcated. They form oval platforms that correspond to the general proportions of houses elsewhere delineated by post molds. In particular, the widths never greatly exceed 25 feet, which approaches the maximum dimension that can be achieved with the saplings available for construction. All of the varied contents are strictly confined to the limits of the stained soil, and all of the artifacts contained therein conform to types that are closely related in time. Many contain domestic artifacts, albeit of a mundane nature.

At Little Silver, in Monmouth County, Ronald A. Thomas and his associates excavated what they interpret to be an aboriginal structure, defined by a number of widely spaced post molds (Thomas, Hoffman, and Sahady 1998:14, 16 [fig. 4]). This is the only prehistoric pole structure so far identified anywhere on the coastal plains. The post molds appear to form an open-ended, oval pattern that measures approximately 16 × 26 feet (5 × 8 m). The construction is unusual in that the posts were quite large, measuring on average about 4 inches (10 cm) in diameter, and widely spaced, between 40 and 60 inches (1 to 1.5 m) apart. In addition, the western end, which would have been exposed to the prevailing winds, appears to have been left open, and interior features are entirely lacking. For these reasons, one may question the true significance of this structure.

Wherever found, each house probably sheltered members of one or more related families. Assuming a requirement of approximately 25 to 35 square feet ($2.3–3.3$ m^2) per person (cf. Dankers and Sluyter in Kraft 1986b:126–127; Ritchie 1965:75), the largest of these houses might have contained from 30 to 50 people at any given time, the smallest not more than 1 or 2.

Rock Shelters

Rock shelters are really small camps that were situated within the recesses of rock formations. Max Schrabisch, who pioneered the exploration of aboriginal rock shelters in northern New Jersey (Lenik 1998), observed: "Manifestly such places can occur only in regions where precipitous rock ledges are common. Here in clefts in the crags, beneath overhanging rocks, in shallow well-lighted caves or in holes under heaps of large boulders the Indian could find the shelter he desired" (Schrabisch 1915:16).

Favored shelters share certain characteristics, including accessibility to water, to trails, and to other settlements. Schrabisch further noted that "most of these are relatively close to other camp sites and are easily accessible except for a little rough climbing. A few are more remote and in one or two instances no other sites are known anywhere in their neighborhood" (Schrabisch 1915: 19). As with other kinds of sites, the availability of water was paramount. Any number of caves and overhanging ledges were not occupied, apparently for want of nearby water, or because the openings were too small. Schrabisch (1917:30) believed that "shelters with a low roof were usually spurned." He also speculated that some enclosures were avoided because the floors were too rocky and uneven. At least for cold-weather use, the Indians "preferred shel-

FIGURE 66. The Skyline Rock Shelter. This overhanging rock formation in Bergen County was home to many generations of natives. Photograph by the author.

ters with a southerly exposure, where the genial warmth of the sun's rays could be felt for the greater part of the day" (Schrabisch 1915:17). At other times, "it apparently did not matter much whether the rock house opened to the south or north" (Schrabisch 1917:30). The entrances may have been secured against the elements with screens of brush, bark, or hides. One unusual shelter—consisting of an opening between two adjacent pieces of a split boulder—almost certainly had an improvised roof (Staats 1991c).

Because of limitations imposed by nature, rock shelters are generally quite small, typically covering no more than 400 square feet (37 m^2), but the internal space is variable owing to the individual characteristics of each enclosure. Schrabisch (1915:19) thought that "[s]ome of these shelters were perhaps places where single families or small parties lived more or less continuously, particularly during the winter, while others were permanent camps well known and resorted to from time to time by hunters and fishermen or periodically occupied by families during their seasonal migrations."

Rock shelters reveal the same kinds of artifacts that commonly occur on open sites, and some, as Schrabisch suspected, show evidence of prolonged or repeated habitation. Commonly found are hearths and shallow layers of

FIGURE 67. The Pompton Plains Rock Shelter. This shelter in Morris County was one of many investigated in the early twentieth century by Max Schrabisch. Courtesy of Edward J. Lenik.

artifacts, refuse bones, shells of freshwater mussels (*Unio spp.*), and other organic debris. Most deposits have little depth because of underlying boulders
or bedrock. Cultural debris may extend some distance from the confines of
the shelter. As Skinner noted, "an interesting feature, common to many rockshelters, is the presence of a dump near at hand where the sweepings of the retreat have accumulated" (Skinner and Schrabisch 1913:14).

Schrabisch, working more or less alone between 1900 and 1917, explored
no fewer than 56 shelters in Sussex, Warren, and Hunterdon Counties (Schrabisch 1915:16, 1917:31). Others have been found in Passaic and Bergen Counties (Chrisbacher 1990; Lenik 1998). A few have been systematically excavated
and reported (Cross 1941:143–149; Staats 1987, 1988, 1991c; Petrosky 1989;
Chrisbacher 1990). Doubtless, others await discovery in remote places. The
distribution of rock shelters extends along the Appalachian Ridge, well beyond the limits of New Jersey (Harrington 1909b:125–138; Schrabisch 1915:16,
1917:29, 1926, 1930; Butler 1947).

Caches

Caches are clusters of implements purposefully buried as a unit, often in neatly
stacked piles or other orderly arrangements suggesting the intention of even-
tual recovery. Caches are most commonly found on large sites (Cross 1941,
1956:68–71; Mounier 1975:3, 1981b:60–61; Kraft 1986b:95; Custer and Morris
1989), but they occasionally occur in apparent isolation (Mounier 1981b:56–
57). Many caches consist of batches of raw material, unfinished implements,
or groups of objects needing reconditioning (Cross 1941, 1956:68). There is
an old tradition—substantiated by modern experimentation (Jack Cresson,
pers. comm.)—that certain lithic materials can be knapped more readily when
damp than when dry. As Skinner noted, "it is assumed that the Indian knew
this, and after having blanked out a number of leaf-shaped forms . . . he buried
them in the earth where they might retain their moisture and await his leisure"
(Skinner and Schrabisch 1913:14).

Often the items in a cache are of similar form—all bifaces, axes, or netsinkers, for example—but variations are not uncommon. For instance, the famous hoard of 127 large argillite bifaces from the Abbott Farm also contained
a large native copper pin and a heart-shaped quartz pebble (Cross 1956:68).
Such combinations cannot be assumed to be merely fortuitous.

Although many caches no doubt reflect artifact storage, with the intention of future use, others almost certainly had ritual or symbolic significance.

For example, the caches of bifaces, bannerstones, axes, and other exotic items found in and around the graves of the Koens-Crispin culture (Hawkes and Linton 1916; Cross 1941:81–90, 117–127) unquestionably reflect mortuary practices.

Trails

Trails must be considered as essential elements of any settlement system. Together with water routes, they were the links that connected the settlements of related people. They were also the routes by which those people traveled and communicated with others beyond the confines of their own territories. However, unlike other sites, trails reveal their presence by little more than trampled ground. As Schrabisch observed, "By their very nature they [were] evanescent and exist[ed] only when in constant use. The moment they ceased to be trodden by the feet of those who made them, vegetation began to obliterate them. Efforts at this late date to determine their location are therefore largely conjectural" (Schrabisch 1917:36). Lacking solid documentation or reliable oral traditions, one can only suppose that trails followed the watercourses, skirted mountains, lakes, and swamps, and crossed rivers at shallow fords to join thousands of locations into a vast network of ancient settlements. It is likely that many modern roads follow the general routes of aboriginal trails, whose exact alignments are now obscure.

Work Stations

Work stations are sites that yield evidence of specialized economic activities, such as fishing, hunting, and stone quarrying. Artifacts and features relating to each of these activities may occur discretely in small sites or commingled in larger settlements. Examples of various kinds of work stations are presented below.

FISHING STATIONS. Historical sources reported that the Indians used a variety of nets, weirs, and projectiles to capture fish (H. Kraft 1992a). Similar devices are detectable as archaeological vestiges. Lost or abandoned fishing gear also marks the distribution of ancient fishing places. Naturally, evidence of vigorous fishing is often concentrated near large villages. Such sites occur all along the Delaware River, both in tidewater and above the falls at Trenton to the New York State line (Schrabisch 1915:14–15 and passim, 1917:48; Cross 1956:70,

104; Kier and Calverley 1957:77; H. Kraft 1975a:112, 1992a:13–18; Cavallo 1987; Staats 1990). Schrabisch (1915:14–15 and passim, 1917:48 and passim) identified several fishing stations around Swartswood Lake, in the vicinity of Stillwater, and at other interior localities in Warren and Sussex Counties. The valley of the Passaic River was said to contain many fishing places (Skinner and Schrabisch 1913:37). A large site on Constable Hook in Bayonne also produced abundant evidence of fishing (Skinner and Schrabisch 1913:42).

The nearly ubiquitous distribution of notched pebble sinkers along the shores of the Delaware gives mute testimony to the importance of net fishing. Indeed, at some sites hundreds of notched weights have been found (Schrabisch 1915:14–15 and passim, 1917:48; Cross 1956:70, 104; Kier and Calverley 1957:77; Kraft 1975a:112, 1992a:13–18; Staats 1990). At others, fishing was apparently undertaken less intensively. For instance, at the Dark Moon site, in the interior of Sussex County, only 45 sinkers were found, scarcely enough for one or two small nets. By contrast, this site yielded thousands of small triangular points, demonstrating a focus on hunting (R. de Vries 1994:109). The Indian Site Survey (1936–1942) recorded a few notched stones at each of fourteen other sites around the state. These sites are about equally divided between locations in tidewater and niches at the heads of freshwater streams (Cross 1941). The researchers assumed that the notched stones were net weights, although other interpretations are possible. Such items could have served as counterweights, as bolas stones, or even as small hand tools. At any rate, fishing at these places must have been of marginal importance.

At the Harry's Farm site in Warren County, Herbert Kraft (1975a:112–113) found a workshop for the manufacture of notched weights as well as six clusters or caches of trimmed sinkers, each containing from 8 to 35 specimens. At the Abbott Farm, four caches of notched sinkers were unearthed, each containing from 9 to 19 weights. These discoveries provide presumptive evidence for the use of individual nets (Cross 1956:70, 104); indeed, considering the apparently deliberate arrangements of the weights, it seems likely that the caches originally harbored carefully folded nets (Kraft 1986a:107). If one assumes 3 to 5 feet (0.9–1.5 m) between each weight along the bottom of the mesh, then these cached sinkers would represent nets that varied in length from 21 to 170 feet (6–52 m). Excavations at the Morrow site in New York State yielded a portion of a carbonized net manufactured from "Indian-hemp fiber, twisted into a cord of small diameter, which was woven into a net with about a two-inch mesh" (Ritchie 1965:185). This example gives an impression of the sorts of nets that might have been employed at New Jersey sites.

Netsinkers are the most pervasive indicators of subsistence fishing, but gorges and hooks—perishable because they were fashioned from bone or thorns—were almost certainly employed. At Raccoon Point, on the Delaware River in Gloucester County, Kier and Calverley (1957:76–77) recovered three double-pointed argillite spikes, which they identified as fish gorges. In New York State, evidence of fishing with hand-held cords and trotlines equipped with hooks and gorges is indisputable (Ritchie 1965:48–50, 276).

The Indians also constructed weirs to trap fish or to cause them to concentrate in shallow waters. Fish weirs are lines of rocks or poles set in streams, often in a V-shaped arrangement, to direct fish to locations where they could be caught by hand or with dip nets or spears. When rocks were used in their construction, the weirs might have doubled as paths for "hopscotching" across shallow streams. The use of weirs among the natives was observed by early European chroniclers (Lindeström 1925:219; Loskiel 1794: pt 1, 94ff.).

Archaeological examples of rock weirs are fairly common. Skinner and Schrabisch (1913:37) reported many relict fish weirs on the Passaic River: "Between Passaic Park and Two Bridges, a distance of about 20 miles [32.2 km], no less than sixteen fords or weirs may be distinguished. . . . [There are] six more up the river to the Falls, four between Totowa and Singac, and two opposite Two Bridges. A peculiar feature of all these fords is that the rocks used in their construction are not laid across the river in a straight line, but are arranged so as to form midstream an angle, with the apex pointing downstream." Allen Lutins and Anthony DeCondo (1999) give a detailed description of a weir that spans the Passaic River between Paterson and Fair Lawn.

According to Herbert Kraft (1992a:12), "stony remains of presumed fishweirs are known from the area above Dingman's Ferry on the Delaware River in Sussex County." Kier and Calverley (1957:96) mentioned, but did not describe, an archaeological weir in the tidal flats along Raccoon Creek, in Gloucester County. The height of the tide and a deep, soft bottom at this location would have favored construction from slender poles and wattles rather than from rocks. In order to ease their passage across the marshy ground, the Indians also built a path—paved with stones, potsherds, and other camp debris—between this weir and the main body of the site (Kier and Calverley 1957:95–96). Henry B. Kümmel, state geologist of New Jersey and general editor of the early state archaeological survey reports, correctly observed that historic populations constructed weirs similar to aboriginal ones and that care is needed in discriminating between them (Skinner and Schrabisch 1913:37n1).

At some locations, large platforms of fire-broken rocks have been interpreted as stages for the roasting, smoking, or drying of fish. At the Harry's Farm site along the Delaware River in Warren County a huge rectangular hearth, measuring 26 × 47 feet (7.9 × 14.3 m), appears to have served this purpose (H. Kraft 1975a:90). Several posts, possibly from drying racks, extended through this platform into the underlying earth, and charcoal from wood fires was scattered throughout (H. Kraft 1975a:50). At the Abbott Farm, Cavallo (1987:157–160) identified several rock clusters, which he initially considered to have been hearths for curing fish. Later experimentation suggested that the "hearths" might have been dumps of "boiling stones" employed in conjunction with rendering fish oils (Cavallo 1987:181).

One supposes that aboriginal fishermen exploited anadramous species, such as American shad (*Alosa sappidissima*), which run annually in great numbers to spawn. Net fishing for shad is still a traditional activity in the middle reaches of the Delaware River. Early in historic times, Indians were observed taking eels (*Anguilla rostrata*) in large quantities with basketry traps (H. Kraft 1986b:151, 1992a:12). Sturgeon (*Acipenser oxyrhyncus*), which grow to great size, were probably speared with harpoons (Willoughby 1935:218; Cross 1956:120). Doubtless, stream- and lake-bound species in New Jersey, such as catfish (*Ictalurus nebulosus*), perch (*Perca flavescens*), sunfish (*Centrarchidae*), and suckers (*Catostomus commersonnii*), were also caught, as they were in New York State (Ritchie 1965:48–50, 55–56, 185).

SHELLFISHING STATIONS. Countless accumulations of cast-off shells confirm the economic importance of mollusks to ancient cultures. Situated near natural shell beds, both in freshwater and marine environments, archaeological middens typically consist of scatters or heaps of shells, or in-filled pits. These deposits contain refuse from food preparation or, rarely, from the manufacture of beads and tools. Shell middens vary dramatically in size from huge masses that covered several acres to tiny spreads containing barely a handful of shells.

As previously observed, freshwater mussels (*Unio spp.* and *Elliptio spp.*) were consumed when available. Among marine mollusks, the oyster (*Crassostrea virginica*) and hard-shell clam or quahog (*Mercenaria mercenaria*) were the principal prey species, but the channeled conch (*Busycon canaliculatum*) and knobbed conch (*Busycon carica*) were taken along with mussels (both *Mytilus edulis* and *Volsella plicatulus*) and the soft-shell clam (*Mya arinaria*). Although they were a dietary staple in southern New England (Ritchie 1969), bay scallops (*Pectan irradians*) rarely occur in New Jersey shell middens. Perhaps ancient environmental conditions did not favor their abundance, or perhaps these capable swimmers were simply more difficult to gather than sedentary bivalves and slow-moving conchs.

Crustaceans—even easily captured species, such as the common blue crab (*Callinectes sapidus*)—are almost never recovered from archaeological sites. This situation suggests the possibility of a culturally prescribed food prohibition rather than a lack of organic preservation.

The following paragraphs offer brief descriptions of several shellfishing sites. The order of presentation roughly follows the arrangement of the sites from the Delaware Bay, around the Cape May peninsula, and northward along the coast toward Staten Island.

Near the mouth of the Maurice River in Cumberland County, I found several large but shallow spreads of oyster shells associated with refuse bones of various mammals, reptiles, and birds, along with flat-bottom pottery and bifaces of Early Woodland origin (Mounier 1974b). A platform of fire-broken rocks, which measured 5 × 7½ feet (1.5 × 2.3 m), was probably used for roasting or baking shellfish. On the nearby East Point site, excavations in 1939 revealed subterranean pits containing oyster and clam shells, pottery, stone tools, animal bones, and human skeletal remains (Cross 1941:41–44).

Skinner observed a variety of shell heaps near Cape May Court House, noting that certain shell piles contained many small, angular shell fragments resulting from the manufacture of wampum beads (Skinner and Schrabisch 1913:53). In the course of unpublished research near Swainton, Cape May County, Alan E. Carman (pers. comm.) excavated 33 pits filled with oyster and clam shells. One remarkable feature of this site was a shell-paved causeway that traversed the marshland between the fast ground and the shell beds. Later investigations in the vicinity revealed additional deposits of refuse shells a short distance inland (Mounier 1988, 1999c). Two other nearby sites disclosed pits filled with clam and oyster shells, Middle and Late Woodland pottery, stone tools, animal bones, and charcoal, which has been dated between A.D. 710 and 1240 (Mounier 1997:13, 15).

I also found shell scatters and pits well inland near the head of the Cedar Swamp Creek in Upper Township, Cape May County (Mounier 1989b). Here, 10 small deposits of oyster, clam, and mussel shells were discovered, along with refuse bone and pottery of Late Woodland derivation. This site is of considerable interest because the tidal waters, from which the mollusks must have been collected, lie no closer than 3,000 feet (914 m) under present conditions, and the distance was probably even greater in antiquity, when sea levels were lower. The discrete character of these small middens strongly suggests transportation to the site in batches, presumably by watercraft.

Andrew Stanzeski excavated a late prehistoric shell deposit at the Steel site, near Beesley's Point in Upper Township, Cape May County (Stanzeski 1996). The Archaeological Society of New Jersey funded a C^{14} assay, which dated the site to A.D. 1390. On the opposite shore of Great Egg Harbor, near Somers Point in Atlantic County, shell heaps of undetermined composition are said to occupy the fast ground adjoining the meadows (Joseph Arsenault, pers. comm.).

During the course of a survey along Patcong Creek, near Bargaintown, Atlantic County, I found oyster shells and fire-broken rocks in two features (Mounier 1989a). Other artifacts and features nearby indicated a late prehistoric origin for the shell deposits. A small clutch of clam shells, stone flakes, and Middle Woodland pottery came to light during another survey along Doughty's Creek in Galloway Township, Atlantic County (Mounier 1990b).

Large shell heaps of uncertain age and composition once occupied the tide meadows around Absecon, Pleasantville, and Leeds Point in Atlantic County, and around Manahawkin in Ocean County (Cook 1868:362, 501; English 1884:13; Skinner and Schrabisch 1913:52; Mounier 1990b; Joseph R. Arsenault, pers. comm.).

Several deposits of shells are known from the vicinity of the Great Bay in Little Egg Harbor Township, in Ocean County (Cook 1868:362, 501; Blackman 1880:237; Jordan 1906; Skinner and Schrabisch 1913; Cross 1941; Mounier 1990a; Stanzeski 1996). Excavations on Wells Island by Stanzeski (1996) yielded quantities of oyster shells, triangular points, perforators, and scrapers. Although much of this work remains unpublished, a C^{14} assessment funded by the Archaeological Society of New Jersey determined the date of the site to be about A.D. 1300.

The society also obtained two carbon dates from the nearby Pennella site, where excavations by Stanzeski in the mid-1970s (Stanzeski 1981:17, 1996) were never followed by thorough publication. This site contained numerous pits and other features, which were expressed as black earth mingled with clam shells and abundant refuse bone. Several late prehistoric human burials were also found. According to the carbon dates, the occupations at this site occurred between A.D. 140 and 420.

Skinner noted the presence of very large aboriginal shell mounds on the tidal meadows surrounding the Great Bay (Skinner and Schrabisch 1913:11). Apparently, the only surviving example is the famous Tuckerton Shell Mound

FIGURE 68. The Tuckerton Shell Mound. This mound is a huge accumulation of clam shells, the refuse of intensive shellfish collection about 1,500 years ago. This photograph was recorded by the Indian Site Survey in 1939. Courtesy of the New Jersey State Museum.

(Cook 1868:362, 501; Blackman 1880:237; Abbott 1881:447; Jordan 1906:12–17; Cross 1941:39–40), which appears to be about 1,500 years old (Stanzeski 1981:17, 1996). This mound is a massive accumulation, mostly of quahog shells, with lesser quantities of oyster and conch shells. It covers about one-tenth of an acre above ground, but extends laterally under the marsh for an undetermined distance. At present, it rises about 10 feet (3 m) above the tide meadow. Ongoing research by the Archaeological Society of New Jersey demonstrates that the shell deposits extend as much as 14 feet (4.3 m) below the present marsh surface. Evidently, owing to rising sea levels, the meadow has encroached upon the mound since the natives first discarded shells at this location.

Near the mouth of Oyster Creek, Joseph R. Arsenault found a very large oyster shell midden that contained stone flakes and tools. Because no pottery was found there, this site is assumed to be of Archaic origin. Moreover, the ancient shells are much larger than any from oysters that grow in the region today.

Nearby is a remnant of another spread of oyster shells, among which were found crude cross-corded pottery and a human skeleton (Cross 1941:36–37). Cultural associations with the shells are uncertain. If the pottery and shells were laid down contemporaneously, an accumulation during Middle Woodland times may be assumed.

Woolley (1948) noted several shell heaps and spreads around Mosquito

Cove and along the shores of Cedar Creek. Similar sites were explored along the Shrewsbury River (Fountain 1897) and at Little Silver in Monmouth County (Thomas, Hoffman, and Sahady 1998). Rau (1865) provided a synopsis of a very large shell heap that covered five or six acres near Keyport, Monmouth County. Shells of clam and oyster were piled in batches, with several eminences rising about 5 feet (1.5 m) above the level of the surrounding ground. Associated artifacts were reported but not described in specific terms.

Skinner mentioned a village site on Constable Hook, where several shell mounds or pits were exposed (Skinner and Schrabisch 1913:42). Shell middens formerly dotted Staten Island, particularly along the shores of Arthur Kill and Kill Van Kull (Harrington 1909a; Skinner 1909).

The distribution of aboriginal shell deposits continues both north and south along the coast, well beyond the political and geographic boundaries of New Jersey (C. Smith 1950; Salwen 1962, 1966; Ritchie 1965; Thomas and Warren 1970; Custer 1988; Lavin 1988). It has been noted that the composition of shell heaps and spreads varies through space and time. Where adequate data exist, it is clear that both oysters and quahogs were heavily exploited from an early time. Brennan (1963) has produced ample evidence of large-scale oystering in the Hudson estuary during Late Archaic times. Archaic and Early Woodland use of oysters is well represented in coastal New York (C. Smith 1950; Salwen 1962, 1966; Ritchie 1965) and southern New England, where quahogs and scallops were also heavily exploited (Ritchie 1969; Braun 1974; Lavin 1988).

With the relative rise of sea levels in postglacial times, the habitat of oysters was supplanted by a more saline and silty regime favored by other species, most notably the quahog. Thus a corresponding dependence on clams is seen in late prehistoric shell heaps at various points along the New Jersey coast. Intense human predation on mollusks—adding to a diminution of targeted stocks—may have played a role in the proportions of different shellfish revealed in archaeological sites.

HUNTING AND FORAGING SITES. The nearly ubiquitous distribution of stone weapon tips, knives, and scrapers suggests the importance of hunting in prehistoric times. When they occur outside of ceremonial contexts, bannerstones or atlatl weights also indicate hunting, as do deposits of refuse bone—especially of large game, such as deer, elk, and bear. Smaller creatures—rabbits and furbearers, for example—were probably taken in traps, snares, or nets. Hunting and foraging are intimately intertwined, and for this reason hunting camps are likely to contain a variety of general-purpose tools, such as choppers, hammerstones, and axes, as well as the weapons and tools specifically needed to kill and butcher game.

Clusters of projectile points and related tools reveal the camps from which hunters departed during the chase and to which they returned to butcher the kill and to repair damaged equipment. This pattern is especially apparent in smaller hunting camps, which are not cluttered with the remains of other activities.

Up to the beginning of Late Woodland times, about 1,300 years ago, hunting was accomplished simply by hand or with javelins or darts hurled from an atlatl or throwing stick. The related weapon tips—commonly, large notched or stemmed forms—were generally bigger and heavier than those used later by archers. Arrow points are frequently small triangular or pentagonal bifaces, which were sometimes notched for hafting.

Weapon tips, commonly known among archaeologists as projectile points, necessarily adhere to certain formal conventions. They must be sharply pointed and have keen edges to penetrate the body of the quarry and to cause internal bleeding. The optimum tip angles for stone points range between 20° and 55°, while the cutting edges might vary from 35° to 90° (Rothchild and Lavin 1978:374–375; Cresson 1990:121–124; Mounier 1998c:37). Accordingly, any biface that meets these criteria might be regarded as a projectile point. However, there is a complication: experimental studies show that many bifaces probably served as knives and not as weapons. Therefore, the ability to identify hunting points in archaeological assemblages becomes essential for understanding site function.

Because projectile points and knives tend to break in different ways, this discrimination can be achieved by a careful examination of broken specimens (Ahler 1971; Dunn 1984; Truncer 1990:12–23). It often happened that a projectile speeding toward its mark would strike a hard object, such as a large bone in the prey or, in the case of an errant shot, a rock or tree. When this occurred, the tip was likely to chip, crush, or snap off entirely. Such tip-initiated failures are known as "distal impact fractures." By contrast, bifacial knives tend to break transversely, across the middle of the blade, from stresses applied during cutting.

When available, data on impact fractures give the best indication of the extent and intensity of projectile hunting at sites where the broken points were discarded or lost, but surprisingly few archaeologists have taken advantage of this kind of analysis. Often, hunting has been inferred simply from the density of well-formed bifaces in archaeological deposits (R. Stewart, Hummer,

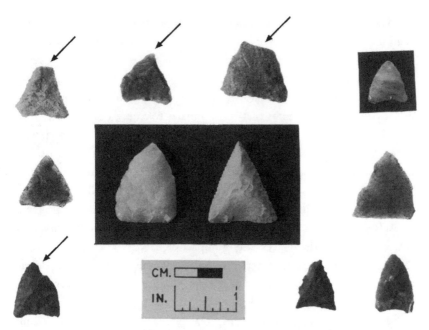

FIGURE 69. Triangular bifaces. Several specimens show impact fractures, demonstrating use as projectile points (top row, three at left; bottom row at left). Photograph by the author.

FIGURE 70. Transverse fractures on knives. These stemmed bifaces show blade snapping characteristic of failure from use as knives. Photograph by the author.

and Custer 1986:85). Yet we now have demonstrable evidence from fracture analysis that hunting was very important at some sites and inconsequential at others (H. Kraft 1975a:156; Cavallo 1987:208; Perazio 1988:66; Cresson 1990:121–124; Mounier 1998c:37).

Comparative data from various sites around the state show a broad range in the proportion of bifaces that reveal impact fractures. For example, at the Frenche's Pond and Dark Moon sites in Sussex County (Hall 1970:13; R. de Vries 1994:109) upward of 90 percent of the triangular points show tip fractures that strongly suggest failures from impact (Jack Cresson, pers. comm.). The West Parkway site in Morris County contained a small assemblage of hunting gear, including projectile points, two-thirds of which were broken by impact (Perazio 1988:66). At the Cherry Hill site in Camden County, more than 61 percent of the bifaces exhibit impact damage (Cresson n.d.a). Clearly, the occupants of these sites were hunters. By contrast, at the Area B site, located near the Delaware River in Mercer County, only 3.2 percent of the points revealed impact fractures. Cavallo (1987:208) has correctly concluded that hunting was unimportant at this site, which was probably a fishing camp. Analyses of point failures from several other sites in Hunterdon, Burlington, and Gloucester Counties show a nearly continuous range of variation between these extremes (Mounier n.d.b). Herbert Kraft's (1975a:156) researches into the archaeology of the Tocks Island area yielded "numerous projectile points, both whole and point-impact fractured," but comparative figures are lacking.

That hunting varied in intensity from place to place is scarcely surprising; some locations are simply better suited to hunting than others. The bustle of human activity around larger settlements would tend to scare off local game animals, while continual human predation would reduce their numbers. In addition, the occupants of larger settlements often concentrated on economic and social activities that had nothing to do with hunting.

For these reasons, many stations that focused mainly on hunting were situated in the mid-reaches or headwaters of river systems, some at considerable distances from large village sites. Indeed, Johannes Campanius, writing in the middle of the seventeenth century, observed that the Lenape spent their winters "up in the country [away from the Delaware River] where they find [an] abundance of venison" (transcribed by Holm in DuPonceau 1834:123).

Herbert Kraft (1982:61) has described typical hunting sites in northern New Jersey as "smaller inland stations, rockshelters, and bluff locations, where projectile points make up the bulk of the artifact inventory." Littered with thousands of projectile points, the Dark Moon site in Sussex County appears to be a good example of a hunting station.

Site 28-GL-123, located on the Inner Coastal Plain near the head of tidewater in Almonesson Creek, revealed evidence of episodic hunting (Mounier 1991:IV-44, V-15). One part of this site was occupied by a small group, possibly during the winter, while taking small furbearing mammals. A dense accumulation of Late Woodland artifacts—including broken weapons, pottery, and stone tools—was found with refuse bone in the confines of an apparent shelter.

Site 28-GL-171, situated in the head of the Maurice River on the Outer Coastal Plain, revealed a variety of stone weapon tips, along with other hunting gear, small hearths, and several fragmentary clay smoking pipes, which were probably used in hunting rituals (Mounier and Martin 1992:V-8). This site was a staging area, where perhaps as many as 50 men gathered to prepare themselves, both logistically and spiritually, for a hunt. Refuse bone and tip-broken points, discarded after the hunt, were found in some quantity.

Numerous small sites have been identified in the hinterlands of what are now Atlantic, Burlington, Camden, Ocean, and Monmouth Counties. Many of these stations contain only a stray point or two, some simple flake tools, and perhaps a few potsherds and hearth rocks. In some cases, a small clutch of stone flakes is the only vestige (Skinner and Schrabisch 1913:15; Mounier 1976a; Joseph R. Arsenault, pers. comm.). At such locations, one may envision a solitary hunter pausing to sharpen a quiver of arrows or to fashion a flake knife to skin a freshly killed deer.

Isolated projectile points and hand tools, which sometimes occur upon the divides between drainage basins, are quite probably the exact locations at which hunters killed or attempted to kill their quarry. These tiny sites are almost always found by chance and are very seldom reported in the archaeological literature (Mounier 1998c). Research on the coastal plains has revealed projectile points, scrapers, and other hunting equipment from Paleoindian, Archaic, and Early Woodland cultures around the rims of natural depressions, which are largely independent from flowing streams (Bonfiglio and Cresson 1982; Mounier 1999b, 2000a).

The importance of hunting varied across time and culture as well as in space. Paleoindian and earlier Archaic cultures seem to have placed greater reliance on hunting than later Archaic groups, who are known from archaeology to have exploited a variety of edible plants. Hunting returned to greater prominence in late prehistoric times. Thus, it seems that most archaeological cultures consisted primarily of hunters and gatherers.

If we assume that faunal remains in archaeological situations are representative, we can say that the favored prey was the white-tail deer (*Odocoileus virginianus*). Yet the inventory of exploited species was broad and included elk (*Cervus canadensis*), black bear (*Ursus americanus*), squirrels (*Sciurus carolinensis*), raccoon (*Procyon lotor*), and beaver (*Castor canadensis*), among many others. On occasion, extinct or locally extirpated species have been recovered from archaeological deposits in New Jersey. A tooth of the giant beaver (*Castoroides*) was recovered from the Fairy Hole cave in Warren County (Cross 1941:148), and a bison bone (*Bison bison*) was found, pierced with a stemmed stone point, near Bridgeton, in Cumberland County (Kier 1949).

At two sites in the tidewater reaches of the Delaware River, the Indian Site Survey found bones of humpback or finback whales (Cross 1941:60–61). That whales were actively hunted seems unlikely, given our knowledge of traditional cultures and technology, but it is entirely possible that accidentally beached whales could have been butchered and eaten.

The range of hunted species was probably limited by cultural preferences and prohibitions as well as by local availability. Ethnographic data show that humans will accommodate themselves to meager conditions by hunting animals not ordinarily regarded as food. For instance, in the Carolinas, the Catawba sometimes found it necessary to pursue small birds, such as robins and blue jays, to escape starvation (Speck 1946:13). The taking of songbirds for food has also been recorded among nineteenth-century whites in Cape May (Buchholz 1999:91). In this regard, it is interesting to note the presence of snakes, mice, and other nontraditional prey species among the refuse bones in archaeological sites (Cross 1941:147–148; Stanzeski 1996; Mounier 2000b). Although such creatures might have perished naturally in their dens, the possibility that they were consumed in times of hunger cannot be dismissed out of hand.

Archaeological cultures probably organized their hunting activities within broadly recognized territories, which in historic times were still defined by geographic elements (Speck 1940:203, 206). In the negotiations of 1758 with the English over disputed land titles, "the Indians informed the commissioners, that the lands they claimed, could not be by them described by lines, very intelligible to persons not on the spot, as they went to hollows, and small brooks, which had no certain names" (S. Smith 1765:443). MacLeod (1922:463) and Wallace (1947, 1957) indicated that, among the historic Lenape, related families resided in the same village and owned contiguous hunting territories, control of which was exercised by family elders.

Historical accounts indicate that hunting was practiced both by organized parties and by individuals, and this behavior can be projected back at least into late prehistoric times. In the middle of the seventeenth century, Peter Lindeström recorded a communal hunt that employed a technique known as the "fire-surround" (Lindeström 1925:213–215). An undisclosed number of hunters encircled a large area with fire and drove game animals toward the center. When the animals were concentrated in a confined space, the hunters attempted to kill as many as possible. After this hunt, which occurred in the spring, the Indians dispersed to hunt individually.

In the winter of 1632, while sailing into Delaware Bay, David Pietersz de Vries, a Dutch navigator, claimed to have "smelt the land" before sighting it. As he explained, "This comes from the Indians setting fire, at this time of year, to the woods and thickets, in order to hunt. . . . When the wind blows out of the northwest, and the smoke is driven to sea, it happens that the land is smelt before it is seen" (D. de Vries 1912:15).

In setting fires, the Indians were, in fact, practicing a form of wildlife management. Burning was followed by a renewal of shrubby vegetation, which served not only as food but also as cover for game animals. The same technique, with refinements, is still practiced in New Jersey today (Menzer 1977).

Moreover, the deer drive survives in New Jersey as a popular hunting technique among numerous gun clubs, which are largely composed of elder males, their sons, nephews, and close friends. To such groups, hunting is as much a traditional social function as it is a matter of food getting (Moonsammy, Cohen, and Williams 1987:18–19, 115–118). The social organization and protocols that regulate modern deer hunting by gun clubs harken back to the long-forgotten social relationships and logistics of ancient communal hunting.

HORTICULTURAL SITES. Throughout most of antiquity, the Indians followed an economy based on foraging, or what anthropologists frequently call "hunting and gathering." Archaeology attests to the collection of wild plant foods, such as amaranth and chenopodium, and this practice may have culminated in small-scale gardening late in prehistoric times (H. Kraft 1982:68; R. Stewart, Hummer, and Custer 1986:65). Tantalizing evidence for deliberate cultivation appears in large sites along the Delaware Valley from Trenton northward. At the Miller Field site, in Warren County, Herbert Kraft (1972:42, 51, 1975a:157–158) found numerous corncobs and husks (*Zea maize*) along with pumpkin and squash seeds (*Cucurbito spp.*) and common beans (*Phaseolus vulgaris*). He also reported beans and scattered traces of corn nearby at the Harry's Farm site (Kraft 1975a:157–158).

These sites contained deep storage pits, some of which measured 5 or 6 feet (1.5–1.8 m) in diameter and as much as 7 or 8 feet (2.1–2.4 m) deep (H. Kraft 1975a:157–158, 1982:154). The walls were puddled with clay to prevent infiltration of ground water, and post molds in the pit bottoms indicate the presence of ladders, racks, or roofing. These pits were repeatedly used. Charred corncobs and wood suggest that fires were intentionally set to harden the clay walls and to stem infestation by vermin (H. Kraft 1986a:112).

Even though cultigens (cultivated plants) are in evidence in the upper Delaware Valley, agricultural production was apparently limited. For example, at the Minisink site fewer than 1 percent of the pits contained seeds of maize, beans, or squash, and those pits all reflected occupations in very late prehistoric or early historic times (H. Kraft 1978:44–45; R. Stewart, Hummer, and Custer 1986:85). South of the Water Gap, the evidence for gardening is even more tenuous. Chris Hummer retrieved carbonized maize kernels from the Williamson site near Frenchtown, in Hunterdon County. Some of these seeds have been dated by C^{14} analysis to the period between A.D. 1220 and 1300 (R. Stewart, Hummer, and Custer 1986:79, 85). John Martin (1991:24) reported the discovery of a single kernel of corn at the Old Barracks in downtown Trenton, again in what are apparently late contexts. Despite all of the excavations at the Abbott Farm, spanning more than 120 years, not a single seed of any domesticated plant has ever come to light (R. Stewart, Hummer, and Custer 1986:79). Indeed, the only evidence of cultigens on the coastal plains comes from the Turkey Swamp site, in Monmouth County, where John Cavallo reported the discovery of a few carbonized corn kernels (R. Stewart, Hummer, and Custer 1986:79).

The paucity of the archaeological record is at variance with the accounts of early European visitors, who observed Indian gardening at large settlements in the middle and lower reaches of the Delaware Valley. Between 1654 and 1656 Peter Lindeström reported seeing maize and other vegetables growing in prepared hills. He stated that the banks of the Delaware near the falls, around Trenton, were "occupied by a large number of plantations," while at the falls of the Schuylkill the land was "cultivated with great power" (Lindeström 1925:179). Lindeström also described the Indians at Haertkill (Whorekill River in Delaware) as "a powerful nation rich in maize plantations" (Lindeström 1925:154, 166, 170). In this light, it is curious that there is no solid archaeological evidence of horticulture from any sites around Trenton or, indeed, from other locations in the lower Delaware Valley.

Twenty years ago, I attributed this situation to a lack of preservation due to adverse soil conditions or to the use of gross excavation techniques, which characterized much of the earlier archaeological work in this region (Mounier 1982:162). Yet, after many careful excavations in the ensuing years, direct evidence of horticulture on the coastal plains remains as weak as ever. Even in the north, where the data are stronger, there is no indication that the Indians ever became dedicated agriculturalists.

Marshall Becker's excavations in Pennsylvania and Delaware and, particularly, his painstaking study of early historical documents help to explain this discrepancy. Like their ancestors, the historic Indians were foragers who supplemented gathered foods with summer gardening. According to Becker, between ca. 1640 and 1660, when several important early historical accounts were recorded,

> [S]ome Lenape bands were cash cropping maize from an unusually clustered series of summer stations. This activity was an economic response to the Swedish colonists' need for grain. When the colonists could grow sufficient grain to feed themselves by 1660, the market for Lenape grown maize disappeared. At no time during this episode did the Lenape store maize nor did they alter their normal collecting strategies. (Becker 1988:80)

Apparently, the Indians took to horticulture only on the eve of the European onslaught, and then principally as a means of bolstering trade. The power of cultural traditions is very strong, and these very mobile foragers apparently did not feel compelled to abandon an age-old and very successful way of life in favor of a sedentary existence as farmers. Thus, it seems increasingly likely that the native populations never embraced gardening with any enthusiasm.

QUARRIES OR LITHIC WORKSHOPS. Aboriginal quarries are found wherever erosion has exposed suitable raw materials. Characteristic locations include rock outcrops, exposed hillsides or valley walls, and gravel bars. In geological terms, two kinds of exposures were exploited, primary and secondary. Primary deposits are those that reside where they were first formed, for example, chert nodules in limestone formations. Secondary deposits contain materials—usually cobbles and pebbles—that have been transported from primary sources by natural agencies, such as glaciers or floodwaters.

Usually, primary sources yield relatively large masses of material from which large weapons and tools can be fashioned (Knowles 1941a:154; Cross 1956:75). Such materials lend themselves to reduction through a series of useful forms, beginning with large bifaces suitable for use as choppers or cleavers, through progressively smaller and more refined pieces, such as hafted knives, and ending with projectile points, scrapers, and drill bits. This sequential progression—or "staged biface reduction"—is typical of certain Late or Terminal Archaic knapping systems, such as those practiced by the various cultures of the Susquehanna tradition (Witthoft 1949, 1953; Ritchie 1965:149–155; Cresson 1990; Truncer 1990). The Middle Woodland Fox Creek and Jack's Reef cultures also employed staged biface reduction strategies (Cresson 1984, n.d.a, and pers. comm.). The "cookie-cutter" exactitude of biface production among these cultures has inspired some archaeologists to postulate the rise of an elite class of expert knappers (R. Stewart 1987:40–42; Cresson n.d.b and pers. comm.).

On the other hand, the relatively small size of cobbles and pebbles in secondary deposits limited their use to implements of small proportions, virtually eliminating the potential for developing a system of staged biface reduction by knapping (Knowles 1941a:154; R. Stewart 1987; Jack Cresson, pers. comm.). Rather, weapons and tools were fashioned directly from cobbles or from cobble-derived flakes. Much of this work—well within the grasp of the general populace—was decidedly inelegant, especially toward the end of the prehistoric era (R. Stewart 1987:42; Jack Cresson, pers. comm.). The complex of small triangular points, flake tools, and scrapers that characterizes most Late Woodland assemblages is typical of this approach to knapping.

Most aboriginal quarries are really workshops, where pieces of workable stone were tested for quality, reduced to manageable proportions if needed, and rendered into useful implements. Aboriginal knappers attempted to select the very best materials from those that were readily available. In the northern Highlands, Lenik (1991:15) has noted that "some time and energy were expended in sorting and selecting particular cobble materials by prehistoric people during their seasonal rounds." In independent research around the state, Jack Cresson (pers. comm.) has observed many outcrops and gravel beds that are littered with "tested" nodules, tablets, or cobbles. These are stones from which flakes had been removed to expose a fresh inner surface for inspection. This clever practice presaged by several millennia the modern technique of prospecting with a geologist's rock hammer. Tested cobbles frequently show up on habitation sites on the coastal plains (Mounier 1999b, 1999d, 2000b).

Once suitable materials were located, they had to be broken into pieces that allowed for transportation. Thus, at many source locations, "blocks of material lie detached, and with them the chips, cores, rejects, and failures of the process of arrow making. Stone mauls and hammers nearby also tell of the quarryman's industry, but usually there are no perfect examples of the tools at which he toiled, for he took them away as the fruits of his labor" (Skinner and Schrabisch 1913:15). This description is typical of the many native quarries that have been found around the state (Skinner and Schrabisch 1913; Schrabisch 1917; Kier 1949; Hall 1970:12).

Despite occasional references to the contrary (Hall 1970:12), extensive pitting or shaft mining has not been confirmed from the prehistoric era in New Jersey (Lenik 1991:14; Jack Cresson, pers. comm.). Most of the numerous open-face mines, especially in the northern parts of the state, were excavated by historic peoples in search of metallic ores, building blocks, or fill materials. Aboriginal stone mining appears to have been limited to working around partially exposed pieces to aid in their manipulation or removal.

Settlements often occurred near workable lithic sources, thereby leaving evidence not only of lithic processing but also of other cultural activities. Villages or camps occupied locations that offered advantages for long-term settlement in addition to nearby lithic sources. The late prehistoric site at Frenche's Pond in Sussex County is but one example (Hall 1970). Less favorably situated workshops might still show evidence of at least transient occupation (Cross 1941:132; Mounier 1999a; Jack Cresson, pers. comm.).

The gathering and processing of stone was likely to have been integrated into an annual cycle so as not to conflict with other necessary activities, such as hunting, fishing, and nut collecting. Cresson, who has studied many ancient quarries and aboriginal stoneworking techniques, has concluded that stone procurement and processing was probably scheduled for the spring of the year in conjunction with traditional "renewal rituals" (pers. comm.).

The diversity of stone used in antiquity reflects the natural occurrence of various materials around the state. In the mountainous sections of northern New Jersey, flints and cherts abound in limestone formations and in cobble deposits outwashed from the Wisconsin glacial moraine (Schrabisch 1915:25, 1917:46; Richards 1941:20; Hall 1970:12; H. Kraft 1982:69; Marshall 1982:22–23; LaPorta 1989; Lenik 1991:14). Numerous aboriginal quarries have been found in this region. Indeed, LaPorta (1989, 1994) discovered more than 300 chert quarries just in the valley of the Wallkill River in Sussex County and adjoining parts of Orange County, New York. Hall (1970:12) observed that black, gray, and white cherts or flint were the dominant materials for flaked stone tools in Sussex County. Often settlements were situated near chert or flint outcrops. For example, the thousands of small triangular points from a site on the shore of Frenche's Pond appear to have been made from a dark gray flint obtained from a local exposure (Hall 1970:12). In addition, Schrabisch (1915:25) reported that "flint pebbles are also more or less common in many gravel deposits of the county, so that there was a great abundance of this material which was highly prized by the Indian and much used particularly for arrow-points." Research in the Highlands indicates the extensive use of local pebble cherts for stone weapons and tools (Chrisbacher 1990:71; Lenik 1990:36, 1991).

In the Piedmont, masses of argillaceous shale and argillite occur in formations of Triassic age, especially along the Delaware River below Rieglesville in Hunterdon and Mercer Counties (Schrabisch 1915:25–26, 1917; Didier 1975). To a large extent, the widespread distribution of argillaceous artifacts throughout New Jersey and adjoining states can be tied to the quarries and work stations in and around Flemington. Schrabisch noted:

> Ledges and boulders of argillite occur abundantly along the streams, which have cut deep valleys in the edge of the tableland west of Flemington. Ancient workshop sites strewn with chips and rejects are particularly numerous along Mine (Walnut) Brook. . . . It is highly probable that partly-shaped implements from these "quarries" were carried in large numbers to distant camps and villages for finishing. . . . Enormous quantities of chips and many unfinished or rejected blades of argillite indicate the former existence of an industry both intense and long continued. Here were the so-called Indian quarries to which the redman came probably from a relatively wide area to obtain the raw material for his stone implements. (Schrabisch 1917:62)

The use of argillaceous materials is common in central New Jersey, especially near the natural sources, but cobble cherts were also extensively employed (Cross 1941:208; Knowles 1941a:153–154 [table 10]; R. Stewart 1987; Perazio 1988:65; Lenik 1991).

The coastal plains, which themselves are formed of reworked glacial and marine sediments, abound with pebbles and cobbles of chert, flint, jasper, quartz, and quartzite (Salisbury and Knapp 1917; Kümmel 1941:11; Richards 1941:20). Transported boulders of shale are also sometimes found, though often at considerable depths (Salisbury and Knapp 1917:13).

Exposures in streambeds and other deposits were worked for suitable stone. For example, at the Salisbury site in Gloucester County, Cross (1941:56) suggested that partially worked cobbles might indicate the acquisition of stone from the nearby river beaches. A large cobble field in the confluence of Co-hansey Creek and Rocaps Run, south of Bridgeton in Cumberland County, shows evidence of extensive prospecting by aboriginal knappers (Mounier n.d.a). Joseph Arsenault (pers. comm.) has discovered evidence of aboriginal cobble knapping on a hillside near Glassboro in Gloucester County. Simi-lar tailings can be seen on the flanks of the cuesta mounts from Salem to Monmouth Counties, where quartzite and limonitic sandstone were worked in addition to cryptocrystalline cobbles (Mounier 1990a; Jack Cresson, pers. comm.).

Most sites on the Outer Coastal Plain provide at least a hint of imple-ment manufacture from locally obtained cobbles or pebbles of chert, jasper, quartz, or quartzite. Although cobble cherts were used as early as Paleoindian times (Cavallo 1981; Bonfiglio and Cresson 1982:19), the percentage of cobble usage increased in the later cultural periods (Cross 1941; Mounier 1972a, 1974b, 1975, etc.; R. Stewart 1987). Cresson (n.d.a) has calculated that as many as 94 percent of the stone tools of late prehistoric age originated in local cobble sources on the Inner Coastal Plain, on the eastern part of the Outer Coastal Plain, and along the flanks of the cuesta. In the lower portions of the Outer Coastal Plain, especially in drainage basins that flow to the Delaware Bay, Cresson has determined that cobble sources account for as many as 50 per-cent of the stone tools. The use of cobbles is often demonstrated by the pres-ence of residual cortex or "rind" on flakes or, more rarely, on the implements themselves.

A peculiar form of pink or reddish brown quartzite occurs as cobbles and boulders in deposits along the cuesta belt, on the divide between the Inner and Outer Coastal Plains. Jack Cresson has coined the term *cuesta quartzite* to de-scribe this material. At many locations in Evesham Township, Burlington County, aboriginal populations exploited this material as a source of flaked stone tools, especially during Late Archaic and Early Woodland times (Mou-nier 1998a, 1999b; Jack Cresson, pers. comm.). Cobbles of cuesta quartzite also served as hammerstones for working other materials, especially argillaceous shale. A "mining" technique, apparently unique to cuesta quartzite, was the use of fire to detach spalls from very large, water-rounded rocks that could not be reduced in any other way (Jack Cresson, pers. comm.). Another min-eral product of the cuesta region is limonite-cemented sandstone, sometimes known as "ironstone," which was also used to make projectile points, slab tools, and chopping tools (Mounier 1975, 1990a). Like cuesta quartzite, this material was briefly popular during the Early Woodland period.

A fossiliferous quartzite is found between the villages of Fairton and

Greenwich, along Cohansey Creek in southwestern Cumberland County (Skinner and Schrabisch 1913:57; Knowles 1941a:154; Richards 1941:21; Kier 1949). This material, known as Cohansey quartzite, was widely utilized for flaked stone tools during the Early and Middle Archaic periods and again in the Early and Late Woodland periods. It was very widely used in southwestern New Jersey and, more sporadically, across the rest of the coastal plains. An aboriginal quarry of this material was said to exist along the western side of Molly Wheaton Run near Greenwich (Skinner and Schrabisch 1913:57). This quarry was probably expanded during historic times, when quartzite was removed for use in local building foundations. The site is now marked by a large circular depression.

Cryptocrystalline materials from more distant primary sources occur in archaeological sites around the state. Cherts, jaspers, and chalcedonies from isolated locations in Pennsylvania, New York, and Delaware sometimes appear as raw material in archaeological deposits in New Jersey (Kümmel 1941; Custer, Ward, and Watson 1986; Lavin and Prothero 1987). The most notable of these are: the fine "Pennsylvania jaspers" from deposits around Vera Cruz and Macungie, Pennsylvania; Onondaga chert from upstate New York; the Normanskill, Deepkill, and Coxsackie cherts from the lower Hudson Valley of New York; the so-called Newark jasper from the vicinity of Iron Hill near Newark, Delaware; and Broad Run chalcedony, which outcrops in the vicinity of Landenberg, Pennsylvania.

In contrast to the plentiful evidence of lithic resources, we know virtually nothing about the sources of clay used by prehistoric potters. Suitable clay bodies occur widely in New Jersey and were the basis of a thriving ceramics industry during historic times (Twitchell 1913; Kennedy et al. 1963). Until we have definitive data, we can only suppose that most aboriginal pottery was created from locally available clays, presumably gathered from naturally exposed strata.

OTHER WORK STATIONS. Work stations established to collect or process only perishable materials—such as grasses, bast fibers, or wood—have left few detectable archaeological traces. Moreover, such sites would be very difficult to identify archaeologically, especially if the related tools had been removed.

Nevertheless, the assemblages at certain sites hint at the kinds of tasks that might have been performed. For instance, at the Woodbury Annex site in West Deptford Township, Gloucester County, a large collection of small, teardrop-shaped implements show tip damage from a twisting motion, which seems to signify the splitting of small reeds or slender woody plants, possibly for use in baskets. Thus, these implements, at least at this site, were hand tools and not projectile points, as commonly supposed (Mounier and Cresson 1988; Mounier and Martin 1994:131–132, 138).

Some small sites near Center Square, along Oldmans Creek in Gloucester County, have yielded an abundance of heavy woodworking tools, such as axes and celts. These sites are situated on low ground along the creek bank, where work may have focused on the production of log canoes (Mounier 1996a).

A number of sites in Burlington County appear to have been repeatedly occupied in Late Archaic or Early Woodland times for the collection and processing of hickory nuts. Clusters of charred nuts, together with fire-broken rocks, indicate that the nuts were either roasted or boiled for the extraction of oil (Louis Berger and Associates 1987; Hunter Research 1994; Mounier 2000b).

Many other sites of this sort undoubtedly existed but remain archaeologically invisible for want of organic preservation or the presence of distinctive tools.

––––––––

WE HAVE SEEN that the Lenape and their predecessors occupied a variety of sites, both large and small, that were bound together as settlement systems. These sites were arranged on the landscape in virtually any location that would support life. The largest sites tended to concentrate upon the banks of the major rivers, particularly in ecologically rich zones. The smaller camps, which in a sense were satellites of the larger villages, occupied locations with less varied resources. Although direct archaeological evidence is lacking, it is generally supposed that these settlements were interconnected by trails and watercourses. A few sites contain evidence of ancient housing in the form of rock shelters, pole-built dwellings, and living floors, whose superstructures left no lasting imprint on the earth.

The archaeological remains clearly indicate that the aboriginal cultures of New Jersey survived by exploiting the varied resources provided in nature. Lithic materials were acquired directly from bedrock or were collected from gravel deposits around the state. Many of these sources were exploited only for local use, while others, particularly extensive deposits of argillite and argillaceous shale, yielded artifacts that were distributed across the region.

Hunting, fishing, and shellfishing are amply demonstrated, and a few sites appear to show an emphasis on specific economic activities, such as nut harvesting or woodworking. Gardening, though practiced late in the prehistoric era, apparently never assumed a primary role as a means of survival.

In short, thousands of prehistoric sites have been identified in all parts of New Jersey. The inexorable march of progress has obliterated many sites, but vestiges survive, even in our largest cities. Doubtless, many others await the archaeologist in farmlands, forests, and other undeveloped ground. The archaeological record clearly shows that in ancient times, as now, New Jersey was a good place to live and work.

CHAPTER

4

Of Life and Death

So wilt thou recover me, and make me to live.

———

ISAIAH 38:16

Properly disposing of the dead is a necessary function in all human societies. The physical and ceremonial removal of the dead is required to protect the health of the living, to defend deceased loved ones from scavengers, and to minimize, if not eliminate, the risk of haunting. Accordingly, every human society, at least since Neanderthal times, has prescribed acceptable forms and rituals for the burial of the dead. When preservation allows, archaeology can define various aspects of burial practices and from them infer social relationships, economic status, and other elements of past human behavior. Archaeologists, working together with physical anthropologists and medical practitioners, also can learn about the stature, health, and history of trauma of the deceased. Although many ancient societies clearly had highly developed belief systems regarding the afterworld, archaeology can reconstruct ritual practices only tentatively, if at all.

Most of our knowledge of aboriginal burial practices comes from data gathered as much by chance discovery as by active investigation during the late nineteenth and early twentieth centuries. Natural decay, ever-increasing development, and previous archaeological excavations all diminish the sites now available for study. In addition, an increasing sensitivity to the concerns of native peoples for the sanctity of their dead has affected public policy. Even though archaeology offers the single best hope of understanding ancient cultures, the present political climate severely restricts archaeological research.

As Herbert C. Kraft (1978:47) pointed out, opposition from aggrieved ethnic groups and constraints imposed by state and federal laws ever more severely restrict the exhumation and examination of skeletons from archaeological sites. Indeed, the Native American Graves Protection and Repatriation Act of 1998 has effectively banned the excavation of aboriginal graves. Consequently, future advances in knowledge from continuing archaeological and osteological research are in doubt.

This chapter will summarize our present understanding of archaeological burials in New Jersey and what they tell us about the lives and times of those now long dead. I begin with basic information concerning the relative antiquity of mortuary practices in New Jersey and the distribution of burial places around the state. A discussion of archaeologically recognized modes of interment follows, with specific examples from selected sites, generally proceeding from the most ancient to the most modern sites. The elaborate mortuary complexes by which certain cultures are known will be contrasted with the more common and mundane expressions. Where the data permit, I shall offer examples of how archaeology and related sciences help to flesh out the lives of ancient peoples, and how archaeology can be used to place grave sites, and the related societies, into a cultural-chronological framework.

Although this chapter focuses primarily upon the mortuary practices of aboriginal groups, an example from an early-nineteenth-century graveyard will provide interesting points of comparison and contrast. In the end, we shall see that, in their concern for the proper treatment of their dead, widely disparate cultures are very much alike.

ANTIQUITY AND DISTRIBUTION OF BURIALS

The most ancient graves known to archaeology in New Jersey are cremations from about 10,000 years ago (Stanzeski 1996:44–45, 1998:43). Other cremations date back approximately 4,500 years; and beginning about 3,000 years ago, undeniable evidence of burial in the flesh appears with increasing frequency up to historic times (Cross 1941, 1956:57–67; H. Kraft 1975a:88–89, 1976a:47–62). R. Michael Stewart (1995) has argued on geological grounds that some deeply buried skeletons may be in excess of 8,000 years old, but this estimate remains a matter for debate.

The early date for the appearance of cremation does not necessarily imply the primacy of cremation over burial in the flesh. Rather, it may well reflect differential preservation: calcined (incinerated) bone is chemically stable and will last indefinitely in the ground, whereas untreated or "green" bone rapidly decays. Accordingly, many apparently empty pits and isolated artifacts, especially those in caches, may actually represent graves from which the skeletal materials have disappeared through natural decay processes.

Ancient burial places have been identified in virtually all parts of New Jersey and on Staten Island, which by its geography, if not its political boundaries, is part of New Jersey. Over the years, literally hundreds of graves have been found. For example, beginning in the 1860s, excavators removed about 300 skeletons from the large Indian cemetery opposite Minisink Island in Sussex County (Heye and Pepper 1915; H. Kraft 1978:47). Many other graves have been excavated from sites in Sussex, Warren, and Hunterdon Counties (Skinner and Schrabisch 1913; Schrabisch 1915, 1917; Ritchie 1949:168–170; Kraft 1972:7, 1975a:86–91; Marchiando 1972:135–138). The early work of Ernest Volk at the falls of the Delaware below Trenton yielded at least 86 skeletons (Volk 1911), and later excavations in the same vicinity by the Indian Site Survey produced evidence of at least 88 more (Cross 1956). The Indian Site Survey also found 14 skeletons at other locations around the state (Cross 1941). Skinner (1909, 1915:8, 1932:17–19), Skinner and Schrabisch (1913), and Harrington (1909a:6–7) reported many burials from Tottenville and other locations on the western shore of Staten Island, and also at Constable Hook in Bayonne. Several sites near Tuckerton in Ocean County have yielded, in the aggregate, well over two dozen aboriginal graves (Bello and Eisenberg 1988: 45–51; Stanzeski 1996; Ubelaker 1997a). Five more burials were unearthed in West Long Branch in Monmouth County in the 1930s (Richard Veit, pers. comm.), and many others have been discovered elsewhere, frequently with little or no published notice (Fountain 1897; Heye and Pepper 1915:12–14; Blenk 1977b; Thomas 1987, 1990:44, 47).

FORMS OF BURIAL

Among the archaeological cultures of New Jersey, the most common form of burial involved placing the dead body in the ground, either in a specially prepared grave or in some other convenient hollow. Sometimes skeletons were removed from one location and later reburied at another. Finally, cremations have been recorded, as already noted, but such discoveries are quite unusual.

Sometimes, as a matter of necessity, the deceased were placed in pits that were also used for the disposal of refuse. At the Abbott Farm, near Trenton, many human skeletons were found in refuse pits during the Indian Site Survey excavations (Cross 1956:57). Other examples of this type of burial have been noted in the Tocks Island area (H. Kraft 1975a:88–89, 1976a:54–56). Archaeologists assume that this practice was occasioned by frozen ground or some other impediment to digging a separate grave. Because excavation of the grave pit required manual labor, assisted only by rudimentary tools (such as pointed sticks, stone hoes, and scoops fashioned from wood, bone, or shell), most burials were placed at very shallow depths in the earth.

The cremation of skeletal materials occurred in specially prepared fire pits or on platforms of packed earth (Hawkes and Linton 1916; Cross 1956:59–63). Intense heat from wood fires transformed the bones into small chalky, checkered, and sometimes splintered fragments, which could then be gathered up for burial. The process of cremation reduced both the size and weight of the human remains, easing the task of transportation for reburial, which was a common practice, and also decreasing the required dimensions of the grave pit. In addition, thorough cremation entirely eliminated putrefaction of the corpse. Thus, the act of cremation was doubtless central to certain ancient purification rituals.

In prehistoric times, most in-flesh interments involved the burial of the dead in a flexed position, that is, with the body laid on its side, the knees and elbows bent, and the limbs drawn up toward the chest. Posing the deceased in this manner may have had symbolic meaning, but we shall never know whether ancient peoples entertained metaphorical notions concerning burial in the "fetal position" or whether, by hobbling the body, they hoped to prevent the return of the corpse as a ghost. This much is clear: flexed burials, like cremations, economized on the size of the grave chamber.

Prehistoric peoples apparently desired to bury their dead at home whenever possible; if someone died at a distance, the bones were gathered up after decomposition or intentional removal of the soft tissues. This custom, recorded by Samuel Smith (1765:137), persisted into historical times among the natives of New Jersey: "When a person of note died far from his own residence, they would carry his bones to be buried there." John Heckewelder (1819:75–76), a Moravian missionary, recorded a similar practice among the historic Nanticoke Indians, a group closely related to the Delaware Indians or Lenape of New Jersey. In such cases the major skeletal elements, especially the skull and long bones, were transported back to the home territory for interment. Because the bones were packaged for transit, such interments are called

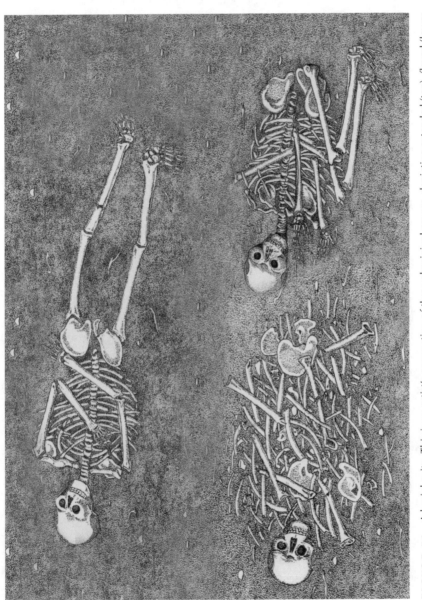

FIGURE 71. A burial suite. This is an artist's conception of three aboriginal graves, depicting extended (top), flexed (lower right), and bundle (lower left) burials. Original art courtesy of Alan E. Carman.

"bundle burials." For obvious reasons, they are also called reburials or secondary burials. Ordinarily, the long bones were arranged in the grave more or less parallel to each other, and the skull was positioned at one end of the parcel. In bundle burials the skeletons were, by necessity, at least partially disarticulated. The extent of disarticulation can be a measure of the time elapsed between death and reburial.

Commonly, the outline of the bone bundle as it appears in the grave describes the shape of the container in which the skeleton was carried and subsequently buried. Apparently, bags or nets were used for this purpose, which might account for the loss of some of the smaller bones. Others may have been lost at the site of the original interment or may have been carried off by scavenging animals.

In some prehistoric burials, the corpse was laid out in a supine position. One writer has suggested that the onset of rigor mortis may have necessitated interment in this position (Volk 1911:53); since rigor mortis is a temporary condition, this conclusion may be more speculative than real. In any case, after the arrival of Europeans, aboriginal peoples increasingly began to adopt the practice of burial in extended postures, sometimes in coffins. This change probably reflects the efforts of Europeans to impart Christian modes of burial. The so-called Munsee cemetery in Sussex County contained at least 28 extended burials, some with trinkets of European manufacture (Heye and Pepper 1915:18–30). At the Pahaquarra site in Warren County, three historic Indian skeletons, dating to the 1750s (Baird 1987), had been buried in coffins, and all were well supplied with European trade goods. One of these graves contained a crucifix and several Jesuit rings (H. Kraft 1976a:56–62).

Skeletons have sometimes been recovered in a "sitting" or partially inclined position. At the Lalor Field, near Trenton, Ernest Volk described one burial in which the "skeleton was found in the posture of one sitting in a reclining chair." Volk (1911:17) was so taken with this burial that he displayed it at the World's Columbian Exposition in 1893. Whether this posture reflects conscious intent on the part of the burial party or the vagaries of placing a body in an irregular, sloping hole is an open question.

On intensely occupied sites, long-forgotten skeletons were quite commonly disturbed by subsequent digging in the course of day-to-day activities. In such cases the bones may have been cast aside or redeposited without regard to keeping the remains intact. Thus, the inadvertent disturbance of previous burials frequently resulted in the scattering of skeletal materials. This phenomenon is also quite common in the older cemeteries of modern societies.

Most often, graves contain solitary interments, but multiple burials in a single grave pit are not uncommon, especially on larger sites. Several multiple burials were noted on sites at the falls of the Delaware River (Volk 1911:31, 62; Cross 1956:63–66). A grave containing the remains of five or six individuals, was unearthed in Gloucester City, in Camden County (Thomas 1987, 1990:44, 47). A minimum of six skeletons from a single grave pit came to light as a result of dredging near Tuckerton, in Ocean County (Bello and Eisenberg 1988). At the Havins site in Sussex County, three bodies had been buried in a single grave and covered with slabs of stone (Dunay 1981:4).

Evidence for the use of coffins is generally lacking in archaeological settings, probably due to decay. A layer of bark, grass, or hide was probably used to line the grave or to wrap the corpse before burial, as suggested by historic and ethnographic analogues. Heckewelder (1819:264, 271) mentioned the use of bark as well as wooden coffins among the historic Delaware Indians or Lenape. Some ancient skeletons appear to have been wrapped in bark or cloth shrouds (Randolph 1983:13).

Occasionally, items were placed in the grave, presumably to sustain the deceased in the afterlife. Some offerings were doubtless tokens of affection left by mourners; alternatively, they may have been the deceased's prized possessions. The presence, quality, and quantity of grave goods may indicate the social status of the deceased or the wealth and rank of the contributors. In the final analysis, the inclusion of grave offerings almost certainly manifests concerns not only with the afterlife but also with the maintenance of individual and group identities as well as social integration among the survivors (Bragdon 1999:89). Funerals, as the saying goes, are for the living.

However, many graves contain no funerary offerings. This condition may denote a low social status for the deceased, a nonmaterialistic worldview in the society at large, or merely the disintegration of offerings fashioned from perishable materials. Valuable goods may have been pilfered, but there is no direct evidence of grave robbing until historical times.

It was not unusual for isolated graves to be placed within living areas or work stations, but in several instances specific locations appear to have been set off for use as cemeteries. At least in some cases, knowledge of cemetery locations was carefully preserved by cultural tradition, as the following anecdote demonstrates: "Dr. Abbott informed the writer [Alanson Skinner] that some modern Delaware Indians, from the west, visiting Trenton with Buffalo Bill some years ago, were in possession of so vivid a tradition of the location of this cemetery [near Biles Island] that they were able to find it, although none of them had ever seen the place before" (Skinner and Schrabisch 1913:65). Aboriginal cemeteries have been discovered opposite Minisink Island, in Sussex County (Heye and Pepper 1915), at locations near Trenton (Skinner and Schrabisch 1913:65; Cross 1956:57), at the Lerro Farm near Pedricktown, in Salem County (Blenk 1977b), and at the Boni Farm near Bridgeport, in Gloucester County (Mounier 1974c, 1978b).

Although grave sites frequently occupy natural knolls, the construction of artificial burial mounds in New Jersey has never been substantiated, persistent rumors to the contrary notwithstanding.

ANCIENT CREMATIONS AT WEST CREEK

Excavations in the late 1980s and 1990s by members of the Archaeological Society of New Jersey near the town of West Creek, in Ocean County, revealed the oldest human burials thus far recorded in New Jersey. The cremated remains consisted of 13 clusters of calcined bone, each covering about 4¼ square feet (0.4 m^2). The interments were confined to an area that covered no more than 400 square feet (37 m^2), thus signifying burial within a recognized cemetery. These burials accompanied an assemblage of Early Archaic weapon tips of the Kirk Corner—Notched type, flakes, and a few small scrapers, all of jasper. Associated charcoal was dated by C^{14} analysis to 9,850 B.P. (Stanzeski 1996:44–45, 1998:43). In 1981, a similar association of Kirk Stemmed points and cremated bone was observed at Site 28-CU-79, near Vineland in Cumberland County, but material suitable for carbon dating was entirely lacking (Mounier n.d.b).

CREMATION BURIALS OF THE KOENS-CRISPIN COMPLEX

Cremation burials also occurred in Late Archaic times (ca. 3,000–5,000 B.P.) in sites of the Koens-Crispin complex, named for the Koens-Crispin site near Medford in Burlington County. Other related burial places have been noted near Marlton (Regensburg 1971; Burrow 1997), on the eastern slope of Arney's Mount, and on the outskirts of Pemberton, all in Burlington County (Jack Cresson, pers. comm.).

This complex featured an elaborate pattern of mortuary ceremonialism that emphasized cremation, the ritual use of red ochre, and, often, the profuse inclusion of valuable, imported grave goods. Some of the fancier artifacts appear to have been intentionally broken or "killed," presumably to release the spirit of the implement for travel with the deceased into the afterlife. This custom, which is common in ancient burial sites, also had a practical side: it deterred grave robbing, because the broken articles were rendered useless. Intentional breakage also increased the rarity of the similar objects remaining among the living and thus augmented their value.

The Koens-Crispin Site

The Koens-Crispin site was discovered early in the twentieth century and explored archaeologically in two episodes widely separated in time. E. W. Hawkes and Ralph Linton (1916) opened excavations at the Crispin Farm in 1915. They discovered 20 artifact caches arranged in concentric lines around the edge of a large fire pit. This fire pit covered at least 60 square feet (5.6 m^2). Although the great hearth contained no artifacts, the intense fire had discolored the earth to a depth of 3 feet. A smaller, circular fire pit, about 3 feet (90 cm) in diameter, lay adjacent to the large hearth. Several smaller hearths were associated with scattered artifacts.

Some of the caches around the large hearth contained winged and perforated atlatl or spear-thrower weights (bannerstones) and other artifacts, such as axes, adzes, celts, and hammerstones. Other caches contained pairs of large, stemmed, broad-bladed points or bifaces associated with crumbling fragments of bone. Still other objects included faceted stones for the production of paint (red ochre?), polished stone crescents (which may have been imperforate bannerstones intended to be affixed to a shaft by lashing), fossil brachiopods, a pecked and polished quartz crystal ball, several white quartz pebbles (possibly from a turtle-shell or bark rattle), so-called earplugs (small cylinders worked from soft stone), and oddly shaped iron concretions. The fossils, earplugs, and concretions bore traces of red paint. Finally, six argillite "hoes" were found outside of the "ceremonial area." These objects may have been used as digging implements.

The various features were assumed to define a ceremonial location of uncertain function. Hawkes and Linton (1916:57–58) speculated that "[t]he difference in the value of the caches may represent a corresponding difference in the wealth and station of those who made the offerings, but as there were no other indications of rank, it is impossible to decide this question. It has also been suggested that the caches were not properly offerings, but marked the

FIGURE 72. Bannerstones *in situ*. This cache of exquisite bannerstones was revealed by the Indian Site Survey excavations at the Koens-Crispin site, ca. 1937–1938. Courtesy of the New Jersey State Museum.

position of dignitaries around the council fire. As a rule, the caches adjacent to the fire pit were the richest." The writers interpreted the osseous material to have been the remains of animal sacrifices.

Drawn to the site by the earlier report of spectacular "ceremonial finds," the Indian Site Survey opened excavations on the property in 1937 and 1938 (Cross 1941:81–90). These excavations revealed 41 additional caches, but no evidence of patterned distribution was noted. The caches contained a variety of artifacts, such as broad-bladed points or knives, "blades" (unfinished points), hammerstones, pestles, celts of chipped and knobbed varieties, shaft-smoothers, weights or sinkers, and a "rubbing stone" (burnisher). Two caches contained three atlatl weights, together with blades of shale, celts, and pieces of steatite. Other unusual items included chipped stone hoes and a quartzite ball about 2¼ inches (5.7 cm) in diameter.

One whole bannerstone and six fragments were found loose in the soil. All of these implements were of the winged and perforated type. These items were fashioned from imported materials: banded slate, steatite, shale, and porphyry. Examples in sandstone, possibly of local origin, were also noted. Meager amounts of bone, of both human and animal origin, were found in pits nearby, but no bones were recovered from any of the caches.

The Red Valley Site

At the Red Valley site in Monmouth County, another series of caches containing bannerstones and other objects was found by the Indian Site Survey during excavations in 1936 and 1937 (Cross 1941:117–127). The caches at this site included a mix of artifacts similar to those noted above: bifaces, hammerstones, knobbed celts, hoes, shaft-smoothers, weights or sinkers, and a rubbing stone. The points at Red Valley were predominately of a narrow-bladed and contracting stemmed style, which contrasts with the broader form of their counterparts at the Koens-Crispin site. Based upon differences in the typology of the points, the assemblage at Red Valley probably predates the finds at the Koens-Crispin and related sites.

The Red Valley site yielded 14 bannerstones, 7 of slate, 2 of sandstone, and 5 fragments of the same two materials. Although not all of these objects had been finished before burial, all were of the perforated variety.

Two caches contained bannerstones. In one deposit two bannerstones were found with a blade of shale and one or more pieces of steatite. Another contained a polished stone weight of banded slate, two broken sandstone celts, and some charcoal. In five caches, unusual implements other than

FIGURE 73. Excavations at Red Valley, June 1938. An unidentified WPA crew is at work for the Indian Site Survey. Courtesy of the New Jersey State Museum.

FIGURE 74. Implements from Red Valley. The Red Valley site in Monmouth County contained artifacts similar to the Koens-Crispin complex in Burlington County. Pictured here (top row, from left to right) are a plain celt, two knobbed celts, a grooved adze, and a full grooved axe. At bottom is a pestle. The scale is in inches. Courtesy of the New Jersey State Museum.

bannerstones were included along with points and more mundane artifacts. One feature contained a polished stone gouge; another had a knobbed celt; and a third had a polished stone axe entirely grooved for fixing to a helve, a pestle, a possible whetstone, and fragments of what appeared to be human teeth. Two caches consisted entirely of points; one contained 15 points and the other 5.

The Savich Farm Site

Between 1966 and 1972 Richard Regensburg excavated part of a large and spectacular cemetery of the Koens-Crispin complex on the Savich Farm site, near Marlton. Associated charcoal was dated by the C^{14} technique to a period between 3,500 and 4,400 B.P. The excavations yielded 41 burials, which were arranged within a cemetery that covered approximately 3,000 square feet (279 m^2). Regensburg (1971:21) and Burrow (1997:36) noted 41 pits with funerary offerings, but two of the features no longer contained skeletal remains. Interments occurred in specially prepared pits or, sometimes, in existing holes that already contained refuse. One burial appears to have been deposited in a shallow wooden container. The fact that few of the grave pits encroached upon others suggests that the locations of burials had been marked or otherwise committed to memory. The orientation of the graves and included offerings demonstrated a general alignment along a north-south axis (Burrow 1997:36), hinting at the existence of the belief, common among many societies, that special arrangement of the grave would facilitate the spiritual entry of the departed into the ethereal world.

Associated with the burials were exceptionally well-made atlatl weights of a winged and perforated variety, predominately broad-bladed projectile points, woodworking tools (knobbed celts and adzes), grooved shaft-smoothers, and a host of other artifacts, as well as fossils. Regensburg's excavations yielded 25 complete bannerstones and 15 fragmentary examples. The lithic materials used in many of the specimens indicate importation from the Midwest or other distant regions (Regensburg 1971 and pers. comm.; Burrow 1997).

An analysis of the human bone by Dr. Douglas H. Ubelaker of the Smithsonian Institution indicated the presence of at least 52 individuals, whose remains had been cremated elsewhere and later brought to the site for burial (Ubelaker 1997b). Most of the graves contained the partial remains of at least 1 individual. Five contained at least 2 individuals; another contained at least 3; and yet another contained at least 4.

The condition of the calcined bones indicated crematory temperatures generally in excess of 700°C (ca. 1300°F). Exposure to the fire transformed the bones into small, brittle, and chalky fragments that displayed marked warping, checking, and bleaching to a gray-white color. These characteristics indicate cremation in the flesh. As judged from the closure of cranial sutures (joints in the bones of the skull) and other factors, most of the deceased were older than 15 years of age at death. Young children and infants are not well represented, possibly due to poor preservation or to exclusion of youngsters from cremation, or both. Among the adults, three females and five males appear to have been present; however, the fragmentary condition of the bones and their distortion from thermal stress make the determinations of sex very tentative.

The early researchers failed to deduce the function of the Koens-Crispin and Red Valley sites as cemeteries, apparently because the human skeletal material was scarce. Some of the bones may have been lost anciently due to periodic reburials, or the excavators might have mistaken human remains for those of sacrificial animals. Regensburg's later discovery of human cremations with a very similar suite of artifacts at the Savich Farm strongly indicates that the Koens-Crispin and Red Valley sites were burial places.

The Koens-Crispin complex is clearly related to other socioreligious manifestations in northeastern North America (Ritchie 1959, 1965:138, 162, 173–177; Dincauze 1968; M. Robbins 1968; Tuck 1976a). Both the diffusion of concepts concerning funerary practices and the procurement of exotic materials and goods for use as mortuary furniture indicate the existence of a well-established network of communication, transportation, and exchange within the region and beyond during Late Archaic times. The various sites of this complex give witness to an efflorescence in the use of nonlocal argillite for knives and projectile points. The allocation of opulent goods among a few select grave sites strongly suggests the rise of a population that was segregated along lines of wealth and political influence. This evidence also suggests the development of mortuary cults, which possessed formalized rituals presumably performed by priests or conjurers, "to insure the safety and comfort of the deceased in the spirit world" (Ritchie 1965:195). Such cults also served the living by maintaining social cohesion in the bereaved group and, quite likely, by protecting them from supernatural danger from ghosts.

MEADOWOOD AND MIDDLESEX BURIAL COMPLEXES

Elaborate burials, sometimes involving cremation, also occurred in the Early Woodland period (ca. 3,000–1,500 B.P.), but with evident rarity. One presumed cremation burial was accidentally discovered about 30 years ago near the Great Piece Meadows in Essex County (H. Kraft 1986b:97, 1989a). This site contained a reworked gorget and a pendant (both of slate), a celt, and several distinctive triangular or notched blades. This deposit has an antiquity of approximately 3,000 years. The artifacts are related by their form, workmanship, and materials to a mortuary cult that archaeologists call the Meadowood complex (Ritchie 1944:125–126, 1965:179–200).

Meadowood blades, of the type just noted, occasionally occur in caches that contain from a few to as many as 1,500 pieces. Some of these caches represent grave furniture, although others apparently do not. Twenty-nine Meadowood blades recently came to light in the collections of the University of Pennsylvania Museum in Philadelphia. An associated note indicated that these blades derived from a cache of 180 pieces found near Lumberton, in Burlington County. Whether this hoard was part of a mortuary feature is not known, but the character of the finds strongly suggests that possibility (Bello, Cresson, and Veit 1997).

Other cremation burials of the Early Woodland period were noted on two sites, the Abbott Farm (Cross 1956:60, 63, 121–123), near Trenton, and the Rosenkrans Ferry site, near Flatbrookville, in Sussex County (Carpenter 1950; Cross 1956:62; H. Kraft 1976b, 1986b:99–104, 1998). The latter site also yielded evidence of in-flesh burials related to the cremations. At the Abbott Farm, direct inhumations and reburials of dry bone, contemporaneous with the cremations but otherwise not clearly related, were also found.

Another spectacular Early Woodland cemetery, apparently containing only uncremated remains, was situated near Beesley's Point, in Cape May County (Cross 1941:228; Mounier 1981b:52–56). Still other sites have produced tantalizing but rather flimsy evidence of possible burials during this period (Mounier 1981b:56–61; Bello, Cresson, and Veit 1997).

These isolated cemeteries form part of the Middlesex complex, so called because of their similarities to burial sites of the Middlesex phase in central and eastern New York State (Ritchie and Dragoo 1960; Ritchie 1965:200–203; Ritchie and Funk 1973:97). All known Middlesex sites contain unusual and exotic artifacts that resemble the grave goods of the Adena culture, whose burial mounds are common in Ohio and other parts of the Midwest. The manufacture of artifacts from nonlocal materials and their limited distribution point to the existence of interregional trade networks, probably controlled by a small segment of an economically stratified society. Related sites occur along the eastern seaboard from the Delmarva Peninsula into the Canadian Maritime Provinces (Ritchie and Dragoo 1960; *Archaeology of Eastern North America* 4 [1976]).

The New Jersey sites are usually situated at high elevations on natural knolls or river terraces. A peculiarity is the apparent absence of related habitation sites: all recognized Middlesex sites in New Jersey comprise mortuary features only. Settlements were almost certainly located near the cemeteries, but strict theocratic control over the acquisition and distribution of wealth apparently kept exotic goods out of habitations, making these sites invisible to archaeology. Radiocarbon dates for this complex from the Rosenkrans Ferry site indicate an antiquity of 2,400–2,600 years (Ritchie 1965:203; H. Kraft 1986b:103).

The Abbott Farm Site

Excavations at the Abbott Farm revealed the cremated remains of at least four individuals in a single mortuary feature. The bones consisted of many small, calcined fragments, each about 1 inch (25 mm) in length and displaying a high degree of splintering. Many were charred, and some were stained with verdigris (copper salts). Most of these fragments were confined to a pit that covered about 30 square feet (2.8 m^2), but others had been scattered upon a hard-packed floor of burned earth. This floor was slightly greater than 1 foot (30 cm) in thickness and measured 9 × 17 feet (2.7 × 5.2 m) in plan. A thin layer of pulverized red ochre covered the bones, and a layer of charcoal, perhaps from a funeral fire, had been deposited over the ochre. Also noted were scattered animal bones and artifacts, including large, well-made chalcedony points, a slate pendant, and numerous items of native copper.

A thick layer of copper beads was discovered beneath the burned earthen floor, and four strands of similar beads encircled a disarticulated wrist. Altogether, more than 1,000 beads were recovered. Some of the original cordage upon which the beads had been strung was preserved by permeation of copper salts. In addition to the beads, three copper "boatstones" (perforated sheets rolled into shallow boatlike forms), one copper disk, and a hammered copper hemisphere were also found.

The beads were formed by rolling strips of hammered copper into small balls or rings. The hollow copper hemisphere also had been worked from a malleated copper sheet. The thick copper disk retained faint impressions from contact with a textile whose weave could not be discerned.

The source of the copper is obscure. Herbert Kraft (1986b:260n) argued that there are no suitable deposits of metallic copper in New Jersey, but more recent research by Levine (1999:193, 195–197) provides contradictory evidence. Currently, however, there is no metallurgical evidence linking the aboriginal copper artifacts from this site to mines in New Jersey. This material might have originated in ore beds in the Great Lakes region, as suggested by Kraft (1986b:104).

One of the bifaces found with the cremations had been elegantly knapped from a translucent stone that strongly resembles Ramah chalcedony, the only known natural source of which lies on the coast of northern Labrador. Soon after its discovery by native peoples about 5,000 years ago, this material began to appear in sites far to the south (Tuck 1976b:52).

The Rosenkrans Ferry Site

Artifacts similar to those at the Abbott Farm were found at the Rosenkrans Ferry site, in the Wallpack Bend of the Delaware River, but these finds were more varied. The cemetery was discovered by amateur archaeologists, who excavated intermittently between 1941 and 1948 without the benefit of formal training or professional guidance. (In fairness to the excavators, it should be noted that requests for assistance from the staff of the New Jersey State Museum were not answered, and the work necessarily proceeded without aid from specialists [H. Kraft 1976b:11].) Consequently, the findings are somewhat confused. Nevertheless, through the dedicated efforts of Edmund S. Carpenter (1950) and Herbert C. Kraft (1976b, 1998), the details of this very unusual and important site have been published, much to the profit of science and public heritage. The following information has been abstracted from Kraft's accounts of the site.

The Rosenkrans Ferry site contained several partial skeletons, some of which had been at least fractionally cremated. Most of the burials were richly supplied with offerings of various types and materials, such as copper artifacts, polished stone pieces, smoking pipes, woodworking tools, hunting equipment, and items of personal adornment, among many others.

The copper artifacts included more than 700 small beads, a boatstone, a plate or tablet, and a celt. The beads were used in necklaces and bracelets. A metallurgical assay strongly suggests that the copper had been imported from mines in Michigan (H. Kraft 1976b:42). The collection of polished stone items comprised eight gorgets, two pendants, four boatstones, and seven blocked-end tubes (an early form of smoking pipe). Two stone celts and an adze were found, along with an antler-tine projectile point, six whetstones, and a steatite cone. In addition, many bifaces were dispersed among the graves. Red ochre was applied in some instances.

Many of the graves contained faunal remains, mostly rendered into useful or decorative items (H. Kraft 1976b, 1998). Seashells were used for beads, some of which were strung on necklaces. At least 90 beads were made by drilling the shells of the minute dwarf olive (*Olivella minuta*), a marine gastropod, whose present-day northern limit extends no farther than North Carolina. Many other beads had been prepared from the central column or whorl of conch shells. Other faunal remains included the skull of a long-tailed weasel (*Mustela frenata*), probably retained as part of a skin pouch or medicine bag. (Small bundles or pouches, commonly worn around the neck or looped over a belt, were widely used by the historic Lenape for carrying tobacco, medicinal herbs, charms, and other personal effects [Harrington 1921:36, 42, 49, 65–66; Speck 1931:42; Newcomb 1956:27; Tantaquidgeon 1972:24–25; H. Kraft 1986b:184]). Bones of elk (*Cervus canadensis*) and turtles (possibly box turtles, *Terrapene carolina*), along with several unidentified large bird or small mammal bones, appear to represent food items for meals in the afterlife.

Floral remains consist of charred hickory nuts (*Carya glabra*), burned reeds of uncertain species, and remnants of textiles produced from bast (inner tree bark) or the fibers of milkweed or nettle. The hickory nuts may have been foodstuff, or perhaps they served as fuel. There is speculation that the reeds were part of a panpipe or whistle, but they may have been used as shafts for projectiles. The manufacture of twined mats and twilled fabrics has been demonstrated by the preservation of charred and verdigris-stained fragments.

An analysis of the materials from which many of the items were fashioned indicates the long-distance acquisition of natural resources or artifacts. Samples of the copper artifacts have been assayed to deposits around Lake Superior. Lithic materials derived from sources in Labrador, Montana, Arkansas, and Ohio. The use of seashells from southern coastal waters has already been mentioned.

The cemetery contained 16 individuals, each apparently interred in a separate grave. The evidence on this point is somewhat conflicting because of the involvement of multiple untrained excavators and the lapse of time. None of the skeletons was complete, although most of the bones of one adolescent skeleton were present. Small complements of bones and, in one case, a single tooth denoted the other individuals. The presence of mostly fragmentary skeletons, together with other clues, strongly indicates attrition from reburial.

The demographic profile was developed by Douglas H. Ubelaker. His age assessments are based upon observations concerning normal stages of development in human bones and teeth. Tentative identifications of sex are based upon skeletal morphology. Nine of the skeletons were adults, up to 50 years of age. Two were adolescents, aged 10–16 years, and one was a child of 9 years, more or less. There were four infants, ranging in age from 6 months to 2 years.

Two adults and both adolescents had undergone at least partial cremation, but the other skeletons consisted of uncremated bone burials. The remains of one adolescent showed differential exposure to fire. Part of the skull had been thoroughly incinerated in a fire exceeding a temperature of 800°C (1472°F). Some portions of the skeleton had been charred but not calcined, and other portions displayed no evidence whatever of thermal alteration. The cremated fragments did not evince warping, which usually occurs when green bones are incinerated. In other words, considerable time had lapsed between the moment of death and the time of cremation. Also, the evidence suggests that the cremation did not occur in the grave pit; rather, the skeleton appears to have been buried elsewhere, disinterred, partially burned as dry bone, and, finally, deposited at the place of discovery.

Several of the uncremated skeletons showed verdigris staining from exposure to copper artifacts, and the bones of one infant retained traces of red ochre. One of the skeletons exhibited extensive copper staining even though no copper artifacts existed in his grave. This situation implies an initial episode of interment with copper grave goods, followed by exhumation and subsequent reburial in the absence of metallic artifacts.

The skeletons generally revealed little evidence of trauma or disease. Many of the teeth showed advanced wear, probably from grit inadvertently incorporated into food, but no dental caries or abscesses were observed. The absence of tooth decay indicates a diet low in starches. One instance of dental crowding was observed.

One adult, whose age at death was estimated to be 40 to 50 years, showed signs of arthritis in the shoulder and spine. The same individual suffered an infection or severe trauma to the face, resulting in the loss of the maxillary incisors (upper front teeth), and the two adjacent teeth on the left side. The central portion of the upper jaw had been destroyed, thus joining the oral and nasal cavities. Despite the apparent severity of this affliction, the individual survived for an indeterminate period afterward.

Herbert Kraft concluded that this skull was evidence of the practice of a special form of conjuring known as "Wolf Man Shamanism." At certain Adena sites in Kentucky and Ohio, human skeletons have been found in intimate association with the trimmed snouts and palates of wolves. In one instance a wolf palate was actually found in the mouth of a man, having been slid into an opening created by the removal of the upper incisors. Presumably the conjurer, draped in wolf fur, made ritual gestures and uttered incantations while the wolf's jaw—teeth and all—protruded from his mouth. Onlookers must have been awestruck. Despite its appeal to the imagination, Kraft's interpretation cannot be verified because wolf bones are entirely lacking from the assemblage. Trauma, followed by infection and bone remodeling, as noted by Ubelaker (1976:47), is a more conservative and satisfying explanation.

The richness of the Rosenkrans Ferry site distinguishes it as the most remarkable expression of the Middlesex complex in New Jersey.

The Scott Site

A few other sites that bear more attenuated expressions of the Middlesex complex have been noted in southern New Jersey (Mounier 1981b). Though scanty, the best surviving record comes from the Scott site at Beesley's Point, in Cape May County. This site stood on a sandy peninsula on the edge of the Great Egg Harbor, occupying an area of 150 × 200 feet (46 × 61 m) on a natural moundlike eminence that rises from all sides to an elevation of about 20 feet (6.1 m) above mean tide. In the winter of 1938–1939, Louis P. Scott discovered human remains and artifacts, apparently in some profusion, while digging a cellar for a house on the highest part of the knoll. This discovery came to the attention of relic collectors, who hastily removed 24 skeletons and associated grave goods. It seems that a detailed written record of this unusual site has not survived; however, Dorothy Cross (1941:228) offered a summary listing of the finds, based on Indian Site Survey notes. Also, regrettably, the collections from this site were broken into several holdings, now long since scattered. Thus, there exist no clear descriptions or enumerations of the burials, mortuary offerings, or other archaeological remains.

A sketch map on file with the New Jersey State Museum shows a total of 15 grave lots clustered near the center of the knoll, which means that some of the skeletons were found in multiple interments. However, the actual distribution of human remains among the particular graves is not known. Likewise, there is no evidence regarding the size, shape, or contents of the graves (save for a few bones and relics), or the postures and orientation of the dead. Modes of preparing the deceased for burial were not recorded, nor are clear artifact associations known. The surviving skeletal remains consist of two skulls and two fragmentary long bones. Consequently, virtually all of the data concerning the age, sex, and general lifetime health of the individuals in the cemetery have been lost to clumsy excavation, the dispersal of finds, and inadequate record keeping.

I had an opportunity to examine the few skeletal materials and the meager remnants of the mortuary offerings. Both of the skulls show good organic preservation, but the bones display extensive postmortem breakage and loss.

One of the skulls was heavily stained with verdigris, evidently from contact with numerous metallic beads or other copper artifacts. This condition gives the skull an eerie, bright green cast.

A series of four narrow scars or creases, which resemble incisions, appear on the frontal bone over the eyes. Because their margins are rounded and smooth, these scars are clearly not of modern origin. Rather, they appear to represent a trauma, perhaps inflicted purposefully under ritual auspices, during life.

With the exception of the upper central incisors, which had been lost in life, all of the permanent teeth are present and show relatively advanced attrition. These characteristics suggest that physical maturity had been attained for some time prior to death. The generally massive features of the cranium and jaw permit a tentative determination of the sex as male.

Whether ritual activity can be imputed from the scarification of the skull seems a moot question. Likewise, the removal of the upper central incisors might relate to the practice of shamanism, but natural tooth loss seems a far more probable cause. In any event, a strong case for Wolf-Man ritualism cannot be advanced; we have only fragmentary remains of the man and none at all of the wolf.

According to the records of the Indian Site Survey, the cultural remains associated with inhumations at the Scott site included gorgets, copper and shell beads, and a few potsherds. To this list can be added blocked-end tubes of Ohio fireclay, projectile points and cache blades of chert from Flint Ridge, Ohio, and red ochre (Charles F. Kier Jr., pers. comm.). Most of the artifacts were sold or traded among collectors. When the author researched the site in 1980, all that remained were 175 copper beads or bead fragments and four small, tabular pieces of hematite of a brilliant orange-red color. The presumed function of these pieces was the preparation of pigment for the adornment of graves.

The Canton Site

In 1949–1950, George Woodruff of Bridgeton excavated an aboriginal burial site near Canton in Salem County. With the burial were found 46 tubular copper beads, and either in the grave or nearby was a cache of seven bifaces of exotic material. Contact with the copper preserved fragments of native cordage on which the beads had been strung. It appears that at least two different cords were present. Both were built up from fine, silky white plant fibers. The stone artifacts found in or near the grave consist of thin, lanceolate blades of a black flinty stone of unknown origin, though it is almost certainly not indigenous to southern New Jersey. One of the blades was notched for hafting.

The commingling of skeletal remains with copper artifacts is indisputable because the bones display heavy verdigris staining. The surviving bones are limited to two fragments of the lower jaw. Both fragments show postmortem breakage, and many of the teeth were lost or broken between the time of discovery and my examination in 1980. The fate of the rest of the skeleton is unknown.

Perhaps this grave represents another partial burial, so common on sites of the Middlesex complex. The presence of copper beads in a mortuary setting indicates burial practices that are very much out of the ordinary for most aboriginal cultures. The spirally wound sheet metal beads from Canton resemble the tubular form that constituted a minority of the ornaments at the Rosenkrans Ferry site. The blades in reported association with the burial at Canton fall within the range of variation observed among specimens attributed to the Middlesex complex elsewhere along the East Coast. The notched blade, in particular, finds an analogue in a specimen from one of the burials at the Rosenkrans Ferry site.

Isolated smoking pipes and other fancy artifacts from various sites around the state indicate the possibility of association with burials in the ensuing Middle Woodland period (Bello 1996; Bello and Veit 1997), whose cultural trappings, for the most part, remain unknown to us.

Aboriginal Grave Goods: Clues to the Past

Although not associated with well-defined mortuary cults, many prehistoric graves contain offerings that reflect on aboriginal material culture, social behavior, and chronology. Several burials near Trenton included sets of deer antlers, which might have been kept as hunting lures or charms, or simply as valuable raw material for use in the afterlife (Volk 1911:78; Cross 1956:60). Others contained the remains of carnivores and turtles. The pelts of carnivores may have served as tobacco pouches, medicine bags, or quivers. Sometimes turtle shells were made into cups or rattles.

The placement of serviceable vessels and utensils with the dead can be taken to mean that a final meal, possibly shared by mourners, had been prepared to give sustenance to the deceased. At the Lerro Farm site, in Pedricktown, Salem County, one of the graves contained five box turtle shells that had been fashioned into cups or dishes (Blenk 1977b). A single oyster shell, possibly used as a spoon or spatula, was found among the turtle shells. Complete or nearly intact pots have also been recovered from a few other late prehistoric graves in central and northern New Jersey (Volk 1911:22; H. Kraft 1976a:50, 54, 1978:89–90).

The practice of mortuary feasting is strongly supported by Kraft's discovery at the Pahaquarra site of a grave containing the bones of a young child atop a mound of food remains, which included the bones of various mammals, birds, fish, amphibians, reptiles, and mollusks. Analysis of the faunal remains indicated that the burial occurred during the spring or summer. One interesting aspect of this burial was the discovery of a small saltwater mollusk and some sand from the seashore inside the skull. This evidence clearly implies the relocation of the skull from a temporary burial site on the Atlantic coast to its final resting place overlooking the Delaware River (H. Kraft 1976a:50–54). Another burial at the Pahaquarra site contained a globular, low-collared vessel of the Munsee Incised type, which dates to the period after A.D. 1400 (H. Kraft 1976a:50, 54, 1978:89–90).

One of the skeletons at the Abbott Farm, was accompanied by several late prehistoric triangular arrowheads and a smoking pipe whose bowl bears two simple human face effigies (Cross 1956:61, 66, 196). On each effigy, two circular punctations represent the eyes and a broad, elongated impression, the mouth. A date between A.D. 1000 and 1350 is likely, given that rudimentary renditions of the human face appear about this time in more northerly districts (Ritchie 1965:274; H. Kraft 1986b:120). This pipe suggests a connection with the Pahaquarra culture of northern New Jersey or the Owasco culture of central New York State. Accordingly, this burial has been interpreted to represent either an episode of trade with people from the north or the interment of a visitor from that region (Cross 1956:61, 196).

European Trade Goods: Cultures in Contact

Over the years, many aboriginal graves have been found with items of European manufacture. Alanson Skinner reported the discovery of "shell beads (wampum) and little bird-shaped shell pendants" from a native cemetery on the banks of the Delaware River, opposite Biles Island, near Trenton (Skinner and Schrabisch 1913:65). Richard Veit and Charles Bello (2001) examined a small but imposing collection of artifacts from this site, now housed in the Peabody Museum of Archaeology and Ethnology at Harvard University. In addition to the shell beads and bird effigies mentioned by Skinner, the collection contains glass trade beads and white clay pipe fragments, as well as bracelets of copper and iron. These artifacts can be dated between A.D. 1640 and 1675 on the basis of their form. One of the burials also contained a small copper snuffbox that dates to the early eighteenth century. This box still contains a twist of tobacco, spared from destruction by verdigris poisoning. Accompanying this piece are similarly preserved fragments of cloth, cordage, and leather, which may have been parts of a satchel (Veit and Bello 2001).

In his work near Trenton, Volk found at least two graves that contained European trade goods (Volk 1911:191, 194, 197). In the burial of a small child were two copper or brass bells, bone and shell tinged with copper stains, and two shell ornaments. In another grave the skeleton of an adult was found with several small white and blue glass beads, shell beads, a white clay pipe, and the broken stem of another; also recovered were an unidentified copper object, a piece of graphite, and a mass of red material, possibly a lump of vermillion or rouge.

The aboriginal cemetery near Minisink Island, in Sussex County (Heye and Pepper 1915:18–30), contained at least 22 graves with associated trade goods. Because this site had been repeatedly opened since the 1860s, often without adequate record keeping, the number of actual burials with European artifacts is unknown. Of the burials reported by Heye and Pepper, 13 were extended, 5 were flexed, and 3 had been so disturbed that the arrangement of the bones could not be determined; nor could the burial posture of one infant be established. The graves were evenly split between adults and children. Of the adults, six were female, three were male, and the sex of two could not be ascertained.

Included in the graves were several smoking pipes (some ceramic and others of pewter), hundreds of glass, shell, and catlinite beads, inscribed shell ornaments, and animal effigies in the form of birds, fish, and furbearers. Also found were brass kettles and bells, pewter spoons, and crudely incised, straplike copper bracelets. Some of the graves also contained mirrors and firemaking kits that consisted of bits of flint and steel. Women and children, in particular, occupied the most lavishly furnished graves.

Three of the clay pipes bear the marks of pipe makers from Bristol, England—EB for Edward Battle and RT for Robert Tippett—who produced pipes from the mid-seventeenth to the early eighteenth century (cf. Walker

1977:1060, 1317, 1406, 1498–1499). The pewter pipes are thought to date between A.D. 1650 and 1755 (Heye and Pepper 1915:53–54). The excavators believed that the cemetery was abandoned by 1720 (Heye and Pepper 1915:76).

Five flexed burials were reportedly unearthed at West Long Branch in Monmouth County in the 1930s. There appear to be no surviving data concerning the age and sex of the deceased. Three of these graves contained articles of European manufacture. The records for the other two are imprecise, apparently because they contained no offerings. The trade items included necklaces made from hundreds of glass beads, metal bracelets, wampum, and animal effigies rendered in shell. Metal jinglers (small cones that make a tinkling sound when moved) decorated a pouch, which contained acorns. The jinglers were probably cut from portions of thin sheet brass kettles. Two pewter spoons were found in circumstances that suggested their use as hair ornaments. A ceramic trumpet pipe, apparently of native manufacture, was also recovered. Glass beads from this site appear to date to a period before A.D. 1700 (Pietak 1995:194–195).

Excavations by the Indian Site Survey in 1938 at the Lenhardt site in Monmouth County revealed eight burials, most of which were accompanied by European trade goods (Cross 1941:111). These graves occurred in part of a larger cemetery that had been dug into by collectors beforehand. The skeletons, all of which were found in flexed postures, represented six adults, one child, and one infant.

White clay pipes of European manufacture accompanied the graves of three adult females and one adult male. The form of these pipes indicates manufacture in the late seventeenth or early eighteenth century (Noël Hume 1969:302ff.). One of the female burials also contained one or more pieces of twisted copper wire. The grave of another adult female contained several red glass trade beads and a disk-shaped pendant fashioned from an oyster shell, possibly by a native artisan. Yet another adult female skeleton had been interred with a trade pipe in her right hand and a copper bracelet encircling her left wrist. Many glass trade beads—both black and white varieties—were found beneath her skull. A chert arrowhead was found near the right shoulder of the child. Whether this piece was a grave offering or an accidentally placed item is not known. The graves of one adult male and the infant had no recoverable grave goods.

At the Boni Farm in Gloucester County, a burial ground was exposed by earthmoving equipment (Mounier 1974c). Because of the rude circumstances of discovery, there is no way to know how many graves might have been present originally. Two were known to have been cut through and destroyed. Members of the Abnaki Archaeological Society, a local club, located three other graves, two of which they systematically excavated and recorded. I excavated the last and later reinterred it out of harm's way nearby.

An examination of the skeletons revealed three adults and one young child. One skeleton had so decomposed that the age at death could not be estimated. The age of the child could be fixed at approximately six years, based on the intact deciduous teeth (so-called baby teeth); also, one of the first molars was visible and unerupted in the mandible. One of the adults was clearly a male, probably of advanced age.

Grave goods intentionally included with the older male comprised one shell bead and three tubular brass beads rolled from thin sheet metal. These beads were found by the left ear and probably formed a composite earring. An illustration that accompanies Lindeström's mid-seventeenth-century account of the Indians in the lower Delaware Valley depicts a very similar earring (Lindeström 1925: opp. 195). Also, a fragmentary beaver incisor was found in front of the knees. This tooth probably represents a knife, given that sharpened rodent teeth were frequently hafted for use as cutting tools (Ritchie 1944, 1965; Tuck 1976a:47–48).

The metal beads were transmitted to the Winterthur Museum in Winterthur, Delaware, for x-ray fluorescence analysis, a nondestructive technique used for assaying the chemical composition of unknown substances. That analysis indicated an alloy of copper, zinc, lead, and tin, with traces of several other metals, a combination that identified the material as brass (Reilly 1974). Native peoples lacked advanced smelting skills; thus, this material must have been acquired from Europeans. The brass may have found its way into aboriginal hands, perhaps through intermediate channels, when European goods were in circulation among the native population, but before acculturation had advanced to the point that Christian burial modes had been widely accepted. It is likely that the beads were fashioned by the Indians themselves from fragments of thin brass kettles. None of the graves showed extended postures, coffin remnants, or any other traces of Christian mortuary practices. Thus, the cemetery was thought to date to ca. A.D. 1550–1600, although a later date cannot be ruled out.

The persistence of traditional flexed burials at other sites of the Contact Period is noteworthy. The West Long Branch and Lenhardt sites—and, to a lesser extent, the Minisink site—all disclosed flexed burials that contained quantities of trade goods. This situation suggests that these cemeteries were established earlier rather than later in the Contact period. Based on historic artifact typology—especially of the glass beads and white clay pipes—these sites appear to date to the middle and end of the seventeenth century, as already noted.

At the Minisink site, as elsewhere in northwestern New Jersey, archaeological research demonstrates a decided preference among the natives to place the heads of the departed toward the southwest, so as to ease entry into the spirit world (H. Kraft 1978:50, 1986b:189). A similar orientation was noted at the West Long Branch site and among several graves near Tottenville on Staten Island (Pietak 1995:193). In contrast, most of the graves at the Lenhardt site were oriented toward the northeast. At other locations, no discernible pattern has been recognized (Cross 1956:60). Pietak (1995:193, 195) has suggested that—when it can be established—patterning in the arrangement of contemporaneous graves provides a means of distinguishing among ancient cultural groups.

BONES AND TEETH: CLUES TO HEALTH AND STATURE

The skeletal population at Minisink Island was sufficiently well preserved to permit evaluation by physical anthropologists and osteologists regarding the health and stature of the deceased (Hrdlička 1916; Clabeaux 1972, 1976, 1978). The population was generally healthy, but several instances of arthritis were observed, along with dental attrition. Dental caries was fairly common, probably owing to the consumption of starchy foods in late prehistoric times. This change in diet suggests an increasing dependency on maize (corn) and other horticultural produce. The practice of horticulture has also been inferred from patterns of tooth wear in other late prehistoric populations (A. Robbins and Hummer n.d.).

Many benign genetic anomalies in the bones and teeth suggest a lengthy period of residency and intermarriage among related populations in the region. About half of the skulls showed artificial deformation, resulting from the practice of binding newborn children to cradle boards (Hrdlička 1916:16; Clabeaux 1972:99). William Penn observed the use of cradle boards among the historic Delaware Indians: "Having wrapt them [the infants] in a Clout, they lay them on a straight thin Board, a little more than the length and breadth of the Child, and swaddle it fast upon the Board to make it straight; wherefore all Indians have flat Heads; and thus they carry them at their Backs" (Penn, in

Myers 1970:26). Herbert Kraft (1986b:137) indicated that infants were thus restrained until they could walk. This practice, which was common among Indians of the American West, enabled mothers to carry their babies, much as modern-day hikers might use a backpack or knapsack.

By reference to certain critical dimensions of the femora (thigh bones) from this cemetery, the height of the adult males was estimated to be about 5′6″ feet (167 cm), and the height of females, about 5′1″ (156 cm). An adult male whose skeleton was found in a late prehistoric grave near Tuckerton, in Ocean County, was estimated to have stood approximately 5′9″ (176 cm) tall (Ubelaker 1996). These data substantiate William Penn's observation that the Indians were "generally tall, streight, well-built, and of singular Proportion" (Penn, in Myers 1970:21).

It is well worth mentioning that bare skeletons often appear extraordinarily large to the untrained eye, especially if reassembled without proper tolerances between the members (Brothwell 1965:101; Bass 1971:22). This phenomenon has given rise to specious but persistent tales of an ancient race of giants at Tuckerton. One early writer, commenting on Indian skeletons found near this place, reported that "[o]ne of the skeletons measured over seven feet and was that of a veritable giant" (Jordan 1906:14). This legend has persisted among local residents down to the present. Although they exist only in the imagination, these giants are with us still.

DEADLY VIOLENCE

Archaeologists and physical anthropologists have found little evidence on prehistoric skeletons to suggest injuries from violence or warfare. However, there is one stark and noteworthy exception from nearby Staten Island. Three late prehistoric skeletons, excavated in 1895 near Tottenville, were riddled with no fewer than 26 arrowheads (Skinner 1909, 1932:17–19). Nine points had penetrated the body of one of the victims, another bore 6 points, and the last, 11. Many of the projectiles had lodged in or near the spine, rib cage, shoulders, hands, and legs. Others were found loose amidst the skeletons, obviously having been embedded in soft tissues when the bodies were interred. One of the arrowheads had fractured, evidently from impact with one of the skulls. In addition, a scapula (shoulder blade) bore an injury possibly delivered by a blow with a handheld weapon. All three skeletons appeared to have been haphazardly thrown into a single grave. Alanson Skinner observed that, "taking into consideration the number of arrows which must have been imbedded in the bodies of the warriors, it is perhaps probable that the majority of the projectiles were driven into the victims at close range after death" (Skinner 1932:19). Surely this scene represents an instance of extreme violence; but whether this brutality resulted from interpersonal conflicts or from warfare, as Skinner suggested, cannot now be known.

This multiple grave is also interesting from a strictly technological viewpoint. Skinner was altogether correct in asserting that "the longbows of the local Indians must indeed have been formidable weapons," capable of propelling arrows with great force. Arrows tipped with antler, bone, and stone had been used in the assault. Nineteen of these points were specifically identified according to the kind of material used in their fabrication. Five were triangular stone points, typical of late prehistoric arrowheads. Points of this form were introduced around A.D. 900 and persisted well into historic times. Ten arrowheads had been fashioned from antler tines, and four from pieces of worked bone. Thus, nearly 75 percent of the projectiles had been armed with tips rendered in organic substances. The relative abundance here of projectile points fashioned from perishable materials is highly unusual and illustrates how differential preservation can influence our understanding of aboriginal material culture.

Man's Best Friend

Numerous well-documented examples from across eastern North America attest to a relationship between dogs and humans going back at least to Archaic times (Ritchie 1944, 1965; Haag 1948; Lopez and Wisniewski 1958; T. Stewart 1963; Tuck 1976a:77–78). Dogs may have first appeared as camp scavengers, later to be domesticated and trained for use in hunting. Doubtless, they eventually became watchdogs, pets, and beloved companions, although not always spared from final service as a meal in times of want. Thus, it is hardly surprising to find that dogs were frequently accorded burial in prehistoric times.

Specially prepared dog burials have been observed at various locations throughout New Jersey, mostly on late prehistoric sites, although the apparent relative modernity of canine interments is probably a function of differential preservation. Some years ago, while excavating aboriginal shell middens (dumps) near Swainton, in Cape May County, Alan E. Carman (pers. comm.) discovered a canine grave that contained the mortal remains of a bitch and two pups. (Given good preservation, the sex of dogs can be identified because the males possess a *baculum* [penis bone].) Carman believes that these dogs may have been slain when the Indians left the site with loads of processed shellfish, because transporting the whelps would have hindered the move. There are other possible explanations—such as ritual killing—but we shall never know the circumstances for certain. At the same site, the bodies of two other dogs had been draped over human corpses, apparently as sacrificial offerings. Carman carefully exposed and recorded these two graves, but, out of deference, he removed neither the canine nor the human skeletons. Another carefully buried canine was disinterred at the Havins site in Sussex County (Dunay 1981:5).

Despite affectionate relationships with humans, dogs were commonly eaten. I excavated the shattered remains of at least one dog in refuse deposits at the Cadwalader site, near the mouth of the Maurice River in Cumberland County (Mounier 1974b:47; White 1974:69–70). Herbert Kraft found canine bones in trash pits at the Harry's Farm and Pahaquarra sites in Warren County, as well as at the Minisink site in Sussex County (Kraft 1978:32–33). The nearby Munsee cemetery (Heye and Pepper 1915:59), the Bell-Philhower site (Ritchie 1949:170), and the Bell-Browning site (Marchiando 1972:137) all yielded broken dog bones along with other food refuse.

The osteological evidence indicates that the prehistoric dogs were relatively small, ordinarily ranging in size from that of a small terrier to a collie or retriever. The dogs from the Cadwalader and East Point sites, in the Maurice River tidewater area, were particularly small, whereas those from sites in the central and northern portions of the state were much larger (White 1974:69). A skeletonized canine exhumed from a site along Raccoon Creek near Bridgeport, in Gloucester County, was about the size of a beagle (Mounier 1998b:IV-46). Volk reported the interment of small dogs or foxes from excavations near Trenton (Volk 1911:83).

Occasionally, the intentionally interred skeletons of other mammals appear in archaeological sites. Sites on which I have worked variously contained the skeletons of horses, hogs, and cats. In all cases, the historical background of these sites, as well as the circumstances of deposition, point to burial during historic or modern times.

HISTORICAL CEMETERIES: AN EXAMPLE FROM HAMMONTON

Although this chapter principally concerns finds of the prehistoric era, it is important to note that archaeology can be used to study historical and modern burial practices as well. In one instance, I was able to identify the location of the long-lost cemetery of an early Methodist congregation near Hammonton, in Atlantic County (Mounier 1988). Careful excavation revealed that the grave markers had been removed from their original positions and placed horizontally in shallow trenches a foot or so beneath the surface of the ground. Apparently, this work was accomplished by farmers who were eager to add a little acreage to tillage.

The burial ground contained a total of 31 graves: 21 adults and 10 small children or adolescents. The parallel, non-intersecting arrangement of the graves indicated that the interments had been placed in relation to existing burials. The prevalent use of pinch-toed hexagonal coffins showed that the burials were aligned with the heads to the west and feet to the east. Traditional Christian burials were oriented in this way so that the deceased could rise to face the sun upon hearing the trumpet sound on the morning of Judgment Day.

The local tax map showed incorrect boundaries for the burial ground. This discrepancy indicates that the exact location and orientation of the burial ground had passed from living memory by the time the tax maps were drawn. Although the historical accounts of this cemetery were vague and inaccurate, detailed information was quickly revealed by careful archaeological investigation.

———

THIS VICARIOUS EXCURSION into some of the archaeological burial grounds in New Jersey has provided a glimpse of the variety of ancient mortuary customs. Aboriginal graves have been reported from all parts of the state and date from the historic period to nearly 10,000 years ago. We have seen certain broad similarities—as well as spectacular differences—in the modes of dealing with the necessary task of burying the dead. As far as can be inferred from archaeological evidence, most aboriginal cultures appear to have developed fairly mundane burial customs. From time to time, other cultures, perhaps more properly called cults, devised elaborate systems for disposing of at least a select few among their dead. These mortuary practices were obviously charged with ritual and symbolism as well as a desire to bestow wealth and eternal life upon the deceased. In addition, analysis of skeletal remains gives us a sense of the stature and health of prehistoric peoples. We know that they usually lived healthy and peaceful lives, punctuated on occasion by instances of painful disease or horrible violence.

We also know a good deal about their technological abilities and material culture. We see from grave furniture that they were in contact with people and places well beyond their own territorial limits. Some late prehistoric cemeteries also contain trade goods that reflect dealings with Europeans or aboriginal traders. Various native burials show different levels of acculturation to European lifeways.

The common practice of orienting the graves in particular directions demonstrates the existence of religious belief systems and a concern to speed the deceased on their journey into the afterlife. The careful burial of dogs bespeaks the special relationship that developed anciently between humans and canines.

The people who are known solely from archaeology left no written accounts of their existence, but archaeologists have written, with varying degrees of clarity, the story of their lives. We have seen that archaeology can shed light on more modern situations as well by dispelling deeply entrenched historical myths and by clarifying historical inaccuracies. Archaeology cannot restore life to the dead, but it can facilitate an understanding of lives and times long since past.

5

A Journey of Archaeological Exploration

*Then shalt thou inquire, and make search,
and ask diligently.*

———

DEUTERONOMY 13:14

In this chapter we shall journey across New Jersey, pausing at various sites to see what kinds of information archaeological exploration has brought to light and what it all seems to mean. As befits a science that concerns itself with cultural expressions in time and space, we shall examine sites in a variety of chronological and geographic settings. The archaeological record is far too abundant and complex, however, to consider all of the sites that have been investigated, or even to consider any of them in great detail. I have intentionally avoided delving into some of the larger, more complicated sites, preferring to focus on smaller examples that present a less cluttered view of ancient life. To avoid repetition, I have not included investigations that have been treated in some detail in earlier chapters. Finally, I have chosen to highlight the work of dedicated individuals, especially avocational archaeologists, whenever possible. The following vignettes—organized in chronological order—give a glimpse of the typical, the unusual, and the sometimes amazing discoveries that constitute our archaeological heritage.

Paleoindian Sites (ca. 8,000 –12,000 B.P.)

As we have already seen, the earliest known inhabitants of New Jersey appeared about 12,000 years ago, or somewhat earlier. Their signature artifact—the fluted point—is among the most recognizable of relics, owing to its graceful shape, its exquisite workmanship, and its celebrity, arising from its relative antiquity.

Because of environmental changes since Pleistocene times, evidence of Paleoindian settlement in New Jersey is not especially strong. Many Paleoindian sites may now lie miles offshore, on portions of the continental shelf that have been inundated by rising sea levels. Although many sites are known, most are locations at which only a handful of relics has been found, and then only in disturbed contexts. The following sections will discuss some of the better-known Paleoindian sites in New Jersey.

The Zierdt Site

The Zierdt site in Montague, Sussex County, sits atop a high sandy terrace overlooking a small stream in the headwaters of the Delaware River (Werner 1964; Marshall 1982:31). The deepest geological stratum at this site yielded a single fluted point and another 17 distinctive Paleoindian tools, along with flaking debris. A small hearth constructed of river cobbles and two charcoal stains were also identified by the excavator. The site was apparently a short-term hunting encampment.

The Plenge Site

The Plenge site, now an agricultural location in the Musconetcong Valley of Warren County, is unique in yielding more than a thousand Paleoindian artifacts in a variety of styles, which suggests uncommonly prolonged settlement on a single site. The fields here have also given up thousands more artifacts of many different archaeological cultures, all as surface finds. Although the site was well known to artifact collectors, only a few avocational archaeologists seemed to recognize the presence and importance of the Paleoindian remains. Leonard Ziegler and his sons Pence and Gary, F. Dayton Staats and his brother Harold, along with Jack and Bill Stanley, are credited with bringing this unusual site to scientific scrutiny (H. Kraft 1973:59).

These enthusiasts collaborated with Herbert C. Kraft in compiling a comprehensive catalog of more than a thousand Paleoindian artifacts from the Plenge site. Kraft's (1973) analysis identified nearly 120 fluted bifaces in a wide variety of styles. This discovery alone is unusual, because most Paleoindian sites yield relics sparingly and in a very restricted typological range. In addition to six styles of fluted points, the archaeologists found hundreds of bifacial knives, drills, and specialized tools. Among the specialized implements were flaked tools and wedges.

In a series of test excavations, Kraft attempted to locate portions of the site that might contain artifacts in undisturbed earth beneath the level of plowing. After a prolonged and diligent search, Kraft (1973:112) despaired that his "excavations . . . have been frustratingly barren of undisturbed features and devoid of charcoal suitable for radiocarbon analysis. Almost all of the Paleoindian remains are within the now heavily cultivated tilth zone or in the eroded gulleys." Nevertheless, through the unstinting cooperation of knowledgeable avocational archaeologists, the site's contents have been announced to the scientific world. The search goes on.

Site 28-OC-100

In 1991, in the now dry headwater gullies of Kettle Creek, in Ocean County, a crew in my employ uncovered another Paleoindian site (Mounier, Cresson, and Martin 1993). The circumstances were unusual. The site was discovered in the course of a routine survey in advance of commercial development. Our findings emerged by dint of persistent testing, fueled by the belief that, given sufficient effort, some sort of prehistoric remains would be found here. This belief was grounded in years of experience in testing similar landscapes, many of which have yielded evidence of prehistoric settlement.

Frequently, the sites found in the interior of New Jersey's Outer Coastal Plain are small, apparently ephemeral stations of uncertain age and cultural association. Even though we had fully expected to find evidence of aboriginal occupation at this location, we had not anticipated the discovery of Paleoindian remains, particularly in a site largely unmixed with other cultural residues and, thus far, undisturbed by the incursions of modern society. Therefore, our discoveries brought both reward and surprise.

The fieldwork involved both surface inspection and subsurface testing. All exposed ground surfaces were closely examined for traces of archaeological materials. Surface exposures were limited to two narrow dirt trails and numerous sandy patches among the scrubby oaks and pines that prevail in the region. This search revealed only modern trash.

The crew also excavated more than 345 test holes with shovels, screening all spoil through sieves fitted with ¼-inch mesh hardware cloth. These test units were small circular holes not larger than 1 foot (0.30 m) in diameter. Initial testing occurred at intervals of approximately 50 feet (15.24 m) across the property under survey. This work continued at increasingly tighter intervals in the suspected site area, until the test holes were only a few feet apart. The intention was to place enough test units to yield a positive finding or to warrant discontinuing the effort. The discovery of a single, very small jasper flake during preliminary testing led to intensified prospecting around the findspot.

At this point, we opened a 5-foot (1.52 m) square at the location of the original find, using flat shovels and screens. The initial square yielded a variety of flaking debris distinctive of Paleoindian flint-knapping techniques. Jack Cresson called my office and said that he had just found channel flakes, which are distinctive by-products of Paleoindian knapping. I asked if he had his glasses on to make sure. I'll never forget his response: "I don't need my glasses . . . I can feel the flakes!" His years of tireless research into aboriginal knapping techniques had prepared him to identify these little relics by touch alone.

Even though the survey budget had by now been exhausted, the exploratory excavation continued on a volunteer basis, following the trend of the artifacts in the ground. The work focused on an irregular excavation block covering 125 square feet (11.6 m²). The exploratory excavation yielded more than 300 artifacts, including one very small fragment of a fluted point, 30 channel flakes, and several other kinds of flakes, almost all rendered in a high-grade, nonlocal jasper. Interestingly, we also found a small quartz crystal, which may have been a charm.

In the laboratory, the artifacts were cleaned by gentle brushing. Then the inventory notes compiled in the field were compared with the actual assemblage. All of the artifacts were classified by type and quantified. Measurements of all channel flakes were recorded, along with the dimensions of typical examples of other flake types.

Channel flakes were reconstructed by joining matching pieces. This process permitted the measurement or, in some cases, the estimation of the original size of the flakes at the time of detachment. The reconstructions also allowed inferences about the sizes of the bifaces from which these flakes had been removed and provided key insights into Paleoindian knapping techniques.

Cresson's analysis of the flakes revealed that most of the knapping took place using pressure flaking rather than percussion to shape the implements.

The flakes are remarkable for their length, thinness, and highly regular form. These characteristics indicate very well developed motor skills on the part of the ancient knapper, whose mastery of flintwork is further exhibited by a low level of failure. Only one fragmentary biface was found on the site.

The analysis of the artifacts from this site identified an approach to biface fluting that had not been explicated before. One fluting flake was removed from one face of the implement while two or more were taken from the opposing face. Because the multiple flakes were removed in sequence, one superimposed upon the next, we have dubbed this technique "piggy-back fluting." Many of the flakes were later used as cutting tools. Even though the only formalized biface was represented by a small fragment, detailed analysis of related flaking debris allowed a reasonable estimate not only of the overall form but also of the size of the implement.

The process of fluting may have involved more than the physical thinning of the biface for mundane, technological purposes. Some researchers have suggested that the act of biface fluting may have been part of a pre-hunt ritual, portending success or failure in the chase (Frison 1991:377–379). The knapper may have invoked supernatural powers to assist in successful fluting and, by extension, successful hunting.

We believe that the quartz crystal from this site was part of the Paleoindian assemblage and that it may have been used in hunting magic. The archaeological and ethnographic literature for eastern North America contains many references to the ritual use of minerals, pigments, crystals, oddly shaped stones, and fossil casts (Skinner 1913; Hawkes and Linton 1916:76; Cross 1956:162–163; Ritchie 1965; Tantaquidgeon 1972:25; Tuck 1976a:60, 1976b:35). Such items cannot be dismissed as mere curiosities.

Our work at this intriguing site has given us a peek at an ancient technology and possibly related ritual behavior, both of which have been extinct for thousands of years. Our initial study was followed by another survey, which tended to confirm our findings (Pagoulatos 1992). Sadly, since our discoveries were first announced, someone has clandestinely, but systematically, looted the site. The extent of the loss to science and heritage has not been assessed. As of this writing, the property still awaits development.

EARLY AND MIDDLE ARCHAIC SITES (CA. 5,000 – 8,000 B.P.)

Like sites of Paleoindian times, Early and Middle Archaic sites are relatively rare and usually yield only a handful of artifacts. Also like their predecessors,

Early and Middle Archaic stone knappers tended to craft carefully made bifaces and specialized tools from high-quality lithics. Characteristic bifaces are broad-bladed stemmed or notched points, often sharpened to produce serrated blades. The lack of large, artifact-rich sites may well reflect the loss of coastlands to continually rising sea levels. As we visit some of the known locations, we shall hopscotch around the state.

The West Creek Site

The West Creek site is located on the mainland behind Little Egg Harbor, near the village of West Creek in Ocean County. Working for several years—on borrowed time and with borrowed equipment—Andrew Stanzeski, Bill Absalom, Tom Radlov, and other members of the Archaeological Society of New Jersey excavated 225 5-foot squares at this site. Rat-holing collectors had earlier destroyed most of the later archaeology at this site by digging randomly at shallow depths in search of relics. By systematically excavating more deeply, the Archaeological Society crew came upon a remarkable Early Archaic encampment having an antiquity of nearly 10,000 years.

Three clusters of Early Archaic artifacts, including Kirk Stemmed, Kirk and Palmer Corner-Notched points (Coe 1964), and a variety of formalized scrapers, were found within an area covering about two-thirds of an acre. Among the projectile points and scrapers were hammerstones, small flake tools, and flakes from tool manufacture or repair. As with most Early Archaic toolkits, the materials employed were mainly high-grade lithics, primarily jasper and chert. The discovery of a single fragmentary fluted point demonstrated that Paleoindians had visited the site in former times.

One of the artifact clusters yielded several clutches of incinerated bone, which have been interpreted to be human cremation burials (see chapter 4). An associated radiocarbon age assessment indicates that the site was occupied around 9,850 years ago. One shudders at the thought that looters had come within inches of destroying this important early component. Stanzeski (1996: 44–45, 1998:41–43) has released two preliminary accounts of his excavations. The scientific world awaits the full report of findings from this intriguing site.

Site 28-CU-79

Situated along the banks of the Maurice River, this site has yielded a number of broad-bladed Early Archaic Kirk and Palmer points, mostly at fairly deep levels within the soil column. In one area, a dense cluster of calcined bone occurred with a pair of Kirk points, suggesting either the ritual disposal of animal remains or possibly a human cremation (Mounier n.d.b). Research has also demonstrated the presence of smaller, later bifurcate-base points, which are characteristic of certain Middle Archaic cultures. Unlike the Early Archaic forms, which are generally produced from large blocks of quarried stone, all of the smaller bifurcate-base points were fashioned from locally available crypto-crystalline pebbles.

The Turkey Swamp Site

Located near Freehold, in Monmouth County, the Turkey Swamp site occupies the floodplain of a headwater to the Manasquan River. Several archaeological cultures are present. The earliest assemblage has an assessed antiquity of eight millennia (Cavallo 1981). John Cavallo, the excavator, classed these remains as elements of a late Paleoindian assemblage, but most researchers now believe that they more properly belong in an Early Archaic component. This opinion is based on the absence of true fluted points and the lack of the specialized tools, such as formalized end- and side-scrapers, typical of the Paleoindian period.

The early remains occupy the basal levels of the site. Although not confined to visible strata, these artifacts occur discretely beneath more recent cultural deposits. A total of 150 artifacts were recovered from this component. Among the finds were projectile points, bifacial knives, scrapers, perforators, spokeshaves, hammerstone fragments, a chopper, an anvil stone, cores, chipped stone adzes, wedges, abraders, and utilized flakes.

The projectile points, which are fashioned entirely from pebble-derived chert or jasper, are basally thinned triangles. In general form, they superficially resemble later triangular bifaces, but the distinctive basal thinning and their location deep within the site clearly demonstrate their early origin. Cavallo (1981) concluded that the site was a revisited hunting camp.

Since the discovery of "Turkey Swamp points" by Cavallo, other similar (but undated) examples have been identified elsewhere upon the coastal plains of New Jersey in contexts that seem to support the early origin of the type. A noteworthy and lamentable example was the Larchmont site, near Hartford, Burlington County, whose earliest component—apparently comparable to that at Turkey Swamp—was destroyed by heavy earthmoving equipment before an adequate archaeological evaluation could be obtained (Mounier 1985).

The Abature Site

Now lying beneath the concrete ribbons known as Route 18, near Eatontown in Monmouth County, the Abature site contained cultural material representing several thousand years of human settlement (Fimbel et al. 1984; Fimbel 1985; Mounier 1990a). Some of the earliest artifacts are bifaces relating to one or more Early-Middle Archaic components. Among the excavated remains are three bifurcate-base bifaces that resemble the LeCroy type (Broyles 1966, 1971) and a dimpled-base point similar to the Stanly (Coe 1964) or Neville styles (Dincauze 1971). Also present are two early corner-notched bifaces that resemble Kirk and Palmer points (Coe 1964). For the most part, these artifacts and associated lithic debris were found concentrated in relatively deep deposits, as much as four feet beneath the surface.

The early assemblage also included two grooved ironstone (limonite-cemented sandstone) abraders. The most complete and impressive example is a rounded tablet that has a series of grooves worn more or less radially across both faces. Superficially resembling a shaft-smoother, it differs in having grooves that tend to be V-shaped rather than U-shaped in cross section. Whereas U-shaped grooves result from the abrasion of a shaft held parallel to the face of the stone, V-shaped grooves are achieved by holding the work piece at a slight vertical angle (up to about 45°) while alternately drawing and pushing the implement across the face of the stone. The effect is to work the end of the shaft into a conical point.

Pointed rods of wood and bone were produced experimentally in the field by this technique (Mounier 1990a:IV-7—9). The experimental tablet quickly developed V-shaped grooves consistent with those observed in the archaeological specimen. From this evidence, we conclude that the early occupants of this site made and used pointed weapons or tools of perishable materials.

On the basis of published chronologies from the southern United States, the Early-Middle Archaic components might date to 9,000 B.P. (Coe 1964; Broyles 1966, 1971; Dincauze 1971). However, if the style originated in the South and diffused northward, as seems likely, the appearance of similar points in New Jersey probably occurred somewhat later.

Some of the deeply buried lithic remains from the eastern end of the site are interpreted to be the residue of Paleoindian occupation. These remains consist of a few jasper and chert tools, along with fragments and associated lithic debris. Although no fluted points were found, the depth of occurrence within the site, as well as lithology and overall artifact form, suggests an early

FIGURE 75. A grooved tablet and hammerstone. Experimentation shows that the grooved limonite tablet was used to sharpen points on implements of wood, bone, or antler. Photograph by the author.

cultural origin. In particular, the use of nonlocal lithic types appears to contrast with a later emphasis on the exploitation of locally available pebbles for raw material.

The High Bridge Sites

In the spring of 2000 archaeologists excavated portions of Sites 28-BU-225 and 28-BU-226, which occupy a series of sandy ridges on the divide between the Rancocas and Mullica Rivers in Burlington County (Mounier 2000c). This location is situated squarely within the region known as the Pine Barrens. The uplands support a secondary pine/oak/hickory forest that has been cut repeatedly in historic times for the production of charcoal. The low ground, which grades off to wetlands, contains swamp hardwoods, such as red maple.

An unusual characteristic of these sites is the appearance of Middle Archaic points of bifurcate-base form that generally fall within the type description for LeCroy points (Broyles 1966, 1971). Eight points of this style were found at Site 28-BU-226. These artifacts occur in cryptocrystalline and argillaceous materials in about equal proportions. Two corner-notched bifaces of early form, resembling the Palmer points described by Coe (1964:67–69), were also noted on the same site, one in chert and another in metasediment.

More numerous are contracting stemmed points of Middle to Late Archaic age. Typologically, these bifaces fall within the continuum of styles known as Morrow Mountain points, Poplar Island points, and Rossville points (Ritchie 1961:44–46; Coe 1964:37–43). Three specimens were found on Site 28-BU-225, along with several, probably related, fragments. On Site 28-BU-226 15 complete early stemmed specimens were found together with numerous fragments. This style of point was rendered mostly in metamorphosed materials, such as argillite, argillaceous shale, and various forms of quartzite.

At both sites, Archaic occupations were noted in small, isolated clusters that appeared from 12 to 18 inches (30–46 cm) below the surface. The earliest manifestation consists of a Middle Archaic component whose presence was clearly signaled by the discovery of several bifurcate-base projectile points. These points were found in the lower reaches of the excavation. The second cluster relates to the Morrow Mountain complex, manifested by narrow, contracting stemmed points. At both sites, stemmed and bifurcate-base points sometimes occurred together. Flakes from tool production and rejuvenation were found along with cobble tools of sandstone and limonite. A few incinerated refuse bone fragments were also observed.

By very careful collection of tiny granules of carbonized hickory nuts, we were able to gather enough charcoal to submit two samples from Site 28-BU-226 for radiocarbon analysis. We were careful to select only charred nut hulls, because they were likely to represent aboriginal food residues. The history of the Pine Barrens is largely a history of forest fire (Robichaud and Buell 1973:217–218), and we did not want to risk erroneous results by dating wood charcoal that might relate to natural, rather than cultural, events.

The first sample, which was associated with the stemmed point cluster, indicated an antiquity of approximately 4,010 years. The charcoal from the bifurcate-point cluster dated to around 6,560 B.P. (Beta Analytic 2000). These dates establish temporal benchmarks for the Middle and Middle to Late Archaic cultures in the region.

The functional characteristics of the assemblages indicate hunting, along with generalized foraging for seasonally available resources, such as tubers, nuts, and berries. The nearby swamp would favor the taking of game animals as well as amphibians and turtles, some of which appear to be represented as calcined refuse bone.

The evidence indicates the occasional or seasonal performance of mundane economic activities by small groups, perhaps individuals or, at most, a few members of a single family. Repeated short-term visits are implied by the limited range, variability, and density of artifacts. Apparently prehistoric populations never occupied these sites with the longevity or intensity of the larger settlements on the Inner Coastal Plain.

The sites do not appear to have been used as processing stations for the benefit of populations at larger sites. Rather, one senses almost casual exploitation of resources by small, highly mobile groups. Enough sites of this sort have now been identified to allow archaeologists to state confidently that prehistoric peoples consciously selected swampside settings in the Pine Barrens for ephemeral foraging camps (Mounier 2000c).

The distribution of artifacts at the several sites noted above suggests certain basic consistencies in the spatial arrangement of Early and Middle Archaic components. These consistencies apparently transect chronological, cultural, and geographic boundaries. A fundamental similarity in all early assemblages is a general thinness in artifact density, which may imply a low population density. It seems likely that these early folk followed a foraging regime that involved ephemeral settlement in small encampments.

LATE ARCHAIC SITES (CA. 3,000 – 5,000 B.P.)

Sites of the Late Archaic period are among the most numerous of the prehistoric settlements discovered in New Jersey. They are found in virtually every part of the state, from Sussex County to Cape May. In fact, if the sheer volume of artifacts and the number of sites are taken as evidence, the Late Archaic populations must have been among the largest and most widespread of any in prehistory. We shall look briefly at four Late Archaic sites situated in southern, central, and northern New Jersey.

The Fralinger Site

The unusually stratified Fralinger site is located on the eastern bank of the Maurice River, near Port Elizabeth in Cumberland County. An upper layer of black earth with late prehistoric and historic artifacts overlays deeper and older deposits of Late Archaic age. I first set foot on the Fralinger site in the fall of 1971, and by winter I had secured permission to conduct an excavation (Mounier 1974b). Fieldwork began in December 1971 and continued into

January of the following year. Mostly working alone, I was able to excavate more than 10 5-foot squares to a depth of 5 feet in the sandy soil. The excavation walls, made unstable by episodes of freezing and thawing, collapsed several times without warning, and I eventually abandoned the work out of a prudent and realistic fear of sudden entombment. Besides, each slumping wall destroyed some of the delicate stratigraphy upon which the interpretation of this site depended.

The Late Archaic component lay in bright yellow sand at a depth of approximately 4 feet beneath the surface. This component was manifested by a meager handful of artifacts and a single charcoal-filled pit, the remains of an ancient hearth. The pit was oval in plan and measured 19 × 24 inches (48 × 61 cm). It was basin-shaped in cross section and measured about 1 foot (30 cm) from top to bottom. Analysis of charcoal from this pit indicated an age of approximately 3,830 years, which provided a good chronological reference for the artifacts that were found nearby at the same depth.

The artifacts included a half dozen large, broad-bladed, square-stemmed bifaces characteristic of the Susquehanna tradition in the Middle Atlantic states (Witthoft 1953:21–22; Ritchie 1961:47–48; Kinsey 1972:423–426; H. Kraft 1972:30–31). These bifaces were rendered in argillite, quartzite, and limonite-cemented siltstone. Several large flakes of the same materials were found nearby. A number of the bifaces exhibited snap fractures that broke along straight or sinuous lines across the mid-length of the blades. This failure is characteristic of hafted knives. One unbroken specimen had been repeatedly resharpened so that its length was reduced to half of its estimated original size.

Other associated artifacts included an unfinished and broken sandstone adze or celt of a chipped variety and a small fragment of soapstone, possibly from a carved kettle. Other relics, found in place but of uncertain origin, were three small points with very short, broad stems.

The Fralinger site is of critical importance because it provided evidence of a single, apparently unmixed Late Archaic occupation. Associated charcoal gave the first reported chronometric age assessment for this period in southern New Jersey.

The Miller Field Site

The Miller Field site is located along the Delaware River in Warren County, about ten miles above the Water Gap. The site first came to scientific attention through the patient work of the dedicated and skillful archaeologist F. Dayton Staats. Staats shared his knowledge, accumulated over nearly a decade of personal research, with Herbert C. Kraft, the renowned archaeologist from Seton Hall University.

Between 1967 and 1968 Kraft and a crew of students excavated more than 14,000 square feet (1,300 m^2) of the site, taking pains to record the location of every artifact and feature—no small feat, given the dense concentrations of cultural remains. Although various archaeological cultures were present, the existence of Late Archaic remains in the Susquehanna tradition shed new light on what was then a poorly understood aspect of New Jersey archaeology.

Kraft was able to identify a series of related Terminal Archaic or Transitional cultures, marked by the presence of broadspears and fishtail bifaces, related tools (such as drills), soapstone kettles, and early pottery of the flat-bottomed variety. A plentitude of features with charcoal provided a basis for radiocarbon dating. One of the pit features contained six broadspears, a heat-shattered celt or adze, a few lumps of red and yellow ochre, flakes, and charcoal, including more than a dozen charred hickory nuts. Analysis of charcoal from this feature revealed an age of approximately 3,670 years, thus establishing a benchmark for the Susquehanna tradition in northern New Jersey.

One intriguing aspect of this site was the occurrence of four horseshoe-shaped arcs of fire-cracked rocks surrounded by a series of post molds. Covering about 100 square feet (9.3 m^2), the stone arcs were arranged so that the openings pointed toward a common center. This arrangement suggested to Kraft (1972:12–14) that the arcs and surrounding posts had been laid out intentionally, perhaps as a charnel house or mortuary structure. Because of the highly acidic soil, no bone survived at this location, but soil tests revealed unusually high concentrations of phosphates and calcium. The chemical residues, along with the presence of lumps of red ochre—a common element at mortuary sites—make Kraft's argument all the more plausible. No other features of this sort have ever been found.

The Stow Creek Cache

The Stow Creek cache is one of the most remarkable Late Archaic assemblages ever discovered in New Jersey. Alan E. Carman found it in 1999, the crowning achievement in his career of more than 50 years as an avocational archaeologist. James Holder and James Massey assisted in the excavation.

FIGURE 76. Blades from the Stow Creek cache. These bifaces show heat spalling, evidenced by flat-bottomed craters. The scale is in inches. Collection of Alan E. Carman. Photograph by the author.

The small site, a wooded point of ground on the edge of Stow Creek in Salem County, covers less than one-tenth of an acre. Continual seepage of groundwater keeps the clay-rich earth heavy and sticky. Carman found it necessary to knead the excavated soil by hand to isolate individual artifacts, because the wet earth would not pass through a screen without balling up. The results of this extra effort were rewarding.

The cache was contained within a bowl-shaped pit that measured 48 inches in diameter by 30 inches in depth (1.2 × 0.76 m). This feature yielded nearly 200 lithic artifacts, including a large quantity of preforms (or cache blades), formalized bifaces of broad-bladed design, slender cruciform (cross-shaped) drills, choppers, and flakes. The flaked stone artifacts were fashioned mostly from exotic materials, such as argillite, Hudson Valley cherts, and other non-local cryptocrystalline materials.

In addition to flaked stone items, four chipped and ground celts, a hammerstone, and a pestle were recovered. The assemblage also contained four fragmentary soapstone bowls, five grooved sinkers of the same material, and a sandstone netsinker. The total weight of the specimens exceeds 60 pounds (132 kg).

Except for the smaller artifacts, virtually everything in the cache had been broken before interment, either by intentional striking or by exposure to fire. In particular, many of the bifaces show extensive heat spalling, leading to numerous fractures.

Some artifacts were reassembled from parts, but others could not be reconstructed. Many conjoining pieces were widely dispersed within the pit, indicating that the contents had not been interred in any particular order. In fact, the extent of commingling, together with the apparent loss of some fragments, strongly suggests episodic reburial.

Some of the mended artifacts show differential discoloration, evidently induced by heat. In certain cases, the physical boundaries of particular fragments

FIGURE 77. Celts from the Stow Creek cache. These celts were formed by flaking and grinding. The specimen at left was intentionally broken or "killed" and later mended by the excavator. The scale is in inches. Collection of Alan E. Carman. Photograph by the author.

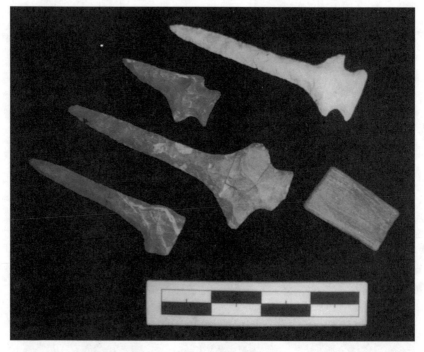

FIGURE 78. Cruciform drills from the Stow Creek cache. Cross-shaped drills reworked from large broad-bladed bifaces are a hallmark of cultures of the Susquehanna tradition. Also pictured is a piece of petrified wood. Photograph by author.

coincided with their respective color boundaries. This situation indicates that some pieces had been more intensively heated than others and that thermal exposure occurred after the artifacts had been broken and scattered.

The large bifaces are typologically related to broad-bladed specimens of the late Susquehanna tradition (Witthoft 1949, 1953; Ritchie 1965:149–163; Dincauze 1968). The presence of long drills—undoubtedly reworked from large bifaces—and soapstone artifacts is also consistent with this attribution. Although no human remains were found, the artifact assemblage is congruent with the contents of cremation burials. The varied elements of the cache await detailed description and analysis.

The Larchmont Site

The Larchmont site was a large, multicomponent site along Parker's Creek near Hartford, Burlington County. A number of archaeological studies were performed there in advance of residential and commercial development in the mid-1980s (Mid-Atlantic Archaeological Research 1984a, 1984b; Mounier 1985). The site covered an area of approximately three acres, which was divided between an abandoned orchard and a maturing woodlot. The wooded portion of the site contained artifacts and features in greater variety and in less disturbed contexts than the orchard, where, it seems, a foot or more of the site surface had been lost to agriculture and erosion in modern times.

Artifacts from this site consisted of several thousand stone flakes and flake tools in various forms. More than 230 bifacial knives and projectile points in stemmed, notched, and triangular styles were found. Also present were rough stone tools such as hammerstones, many of which showed only limited or expedient use in milling or stonework. Fire-broken or otherwise thermally altered rock fragments were numerous, while stone axes and atlatl weights were found in limited numbers. Portions of a soapstone-tempered, flat-bottomed ceramic vessel demonstrates a continuity between the Late Archaic and Early Woodland periods at this site. A fragment of this kettle was submitted to the Alpha Analytic Laboratory in Coral Gables, Florida, for thermoluminescence dating, resulting in an age determination of approximately 2,700 years (Mounier 1985:20).

Nineteen features were represented by clustered artifacts and fire-broken rocks. Several of these features were caches of preforms in argillite, argillaceous shale, quartz, and sandstone. Some caches also contained hammerstones and flaking debris.

Masterful excavations in the woods by Jack Cresson revealed numerous features and individual artifacts, which for a time were left exposed on the ground just as discovered (Mounier 1985). Upon entering the leaf-shrouded woods, visitors were greeted by a wondrous display. The scene left viewers with the impression of having stumbled into a deserted village that somehow had remained untouched for the last 5,000 years. The memory is indelible, but the experience was fleeting. This marvelous ancient camp has now been replaced by modern tract housing.

Early Woodland Sites (ca. 2,000 – 3,000 b.p.)

We tend to think of the introduction of ceramics around 3,000 B.P. or a bit earlier as the hallmark of the Early Woodland period. Yet the Early Woodland was a period of cultural continuity as well as change. It embraced many cultural traits of the preceding Late Archaic period. In fact, the two are very similar in terms of the basic hardware employed—stemmed and notched bifaces, axes, and so forth—and materials common to both often appear on the same sites. That is why some archaeologists use the label "Late Archaic/Early Woodland" to describe sites of this time period. Indeed, locations that can be said to contain nothing but Early Woodland components are quite rare (Hummer 1994). As our story continues, we shall visit both types of sites.

The Williamson Site

Chris Hummer spent more than a decade painstakingly excavating the Williamson site near Frenchtown in Hunterdon County (Hummer 1994). His exertions eventually won him a doctoral degree from Temple University. The Williamson site occupies a natural, sandy levee along the Delaware River in the Piedmont physiographic province. The site is unusual in that it is deeply stratified and has good separation between cultural components. The Early Woodland horizon, which lies at a depth of several feet, is physically distinct from earlier and later cultural deposits.

Several types of stemmed and notched bifaces occur together with cobble tools and flaking debris, ceramic vessels, and a variety of cultural features. The undisturbed context at this site led Hummer to believe that the bifaces and ceramics are essentially coeval, despite the variability in the types involved in these respective groupings.

One biface type, the so-called Hellgrammite point, is rare elsewhere in New Jersey but quite common at Williamson. This long, slender triangular form usually has a serrated blade and modest side-notches just above the base. The type is associated with Early Woodland cultures in the Susquehanna Valley (Kinsey 1959:116–117), and its prevalence at the Williamson site—in contexts dating between 2,800 and 3,300 years ago—confirms this cultural-temporal position in the Delaware Valley as well.

As for ceramics, Hummer identified fragments of at least one conoidal vessel that conforms to the type description for Vinette 1 (Ritchie and Mac-Neish 1949:100). He also found many sherds of flat-bottomed vessels. Some of these fragments derived from a soapstone-tempered ware commonly known as the Marcey Creek type, which is named for a site in Maryland (Manson 1948). Also identified were sherds from at least 18 other vessels of both conoidal and flat-bottomed forms, tempered with gneiss and quartz. Both smooth and corded surface treatments were present.

Careful excavation revealed many cultural features, including 24 pits, a cache of jasper cores, four lithic knapping stations, and 16 hearths or other clusters of thermally altered rock. Some of the pits yielded fragmentary nuts of hickory, walnut, and oak. Of these, hickory nuts were more common than walnuts or acorns. The hearths and rock clusters were fairly expansive.

Looking at his data analytically, Hummer identified four distinct activity areas, each of which contained several pits and non-intersecting rock features. He concluded that the site was occupied as a base camp by discrete family groups on a prolonged basis.

The Raccoon Point Site

In February 1952, Charles F. Kier Jr., an avocational archaeologist, began extensive excavations at the Raccoon Point site, aided by Fred Calverley (Kier and Calverley 1957). This undertaking represented an effort of unprecedented scope by individuals who were neither trained as archaeologists nor affiliated with any supporting institution.

The Raccoon Point site lay near the confluence of the Delaware River and Raccoon Creek in Logan Township, Gloucester County. It was one in a string of very large and productive sites in the lower Delaware Valley. Nearby sites, made famous by WPA excavations in 1937 and 1938 include the Salisbury and Goose Island sites (Cross 1941:52–66), which were similar in some respects to Raccoon Point.

Kier was a man who liked to do things right. He studied archaeology long before he ever sunk a spade into the ground. Before beginning work, he searched out the landowner and secured permission to dig. Rather than starting off blindly, Kier and Calverley cleared the ground of brush, laid out a reference grid, and opened a number of trial trenches to determine the general distribution of cultural remains. Only then did the excavation begin in earnest.

And an earnest effort it was! Working only on weekends, holidays, and in other stolen moments, Kier and Calverley excavated nearly 4,700 square feet (437 m^2) to an average depth of 2 feet (61 cm). In the process they recovered nearly 1,800 artifacts (not counting flakes and fire-cracked rock).

Every step of the undertaking was carefully noted. Artifacts and features were recorded as to provenience (the location of discovery). The relics were cleaned, cataloged, and counted. A base map was drawn, along with details of the excavation profiles. Most important, Kier condensed the results into a comprehensive site report that is now regarded as a classic among archaeo-logical publications (Kier and Calverley 1957).

Most of the artifacts are typical of Late Archaic/Early Woodland assem-blages. Stemmed and notched bifaces were common, and many of these oc-curred in association with soapstone kettle fragments and early ceramics.

Both flat-bottomed ware and conoidal pottery of Early Woodland age were present in large quantities. Kier estimated that no fewer than six flat-bottomed vessels are represented in the collection. These vessels were rectan-gular in plan, and apparently measured about 12 inches in length by 7 inches in width and from 6 to 9 inches in height (30.5 × 17.8 × 15.2−22.9 cm). The capacity was around half a gallon (1.8 liters). Some of the vessels had lug handles. The temper consists of steatite in 87 percent of the sherds, and a mix-ture of steatite and granite in the rest.

Many of the basal sherds bear impressions of mats constructed from plaited cane or from rush twined with cordage. Evidently, the pots were made while resting on these mats, although no one knows why. I suppose that this arrangement facilitated positioning the work during construction. With pots attached, the mats could have been slid or rotated, actions that would have been difficult had the wet clay been positioned directly on an immovable work surface. Whatever the case, the impressions were made permanent when the pots were fired.

Kier and Calverley (1957:87−88) believed that they had found a pottery kiln. This feature comprised a pile of thermally altered rocks, about 4 feet (1.2 meters) in diameter, interspersed with large amounts of charcoal. Sur-mounting the heap was a sandstone tablet that measured 14 inches in length, 10 inches in width, and 2 inches in thickness (36 × 25 × 5 cm). Around the periphery lay several sherds of flat-bottomed pottery.

A good deal of charcoal was obtained from this and other features. With remarkable foresight, Kier saved large samples for dating by the C^{14} technique, which in those days was still in its infancy. The calculated age for a sample of charred white cedar was 1,170 ± 200 years or about A.D. 780 (R. Mason 1959). (This date is several hundred years too recent for the presumed Early Wood-land association, but it is still significant as a pioneering assay.)

After 36 months on the site, Kier and Calverley were forced to depart by the arrival of heavy earthmoving equipment. The site was scooped away to make room for dredge spoil from the Delaware River. Kier lamented the loss: "The Raccoon Point site is more endeared to our hearts now than ever. Now it exists in memory only. As this is being written, Modern Man with his bulldozers, trucks, and shovels is removing every trace of that high ground which was once the home of Early Man. . . . All that is known of this village site has been recorded by us" (Kier and Calverley 1957:61). Indeed! We are very fortunate that Kier took his responsibilities as an archaeologist seriously.

The Cadwalader Site

The Cadwalader site is a coastal station situated on an island of dune sand in the tide meadow near East Point on the Delaware Bay (Mounier 1974b:39–50). In December 1971, Perry A. Brett, then of Vineland, called my attention to scattered oyster shells, dark soil, and surface-borne artifacts. The site is part of the Cadwalader Wildlife Management Area, which is owned by the State of New Jersey and controlled by the New Jersey Division of Fish and Wildlife (formerly the Division of Fish, Game, and Shell Fisheries). A request for permission to test and excavate on the island was filed early in January 1972, and two months later the request was approved. During April of the same year 15 5-foot squares were systematically excavated.

The work revealed a homogeneous lot of artifacts and related features belonging to a single Early Woodland occupation. The artifacts included flat-bottomed pottery, crude side-notched bifaces, and an assortment of bone and antler implements. The features comprised several large spreads of oyster shell, which also contained refuse bone and artifacts.

Two large shell masses were excavated, the smaller of which covered about 50 square feet (4.65 m²); the larger was perhaps twice that size. Both conformed to the hummocky contour of the original ground surface and ranged in thickness from a maximum of 5 inches (12.7 cm) near the center to one-half inch or less at the edges. The deposits consisted overwhelmingly of oyster shell (*Crassostrea virginica*), with the very rare inclusion of hard-shell clam (*Mercenaria mercenaria*) and whelk of uncertain species. These middens clearly represent the detritus of aboriginal oyster harvesting and preparation.

Scattered among the shells were the bones or teeth of various animals, including deer (*Odocoileus virginianus*), gray fox (*Urocyon cinereoargenteus*), and domestic dog (*Canis familiaris*), among others. Various species of turtles and waterfowl were also represented by bones. The buffering of soil acids by the presence of shells fostered the preservation of refuse bone and of artifacts made of bone and antler. The latter included an antler netting needle, bone-splinter awls, a bone spatula, and cut antler tines.

Another feature comprised a platform of fire-broken rocks, which covered

FIGURE 79. An oyster shell midden. This shallow spread of oyster shells was found on an island in the tide meadow near the Delaware Bay. The scale is in inches. Photograph by the author.

a little less than 40 square feet (3.5 m^2). Contents other than rocks were negligible. This feature was considered to be a roasting platform for the preparation of shellfish.

Of special interest is the presence of a peculiar variety of flat-bottomed pottery having a cylindrical or tub-shaped form, rather like a flower pot. This ware is heavily tempered with small, platelike fragments of crushed oyster shell, often expressed as voids caused by leaching or burning. The flat, discoidal bases are only about six inches in diameter. Both the interior and exterior surfaces bear impressions of cordage or twined fabrics. This kind of pottery occurred in direct association with the oyster shell middens.

This pottery is of considerable interest as an early experimental ware whose tempering is directly related to the availability of oyster shells. An earlier ware, heavily tempered with crushed quartz, consistently occurred in the sand beneath the shell layers. This ware—evidently arising before the discovery or exploitation of oysters in this vicinity—is similar to other early mineral-tempered types from the surrounding region.

Stone tools from the shell spreads include broad-bladed, side-notched bifaces rendered entirely in cryptocrystalline materials. These items may have

FIGURE 80. Broad, side-notched bifaces. These Early Woodland tools were probably used as knives. Photograph by author.

been weapons, but the characteristic fractures across the blades strongly suggest their use as knives. Among the other stone artifacts were utilized flakes, a triangular scraper, a rough chopper, and two notched sinkers.

An attempt to date the assemblage by radiocarbon assay of animal bones yielded anomalous results. The best information currently available suggests an antiquity on the order of 2,500 to 2,750 years for the major occupation at the Cadwalader site.

MIDDLE WOODLAND SITES (CA. 1,100 – 2,000 B.P.)

The Middle Woodland period remains somewhat enigmatic. Artisans of this period produced some distinctive artifacts, such as the ornate, zone-decorated pottery at the Abbott Farm, the broad-bladed Fox Creek bifaces, and net-impressed pottery (the latter two types are also hallmarks of the Abbott Farm). Elsewhere, the distinctive pentagonal points of the Jack's Reef phase are unmistakable. Even so, some Middle Woodland components are all but invisible archaeologically because their mundane remains are so similar to earlier and later cultural expressions. The following discussion will present information about two sites whose connection with Middle Woodland populations is demonstrated by distinctive artifact assemblages. A third has been placed in perspective by means of radiocarbon dating.

Site 28-GL-170

Site 28-GL-170 is located in Franklin Township, Gloucester County, on the northwest bank of Little Ease Run, a headwater of the Maurice River (Mounier and Martin 1992:IV-111–IV-132). The site covered about one-half acre on top of an elongated knoll that rises next to the stream. From the crest of the knoll, the sandy ground slopes off in all directions. At the time of discovery, the site lay in a woods of mixed oak and pine. It now lies beneath the southbound lane of Route 55.

Fieldwork involved the excavation of 24 5-foot squares, which yielded several artifacts and three features of Middle Woodland age. Among the artifacts were seven jasper bifaces that conformed to the Jack's Reef type. Two small triangular points, along with a few fabric-impressed potsherds, were also associated with the Middle Woodland component.

One of the features was a shallow, basin-shaped soil stain, about 5 feet (1.5 m) in diameter. A dense concentration of artifacts was recovered from the feature fill, including two Jack's Reef biface fragments, uniface tools, expedient hammers and choppers, and an array of flakes in jasper, chert, chalcedony, and quartz. In addition, a grit-tempered, fabric-impressed ceramic sherd was recovered, along with small amounts of thermally altered rock. The sherd is similar to the Riggins Fabric-Impressed type. An attempt at radiocarbon dating of charcoal from this feature produced anomalous results.

Another feature contained a cluster of fabric-impressed potsherds, a dozen quartz pebbles, and a piece of fossiliferous limestone. The dimensions cannot be stated because the feature was not completely excavated. The fossils were probably brought to the site by its prehistoric inhabitants.

Some of the Jack's Reef bifaces clearly bear evidence of impact fractures from use as projectiles, which suggests that hunting was an important activity at this site. The character of the flakes shows that tool production and maintenance were also practiced here. The relatively confined location, the limited supply and variety of artifacts, and the paucity of features collectively denote a temporary encampment by only a few people. This site is typical of many ephemeral encampments of the Jack's Reef culture that dot the interior of the coastal plains.

Site 28-GL-171

Site 28-GL-171, located a short distance downstream from 28-GL-170 (Mounier and Martin 1992:IV-128–IV-161), occupies a sandy upland that forms the eastern bank of Little Ease Run. During our excavation, stands of oak and pine dotted the upland, and swamp hardwoods covered the nearby floodplain.

A Middle Woodland component of the Fox Creek culture was clearly defined by characteristic argillite bifaces and net-impressed pottery. In all, 18 Fox Creek points were found, along with nearly 120 grit-tempered, net-impressed potsherds. These fragments represent at least two vessels, whose volumes could be calculated from the curvature of the fragments (see Mounier 1987). One vessel has an estimated capacity of 5.5 gallons (21.0 liters), and the other a capacity of 13.7 gallons (51.8 liters).

Most of the Middle Woodland potsherds were found in a single feature that covered an area of only 3 square feet (0.28 m^2). These fragments ranged in depth from 7 to 14 inches (18–36 cm) below the surface of the ground. Also found in the feature were a Fox Creek biface of argillite that had been used as a projectile point, a jasper biface tool, 8 flakes, and 11 thermally altered pebbles and fragments of quartz. A slight discoloration in the soil may represent the vanishing outline of a pit.

Another feature contained charcoal in association with a Fox Creek biface and other related artifacts. A C^{14} assay returned an estimated age of 2,120 years. This result is earlier than most calculated Fox Creek age assessments, which range between 1,100 and 1,600 years ago. However, at least one date from the New Jersey coast places the Fox Creek culture before 1,800 B.P. (Stanzeski 1996:42). An earlier origin for this culture cannot be dismissed out of hand.

The evidence from this site suggests a mixed hunting and foraging existence. The remains are too few and diffuse to indicate long-term occupation or settlement by more than a few people. The excavation of this site provided a tantalizing glimpse of the Fox Creek culture, which remains enigmatic because of its spotty distribution around the state. For every large site, such as the Abbott Farm, there are probably dozens of little sites like 28-GL-171, which attract scant attention because their contents are neither numerous nor imposing.

Sites 28-CM-25 and 28-CM-28

Several years ago, some colleagues and I were called upon to conduct archaeological investigations near Swainton in Middle Township, Cape May County. We found a number of small sites, two of which had important Middle Woodland components as well as other cultural expressions (Mounier 1997). These sites are of interest because some of the contents could be placed without ambiguity in a Middle Woodland time frame by radiocarbon dating. They are also important because the archaeological evidence reveals shifting patterns in shellfishing that can be related to rising sea levels.

Sites 28-CM-25 and 28-CM-28 are two adjacent camps that occupy upland settings near a small stream in the head of Deep Creek. This short coastal stream flows through the tidal meadows between Great Sound and Stites Sound. From these sites it is an easy walk to the head of the stream or to the tidal marshes.

Middle Woodland features at Site 28-CM-25 comprise two pits, which contained cross-corded pottery among layers of mollusk shells. Site 28-CM-28 also revealed artifacts and features relating to the same period. Here the Middle Woodland artifacts were a few cross-corded potsherds, which were recovered from the bottom of a deep shell-roasting pit.

Ecological data confirm that the general environmental conditions at the time of aboriginal occupation resembled those of the present. At Site 28-CM-28, several kinds of animals were represented by fragmentary teeth and bones. These included deer, turtles, fish, and birds. Except for turtle bone, none of the osseous material from 28-CM-25 could be identified as to species.

The meager representation of faunal remains other than shellfish may reflect differential preservation owing to acidic soil conditions. The apparent absence of bony fish is puzzling, given the coastal setting, but may suggest that harvesting shellfish took precedence at these sites and that fishing was undertaken at other locations.

Mollusks are the most numerous and sensitive ecological indicators at these sites. Shifting trends in the exploitation of shellfish through time provide insights into changes in the physical environment and associated cultural adaptations. Substantial exploitation of shellfish first appears during Middle Woodland times, between 1,600 and 1,700 years ago, according to radiometric analysis of charcoal from the shell deposits.

Earth ovens containing large volumes of burned oyster shells occur at both 28-CM-25 and -28. Oysters were found in the bottoms of these features, to the virtual exclusion of other species. Later deposits contain mixed batches of oysters, clam, and conch. The shellfish in the most recent archaeological accumulations, estimated to be less than 700 years old, are almost entirely quahog.

Changes in shellfish harvesting are seen as reflections of necessity rather than of gustatory preferences. The agency inducing this necessity is change in the local environment, resulting from a progressive rise in sea levels. Viewed from this perspective, our data show a decline in the proportion of oysters gathered from deep water and a relative increase in ones taken from beaches and sandbars.

Rising sea levels placed the deepwater oysters beyond reach, because of increasing depths or increasing distance between the land and the oyster beds. Either situation would have raised the risks or costs associated with gathering oysters from relatively deep water. The loss or abandonment of deepwater oysters was apparently offset by more intensive harvesting of shallow-water oysters. At the same time, the collection of conchs, and particularly of quahogs, increased dramatically. These are shallow-water species that prosper in the more saline environments brought on by the encroaching sea. By the end of the archaeological period, the quahog had all but entirely supplanted oysters as a source of food at these sites.

LATE WOODLAND SITES (CA. 500 –1,100 B.P.)

Aboriginal settlements of the Late Woodland period are fairly common in New Jersey. These are sites occupied by natives whose immediate descendants met the European onslaught. Their distinctive assemblages of pottery, pipes, and triangular bifaces—by this time, almost certainly used as arrowheads—make the remains of this period easily recognizable. On the other hand, because of their relative modernity, Late Woodland cultural deposits generally lie nearest the surface, leaving them more vulnerable to destruction than the more deeply buried deposits of earlier times. The following summaries will highlight three Late Woodland sites from central and southern New Jersey.

Site 28-MO-125

An archaeological survey in advance of sewer construction led to the discovery of Site 28-MO-125, a small Late Woodland foraging camp in the Marlin Estates section of Marlboro Township, Monmouth County (Mounier 1984). The site sits on the tip of a sandy peninsula that projects into a swampy expanse in the headwaters of the South River. The cultural material comprised clusters of pottery, flake tools, cores, and bifaces, which were confined to an area of approximately one-half acre. Associated organic materials included wood charcoal and a few calcined bone fragments.

The crew identified scattered relics in a preliminary survey while prospecting with posthole diggers and hand screens. Additional test holes, each about 6 inches (15 cm) in diameter, were placed at close intervals around the original findspots to home in on the principal archaeological deposits. Then seven larger sampling units, each measuring 5 × 5 feet (1.5 × 1.5 m), were manually excavated to the full depth of the cultural deposits. Only shallow digging was necessary because the artifacts extended only about 1 foot (30 cm) below the surface.

An analysis of the cultural remains demonstrated that the site was occupied by a few people on a temporary basis, probably in the course of foraging for berries, roots, or tubers. Non-edible resources, such as wood and plant fibers, might have been collected as well. None of the five bifaces showed any evidence of the impact fractures so characteristic of projectile hunting. Rather, most showed snap fractures, common to stone knives. Many of the 105 flakes also revealed retouched or use-worn edges, indicating their role as knives or scrapers. Some of the flakes betray the reduction of locally obtainable cobbles for the preparation of expedient tools. The pebble cores revealed the same. The remaining lithic artifacts consisted of 208 fire-cracked rocks, some of which were arranged in a hearth that measured about 2 × 4 feet (61 × 122 cm). This feature was probably used in processing plant materials.

Associated with the lithic artifacts were 365 potsherds, which included both corded and fabric-impressed varieties, as well as numerous small fragments. The fabric-impressed sherds strongly resemble the Riggins Fabric-Impressed type, which is very common on late prehistoric sites, especially on the coastal plains.

Particles of wood charcoal, a few charred seeds, and incinerated refuse bone were interspersed among the artifacts. On an archaeological site, charcoal is as precious as it is mundane. By careful excavation, the crew managed to glean a sample of 11 grams (<0.5 oz.) of this ancient fuel for analysis. This sample yielded an estimated age of $1,000 \pm 60$ radiocarbon years, roughly equivalent to a calendrical date of A.D. 950.

Ten small carbonized seeds were retrieved by flotation. In this process soil is placed in a tub of water and gently agitated. The heavier materials, such as sand, settle to the bottom while the buoyant particles float to the surface, where they are removed with strainers. The species of the seeds gathered by this technique could not be identified.

Twenty-four pieces of calcined refuse bone were also collected during the excavation. These specimens had a wide distribution across the site. If it is supposed that this material represents the remains of animals killed and eaten, the very meager sample suggests that the taking of animals did not figure significantly in the prehistoric use of the site.

The archaeological evidence indicates that this site was a small camp occupied for a very short time at the beginning of the Late Woodland period. It

was probably part of a settlement system that included larger villages elsewhere in the drainage of the South River. The results of this brief investigation show that even small sites can contain important archaeological data.

The Bevan Site

Led by Jean Jones of Millville, members of the Maurice River Historical Society conducted a small, but important, salvage excavation at a site near Buck-
shutem in Cumberland County (Jones and Turner 1975). The site occupied a
field on a sandy bluff overlooking the west bank of the Maurice River. The
field had been farmed for centuries, and collectors had gathered many Indian
artifacts from the vicinity. When the proposed construction of a small building threatened the prehistoric remains, permission was secured to excavate the
affected portion of the site.

Work began in earnest in May 1974 and continued mostly on weekends
for several weeks. The archaeologists established a grid of 5-foot squares so
that the provenience of the finds could be accurately recorded. Most of the
plow zone was removed with shovels; then the work proceeded by careful
troweling across the breadth of each square. This work allowed not only the
collection of individual artifacts but also the discovery of any features that
might be present.

In the absence of cultural stratigraphy, the excavation advanced by arbi-
trary 6-inch (15 cm) levels. These levels were excavated in successive horizontal
steps, each about 1 foot (30 cm) wide, all the while maintaining a clean vertical face. The position of each artifact and feature was recorded with reference
to the grid and according to depth. The excavation continued to the apparent
floor of the cultural distribution, about 2½ feet (76 cm) below the surface.

The upper levels contained numerous late prehistoric artifacts. The excavation also revealed one circular, bowl-shaped pit that opened immediately
beneath the plow zone. An organic stain of reddish brown earth clearly defined the feature in contrast to the surrounding yellow subsoil. This pit measured about 32 inches (81.3 cm) in diameter and extended 22 inches (55.9 cm)
into the subsoil. The upper end had been truncated by plowing, and there was
no way to determine how much depth had been lost to farming and erosion.
This feature was probably used initially for storage of foodstuffs and later filled
with refuse. Undoubtedly, other features of this sort were present but could
not be identified owing to spatial constraints placed upon the excavation.

Nestled within the pit were many fragments of Riggins Fabric-Impressed pottery, along with a triangular projectile point and a large amount of wood charcoal. Enough sherds were recovered to reconstruct about one-third of an ovate vessel, whose height can be estimated at approximately 16 inches (40.6 cm). The diameter was slightly greater than 1 foot (32 cm), as calculated from the curvature of the reconstructed portion. A vessel of this configuration and size would have a volume of nearly 5 gallons (18.2 liters).

The age of the charcoal from the feature was calculated to be about 935 radiocarbon years, corresponding to a date around A.D. 1015. This age assessment was the first to place the Riggins Fabric-Impressed ceramic type into a temporal framework that was not based solely on stratigraphic or typological considerations (Mounier 1978b:17–19).

Although the excavation was severely limited in scope, the results indicate that the Bevan site served as a village or base camp in late prehistoric times. The dedicated efforts of a few volunteers have added a short but impressive chapter to the prehistoric archaeology of New Jersey.

The Ware Site (28-SA-3)

The Ware site lies along the southern bank of Salem Creek in Mannington Township, Salem County. Covering less than two acres, this location was occupied with great intensity, especially in late prehistoric times. It has been estimated that more than 100,000 potsherds, not to mention other artifacts, have been collected from this site (Morris et al. 1996:18). Artifacts of the Late Woodland Riggins complex constitute a large portion of this assemblage (McCann 1950; Morris et al. 1996:18, 25–33).

Drawn to the Ware site by the hope of finding a historic Delaware Indian village, Catherine McCann (1950) opened an excavation in 1947. This work, part of the Delaware Project (see chapter 1), continued into the following year. McCann's crew excavated three portions of the site, following standard procedures for maintaining provenience control. In all, the excavations covered 1,110 square feet (103 m²) and yielded several thousand relics. The artifacts in the upper levels—largely fabric-impressed potsherds, triangular points, and small stone tools—are associated with relatively late occupations, which may have extended into the period of European contact. Indeed, the Ware site has yielded a few trade items, such as copper arrowheads.

Between 1940 and 1981, the late Howard K. Urion of Woodstown also dug at the Ware site and amassed a huge collection. After sorting out items of special interest for display, Urion stored the harvest from each episode of digging, separating each in sequence by sheets of newspaper. This practice yielded a curious modern stratigraphy that placed the dates of collection into a rough perspective.

Urion kept few field records, and there is no indication that he took the trouble to differentiate the contents of features from artifacts found loose in the ground. Consequently, a good deal of important data were undoubtedly lost. However, Howard Urion was a generous man who always allowed those of scholarly bent to examine his collection.

With similar kindness, his son, Howard Jr., permitted members of the Archaeological Society of New Jersey to conduct a detailed, long-term study of the ceramic artifacts. For several years, this work required a weekly intrusion into the Urion home, where the collection was then stored. During this time Mr. Urion and his family never failed to show "hospitality, kindness, and support" (Morris et al. 1996:33).

The study was spearheaded by George Morris, Wilbert "Butch" Reed, Cindy Karageanes, and Guy DiGiugno. These tireless investigators were motivated by the belief that this important collection "would yield significant typological and chronological data . . . if the collection could be correlated with McCann's vertical distribution of ceramics and cross-referenced to dated historical types from adjacent regions" (Morris et al. 1996:17). In this endeavor they succeeded admirably. The ensuing report is an important benchmark in New Jersey archaeology.

One by one, the archaeologists sorted more than 100,000 pieces of pottery into 25 discrete types according to paste, temper, surface finish, and decoration. In addition, by comparing measurable or inferred diameters as well as decorative motifs and techniques, they were able to calculate the minimum number of vessels representing each type. The challenging task of reconstructing partial vessels from a mass of fragments also aided in this endeavor. The researchers concluded that the collection as a whole contains fragments from no fewer than 960 vessels. Nearly 780 vessels represent varieties of late prehistoric fabric-marked wares. This information clearly demonstrates the importance of the site in the waning years of prehistory.

The success of the ceramic study emboldened the archaeologists to continue with an examination of the lithic remains. This is a work still in progress, but again, the collection appears to show a strong Late Woodland presence.

The ability of these archaeologists to squeeze important new data from cultural remnants—by digging into collections instead of the ground—foreshadows the future, when few archaeological sites will remain undisturbed in the earth. Morris and his colleagues are true pioneers.

———

AT THIS POINT, our vicarious archaeological journey comes to an end. We have glimpsed an amazing archaeological heritage, composed of the residue of innumerable human acts over thousands of years of unwritten history. Diminished by the passage of time, the inexorable march of human endeavors, and the ravages of greedy collectors, this previously unknown past has been revealed and chronicled by a long line of steadfast scholars, whose curiosity about the past has enlightened our age. Abbott, Volk, Skinner, Schrabisch, Cross, and Kraft have all passed from our midst, but their work lives on. The story of archaeology in New Jersey will continue to unfold as long as archaeologists seek to understand the mysteries of the past.

REFERENCES

Abbott, Charles C. 1872. The Stone Age in New Jersey. *American Naturalist* 6:144–160.

———. 1876a. Indication of the Antiquity of the Indians of North America Derived from a Study of their Relics. *American Naturalist* 10:65–72.

———. 1876b. The Stone Age in New Jersey. In Smithsonian Institution, *Annual Report for 1875*, 246–380. Washington, D.C.

———. 1881. *Primitive Industry or Illustrations of the Handiwork in Stone, Bone and Clay of the Native Races of the Northern Atlantic Seaboard of America.* Salem, Mass.: George A. Bates.

———. 1883. Traces of a Pre-Indian People. *Popular Science Monthly* 22:315–322.

———. 1885a. Palaeolithic Man in America. *Riverside National History* 6:106–109.

———. 1885b. The Use of Copper by the Delaware Indians. In *The American Naturalist*, ed. A. S. Packard Jr. and F. W. Putnam, extra ed. (August): 774–777. Salem, Mass.: Peabody Academy of Science. Reprinted in *Bulletin of the Archaeological Society of New Jersey* 51 (1996): 70–71.

———. 1889a. Descendants of Paleolithic Man in America. *Popular Science Monthly* 36: 145–154.

———. 1889b. Evidence of the Antiquity of Man in Eastern North America. *Proceedings of the American Association for the Advancement of Science* 37:293–315.

———. 1892. Recent Archaeological Explorations in the Valley of the Delaware. In *Publications of the University of Pennsylvania*, Series in Philology, Literature and Archaeology, 2:1–30. Philadelphia: University of Pennsylvania.

———. 1893. A Pre-Columbian Dinner. *The Archaeologist* 1(2): 30–32. Waterloo, Ind.: American Archaeological Association.

———. 1907. *Archaeologia Nova Caesarea.* Vol. 1. Trenton: MacCrellish and Quigley.

———. 1908. *Archaeologia Nova Caesarea.* Vol. 2. Trenton: MacCrellish and Quigley.

———. 1909. *Archaeologia Nova Caesarea.* Vol. 3. Trenton: MacCrellish and Quigley.

Ahler, Stanley A. 1971. *Projectile Point Form and Function at Rodgers Shelter, Missouri.* Missouri Archaeological Research Series, no. 8. Columbia, Mo.

Baird, Donald. 1987. The Indian Trade Gun and Gunflints from Burial 8 at the Pahaquarra Site. *Bulletin of the Archaeological Society of New Jersey* 42:1–8.

Bass, William M. 1971. *Human Osteology: A Laboratory and Field Manual of the Human Skeleton.* Columbia: Missouri Archaeological Society.

Becker, Marshall J. 1980. Wampum: The Development of an Early American Currency. *Bulletin of the Archaeological Society of New Jersey* 36:1–11.

———. 1988. A Summary of Lenape Socio-Political Organization and Settlement Pattern at the Time of European Contact: The Evidence for Collecting Bands. *Journal of Middle Atlantic Archaeology* 4:79–83.

———. 1993. Lenape Shelters: Possible Examples from the Contact Period. *Pennsylvania Archaeologist* 63(2): 64–76.

———. 1999. Cash Cropping by Lenape Foragers: Preliminary Notes on Native Maize Sales to Swedish Colonists and Cultural Stability during the Early Colonial Period. *Bulletin of the Archaeological Society of New Jersey* 54:45–68.

Bello, Charles A. 1987a. A Comment on Edge-Perforated Artifacts. *Newsletter of the Archaeological Society of New Jersey* 142:10–11. Reprinted in *Bulletin of the Archaeological Society of Connecticut* 57 (1994): 55–56.

———. 1987b. An Effigy Pestle from Site 28Me199, Mercer County, New Jersey. *Bulletin of the Archaeological Society of New Jersey* 47:31–32.

———. 1988a. Edge-Perforated Artifacts: Additional Sources of Information. *Newsletter of the Archaeological Society of New Jersey* 145:7–8. Reprinted in *Bulletin of the Archaeological Society of Connecticut* 57 (1994): 57–58.

———. 1988b. An Edge-Perforated Sinewstone from Hamilton Township, Mercer County, New Jersey. *Bulletin of the Archaeological Society of New Jersey* 43:81.

———. 1989. Two Unusually Large Stone Axes from New Brunswick, New Jersey. *Bulletin of the Archaeological Society of New Jersey* 44:73.

———. 1992. A Steatite Spearthrower Weight from Ocean County, New Jersey. *Bulletin of the Archaeological Society of New Jersey* 47:68.

———. 1993. Two Unique Pipes from the Abbott Farm. *Bulletin of the Archaeological Society of New Jersey* 48:65–67.

———. 1995. An "Upside-Down" Pendant from Minisink Island. *Bulletin of the Archaeological Society of New Jersey* 50:18–19.

———. 1996. A Probable Middle Woodland Burial from the New Jersey Shore. *Bulletin of the Archaeological Society of New Jersey* 51:49–53.

———. 1998. A Rejuvenated Plummet from Springfield Township, Burlington County. *Bulletin of the Archaeological Society of New Jersey* 53:117–118.

Bello, Charles A., John H. Cresson, and Richard Veit. 1997. A Meadowood Cache from the Rancocas Creek Drainage, Burlington County. *Bulletin of the Archaeological Society of New Jersey* 52:63–67.

Bello, Charles A., and Leslie E. Eisenberg. 1988. An Analysis of the Skeletal and Artifactual Remains from a Disturbed Coastal Site in Ocean County, N.J. *Bulletin of the Archaeological Society of New Jersey* 43:45–51.

Bello, Charles A., and Richard Veit. 1997. A "Ritually Killed" Platform Pipe from New Jersey. *Bulletin of the Archaeological Society of New Jersey* 52:103.

Beta Analytic. 2000. Report of Radiocarbon Dating Results from Site 28-BU-226. Miami: Beta Analytic Radiocarbon Dating Laboratory. (Lethia Cerda to R. Alan Mounier, 21 June 2000.)

Blackman, Leah. 1880. *History of Little Egg Harbor Township, Burlington County, N.J.* Reprint. Tuckerton, N.J: Great John Mathis Foundation, 1963.

Blenk, Michael H. 1977a. A Birdstone from Salem County. *Bulletin of the Archaeological Society of New Jersey* 34:33.

———. 1977b. The Lerro Farm Site: An Exercise in Cooperative Archaeology. *Bulletin of the Archaeological Society of New Jersey* 34:14–32.

————. 1986. An Unusual Animal Effigy on Pottery. *Bulletin of the Archaeological Society of New Jersey* 40:26–27.

————. 1990. Additional Effigies on Pottery from Cumberland County. *Bulletin of the Archaeological Society of New Jersey* 45:15–16.

Boissevain, Ethel. 1956. The First 25 Years of the Archaeological Society of New Jersey. *Bulletin of the Archaeological Society of New Jersey* 12:1–7.

Bonfiglio, Anthony, and John H. Cresson. 1982. Geomorphology and Pinelands Prehistory: A Model of Early Aboriginal Land Use. In *History, Culture, and Archaeology of the Pine Barrens: Essays from the Third Pine Barrens Conference*, ed. John W. Sinton, 15–67. Pomona, N.J.: Stockton State College, Center for Environmental Research.

Bragdon, Kathleen J. 1999. Ethnohistory, Historical Archaeology, and the Rise of Social Complexity in Native North America: Case Studies in Southern New England. In *Old and New Worlds*, ed. Geoff Egan and R. L. Michael, 84–96. Oxford: Oxbow Books.

Braun, David P. 1974. Explanatory Models for the Evolution of Coastal Adaptations in Prehistoric Eastern New England. *American Antiquity* 39(4): 582–596.

Brennan, Louis A. 1963. A 6000-Year-Old-Midden of Virginia Oyster Shell at Croton Point, Lower Mid Hudson. Paper delivered at the annual meeting of the Eastern States Archaeological Federation, Philadelphia.

————. 1973. *Beginners Guide to Archaeology.* Harrisburg, Pa.: Stackpole Books.

————. 1974. The Lower Hudson: A Decade of Shell Middens. *Archaeology of Eastern North America* 2(1): 81–93.

Brett, Perry A. 1974. The Maurice River Shell Tool Complex. *Man in the Northeast* 7:110–122.

Brothwell, Don R. 1965. *Digging Up Bones.* London: British Museum (Natural History).

Broyles, Bettye J. 1966. Preliminary Report: The St. Albans Site (46Ka27), Kanawha County, West Virginia. *West Virginia Archaeologist* 19:1–43.

————. 1971. *Second Preliminary Report: The St. Albans Site, Kanawha County, West Virginia.* Report of Archaeological Investigations, no. 3. Morgantown: West Virginia Geological and Economic Survey.

Buchholz, Margaret Thomas. 1999. *Shore Chronicles: Diaries and Travelers' Tales from the Jersey Shore, 1764–1955.* Harvey Cedars, N.J.: Down the Shore Publishing Corp.

Burrow, Ian. 1997. The Savich Farm Site: An Archaeological Survey for Phase 1 of the Long-Term Master Plan. *Bulletin of the Archaeological Society of New Jersey* 52:35–50.

Burrow, Ian, Donald Thieme, William Liebeknect, and Joseph Schuldenrein. 1999. Archaeological Data Recovery Investigations at the Derewal Prehistoric Site, Hunterdon County, New Jersey. *Bulletin of the Archaeological Society of New Jersey* 54:12–43.

Butler, Mary. 1947. Two Lenape Rock Shelters near Philadelphia. *American Antiquity* (Menasha) 12:246–254.

Callahan, Errett. 1994. A Mammoth Undertaking. *Bulletin of Primitive Technology* 7:23–39.

Cantwell, Anne-Marie. 1980. Bone Skewers and/or Single Tine Forks from the Pahaquarra Site. *Bulletin of the Archaeological Society of New Jersey* 36:25–26.

Carbone, Victor A. 1976. Environment and Prehistory in the Shenandoah Valley. Ph.D. diss., Catholic University of America. Ann Arbor, Mich.: University Microfilms.

————. 1982. Environment and Society in Archaic and Woodland Times. In *Practicing Environmental Archaeology: Methods and Interpretations*, ed. Roger Moeller, 39–52. Occasional Paper no. 3. Washington, Conn.: American Indian Archaeological Institute.

Carman, Alan E. 1998. The Indian's Sweat Hut. *Bulletin of the Archaeological Society of New Jersey* 53:126.

Carpenter, Edmund S. 1950. Five Sites of the Intermediate Period. *American Antiquity* 15(4): 298–314.

Catlin, Mark, Jay F. Custer, and R. Michael Stewart. 1982. Late Archaic Cultural Change in Virginia. *Quarterly Bulletin of the Archaeological Society of Virginia* 37:123–140.

Cavallo, John A. 1981. Turkey Swamp: A Late Paleo-Indian Site in New Jersey's Coastal Plain. *Archaeology of Eastern North America* 9:1–17.

————. 1987. *The Area B Site (28Me1-B), Data Recovery.* Trenton Complex Archaeology, Report 8. Rev. ed., 1996. East Orange, N.J.: Cultural Resource Group, Louis Berger and Associates.

Cavallo, John A., and Arthur A. Joyce. 1985. Explanatory Models of Late Archaic Culture in the Middle Atlantic Region: An Evaluation. Paper presented at the Middle Atlantic Archaeological Conference, Rehoboth Beach, Del.

Cavallo, John A., and R. Alan Mounier. 1980. *A Regional Predictive Survey of the New Jersey Pinelands—Phase I.* Report to New Jersey Pinelands Commission. New Lisbon, N.J.

Chesler, Olga, ed. 1982. *New Jersey's Archeological Resources from the Paleo-Indian Period to the Present: A Review of Research Problems and Survey Priorities.* Trenton: New Jersey Office of Cultural and Environmental Services.

Chrisbacher, Ernest. 1990. The Skyline Rockshelter, Bergen County, New Jersey. *Bulletin of the Archaeological Society of New Jersey* 45:66–76.

Clabeaux, Marie Striegal. 1972. Osteological Evidence of Disease in the Indians of New Jersey. *Bulletin of the Archaeological Society of New Jersey* 28:19–27.

————. 1976. Analysis of Human Skeletal Remains from the Rosenkrans Site. *Archaeology of Eastern North America* 4:43–44.

————. 1978. An Evaluation of the Skeletal Material from the Bell-Philhower Site. In *The Minisink Site: A Reevaluation of a Late Prehistoric and Early Historic Contact Site in Sussex County, New Jersey,* ed. Herbert C. Kraft, 98–99. South Orange: Seton Hall University Museum, Archaeological Research Center.

Coe, Joffre L. 1964. *Formative Cultures of the Carolina Piedmont.* Transactions of the American Philosophical Society, n.s., vol. 54, pt. 5. Philadelphia: American Philosophical Society.

Cook, George H. 1868. *Geology of New Jersey.* Trenton: New Jersey Geological Survey.

Crane, Eva. 1975. The World's Beekeeping—Past and Present. In *The Hive and the Honey Bee,* 1–18. Hamilton, Ill.: Dadant and Sons, Inc.

Cresson, Jack. 1984. Middle Woodland Lithic Technologies: A Chapter in Deciphering a Unique Extractive Process and Production of Rhyolite Fox Creek Primary Quarry Bifaces. Paper presented at the Middle Atlantic Archaeological Conference, Rehoboth Beach, Del.

————. 1990. Broadspear Lithic Technology: Some Aspects of Biface Manufacture, Form, and Use History with Insights towards Understanding Assemblage Diversity. In *Experiments and Observations on the Terminal Archaic of the Middle Atlantic Region,* ed. Roger W. Moeller, 105–130. Bethlehem, Conn.: Archaeological Services.

————. 1994. Platforms to Prehistory. *Bulletin of Primitive Technology* 7:70–76.

————. n.d.a. Personal Research Notes.

Cross, Dorothy. 1941. *The Archaeology of New Jersey.* Vol. 1. With chapters by Henry B. Kümmel, Horace G. Richards, and Nathaniel Knowles. Trenton: Archaeological Society of New Jersey and New Jersey State Museum.

————. 1953. Delaware and Related Horizons in New Jersey. *Bulletin of the Archaeological Society of New Jersey* 6:7–11.

————. 1956. *The Archaeology of New Jersey.* Vol. 2, *The Abbott Farm.* Trenton: Archaeological Society of New Jersey and New Jersey State Museum.

————. 1986. Canoes of the Lenni Lenape. *Bulletin of the Archaeological Society of New Jer-*

sey 40:25. Reprinted from *Newsletter of the Archaeological Society of New Jersey* no. 3 (January 1941): 10.

Crowl, G. F., and R. Stuckenrath Jr. 1977. Geological Setting of the Shawnee-Minisink Paleoindian Archeological Site (36-Mr-43). In *Amerinds and Their Paleo-Environments in Northeastern North America*, ed. W. S. Newman and Bert Salwen, 218–222. Annals of the New York Academy of Sciences, 288. New York: New York Academy of Sciences.

Crozier, Archibald. 1938. The Steatite Quarry near Christiana, Lancaster County, Pennsylvania. *Bulletin of the Archaeological Society of Delaware* 3(2): 13–15.

Curbishley, David L. 1954. Bone and Antler Implements from New Jersey. *Bulletin of the Archaeological Society of New Jersey* 8:13–22.

Curry, Dennis C. 1980. Burial of Late Archaic Coastal Plain Sites as a Result of Aeolian Deposition. Paper presented at the Middle Atlantic Archaeological Conference, Rehoboth Beach, Del.

Curry, Dennis C., and Jay F. Custer. 1982. Holocene Climatic Change in the Middle Atlantic Area: Preliminary Observations from Archaeological Sites. Paper presented at the Middle Atlantic Archaeological Conference, Rehoboth Beach, Del.

Curry, Dennis C., and Carol A. Ebright. 1989. Buried Archaic Sites in Ridgetop Settings on the Middle Atlantic Coastal Plain. Paper presented at the Joint Archaeological Conference, Baltimore.

Custer, Jay F. 1978. Broadspears and Netsinkers: Late Archaic Adaptations at Four Middle Atlantic Archaeological Sites. Paper presented at the Middle Atlantic Archaeological Conference, Rehoboth Beach, Del.

———. 1984a. *Delaware Prehistoric Archaeology: An Ecological Approach.* Newark: University of Delaware Press.

———. 1984b. The Paleoecology of the Late Archaic: Exchange and Adaptation. *Pennsylvania Archaeologist* 54(3–4): 32–47.

———. 1986. Periglacial Features of the New Jersey Coastal Plain: A Demurrer. *Bulletin of the Archaeological Society of New Jersey* 40:21–25.

———. 1987. *A Management Plan for the Prehistoric Archaeological Resources of Delaware's Atlantic Coastal Region.* Monograph 4. Newark: University of Delaware Center for Archaeological Research.

———. 1988. Coastal Adaptations in the Middle Atlantic Region. *Archaeology of Eastern North America* 16:121–135.

Custer, Jay F., and George J. Morris. 1989. The Beaver Creek Broadspear Cache from Southern New Jersey. *Bulletin of the Archaeological Society of New Jersey* 44:9–16.

Custer, Jay F., H. Henry Ward, and Scott C. Watson. 1986. The Archaeology of the Delaware Chalcedony Complex: A Preliminary Report. *Bulletin of the Archaeological Society of Delaware*, n.s., 26:1–20.

Dankers, Jasper, and Peter Sluyter. 1867. *Journal of a Voyage to New York and a Tour in Several of the American Colonies in 1679–80.* Trans. H. C. Murphy. Memoirs, vol. 1. Brooklyn: Long Island Historical Society.

Davis, Hester. 1971. Is there a Future for the Past? *Archaeology Magazine*, October 1971.

de Vries, David Pietersz. 1912. From the "Korte historiael ende journaels aenteyckeninge," 1630–1633, 1634 [1655]. In *Narratives of Early Pennsylvania, West Jersey and Delaware 1630–1707*, ed. Albert Cook Myers, 7–29. New York: Charles Scribner's Sons.

de Vries, Ralph. 1994. The Dark Moon Site, Sussex County, N.J. *Bulletin of the Archaeological Society of New Jersey* 49:108–110.

Didier, Mary Ellen. 1975. The Argillite Problem Revisited: An Archaeological and

Geological Approach to a Classical Archaeological Problem. *Archaeology of Eastern North America* 3:90–101.

Dincauze, Dena F. 1968. *Cremation Cemeteries in Eastern Massachusetts.* Peabody Museum of American Archaeology and Ethnology, 59(2). Cambridge: Harvard University.

———. 1971. An Archaic Sequence for Southern New England. *American Antiquity* 36:194–198.

Dragoo, Don W. 1963. *Mounds for the Dead: An Analysis of the Adena Culture.* Annals of the Carnegie Museum, 37. Pittsburgh: Carnegie Museum.

Dunay, Robert J. 1981. The Havins Site, Vernon Township, Sussex County, New Jersey. *Bulletin of the Archaeological Society of New Jersey* 37:3–5.

Dunn, Robert A. 1984. Form and Function of the Perkiomen Broadpoint. *Pennsylvania Archaeologist* 54(3–4): 11–18.

DuPonceau, Peter S., trans. 1834. *A Short Description of the Province of New Sweden, by Thomas Campanius Holm.* Philadelphia: M'Carty and Davis.

Edwards, Robert L., and K. O. Emery. 1977. Man on the Continental Shelf. In *Amerinds and Their Paleo-Environments in Northeastern North America,* ed. W. S. Newman and Bert Salwen, 245–256. Annals of the New York Academy of Sciences, 288. New York: New York Academy of Sciences.

English, A. L. 1884. *History of Atlantic City, New Jersey.* Philadelphia: Dickson & Gilling.

Fimbel, Deborah. 1985. Archaeological Survey in the New Jersey Outer Coastal Plain. M.A. thesis, Department of Anthropology, Temple University.

Fimbel, Deborah, Arthur A. Joyce, Jean Meier, David Mudge, L. Rappleye-Marsett, and David Zmoda. 1984. *New Jersey Route 18 Freeway, Section 3B and 3C, Eatontown Borough, Ocean Township, Tinton Falls Borough, Monmouth County, New Jersey.* Technical Environmental Study: Historic and Prehistoric Archaeology. Trenton: New Jersey Department of Transportation, Bureau of Environmental Analysis.

Fountain, George H. 1897. Shell Heaps of the Shrewsbury River, N.J. Reprinted in *Bulletin of the Archaeological Society of New Jersey* 51(1996): 69–70.

Fowke, Gerard. 1896. Stone Art. In Bureau of American Ethnology, *Thirteenth Annual Report,* 57–178. Washington, D.C.

Frison, George C. 1991. *Prehistoric Hunters of the High Plains.* With contributions by Bruce A. Bradley, Julie E. Francis, George W. Gill, and James C. Miller. 2d ed. San Diego: Academic Press.

Funk, Robert E., George R. Walters, and William F. Ehlers Jr. 1969. A Radiocarbon Date for Early Man from the Dutchess Quarry Cave. *Bulletin of the New York State Archeological Association* 46:19–21.

Gladfelter, Bruce G. 1985. On the Interpretation of Archaeological Sites in Alluvial Settings. In *Archaeological Sediments in Context,* ed. Julie K. Stein and William R. Farrand, 41–52. Orono: University of Maine, Center for the Study of Early Man.

Goddard, Ives. 1974. The Delaware Language, Past and Present. In *Delaware Indian Symposium,* ed. Herbert C. Kraft, 103–110. Anthropological Series, no. 4. Harrisburg: Pennsylvania Historical and Museum Commission.

———. 1978a. Delaware. In *Handbook of North American Indians,* vol. 15, *Northeast,* ed. Bruce G. Trigger, 213–239. Washington: Smithsonian Institution.

———. 1978b. Eastern Algonquian Languages. In *Handbook of North American Indians,* vol. 15, *Northeast,* ed. Bruce G. Trigger, 70–77. Washington: Smithsonian Institution.

Griffin, James B., ed. 1952. *Archeology of the Eastern United States.* Chicago: University of Chicago Press.

Grossman-Bailey, Ilene. 2001. "The People Who Lived by the Ocean": Native American Resource Use and Settlement in the Outer Coastal Plain of New Jersey. Ph.D. diss., Temple University.

Gruber, Jacob W., and Ronald J. Mason. 1956. Temple University Excavations at the Buri Site, Burlington County, New Jersey. *Bulletin of the Archaeological Society of New Jersey* 12:9–22.

Haag, William G. 1948. An Osteometric Analysis of Some Aboriginal Dogs. In *Reports in Anthropology and Archaeology* 7(3): 107–264. Lexington: University of Kentucky.

Haggerty, Lewis M. 1980. A Forgotten Wampum Factory in Bergen County. *Bulletin of the Archaeological Society of New Jersey* 36:12.

Hall, M. D., Jr. 1970. An Indian Village Site at Frenche's Pond, Waterloo, Sussex County, N.J. *Bulletin of the Archaeological Society of New Jersey* 25:10–14.

Harrington, M. R. 1909a. Ancient Shell Heaps near New York City. In American Museum of Natural History, *Anthropological Papers*, 3:167–179. New York: American Museum of Natural History.

———. 1909b. The Rock Shelters of Armonk, New York. In American Museum of Natural History, *Anthropological Papers*, 3:125–138. New York: American Museum of Natural History.

———. 1921. Religion and Ceremonies of the Lenape. *Indian Notes and Monographs*, vol. 19. New York: Museum of the American Indian, Heye Foundation.

———. 1924. An Ancient Village of the Shinnecock Indians. In American Museum of Natural History, *Anthropological Papers*, 22(5): 227–283. New York: American Museum of Natural History.

———. 1925. Obituary and Bibliography of Alanson Skinner. In *Indian Notes* 2(4): 247–257. New York: Museum of the American Indian, Heye Foundation.

Hartzell, Warren, and F. Dayton Staats. 1983. Rare Clay Beads from the Dark Moon Site. *Bulletin of the Archaeological Society of New Jersey* 39:11

Hartzog, Sandra. 1982. Palynology and Late Pleistocene-Holocene Environment on the New Jersey Coastal Plain. In *History, Culture, and Archaeology of the Pine Barrens: Essays from the Third Pine Barrens Conference,* ed. John W. Sinton, 6–15. Pomona, N.J.: Stockton State College, Center for Environmental Research.

Hatch, James W. 1994. The Structure and Antiquity of Prehistoric Jasper Quarries in the Reading Prong, Pennsylvania. In *Recent Research into the Prehistory of the Delaware Valley,* ed. Christopher A. Bergman and John F. Doershuk, 23–46. A special issue of *Journal of Middle Atlantic Archaeology* 10. Bethlehem, Conn.: Archaeological Services.

Hawkes E. W., and Ralph Linton. 1916. *A Pre-Lenape Site in New Jersey.* University Museum Anthropological Publications, 6. Philadelphia: University of Pennsylvania.

Haynes, C. Vance, Jr. 1973. Elephant Hunting in North America. In *Early Man in America,* 44–52. San Francisco: W. W. Freeman and Company.

Heckewelder, John. 1819. *An Account of the History, Manners, and Customs of the Indian Nations Who Once Inhabited Pennsylvania and the Neighbouring States.* Transactions of the Historical and Literary Committee of the American Philosophical Society, 1. Philadelphia: American Philosophical Society.

Heye, George G., and George H. Pepper. 1915. *Exploration of a Munsee Cemetery near Montague, New Jersey.* Vol. 2, no. 1. New York: Museum of the American Indian.

Hodge, F. W. 1920. *Hawikuh Bonework.* Indian Notes and Monographs, 3(3). New York: Museum of the American Indian, Heye Foundation.

Hoerler, Alice. 1939. *Selected Pottery from the Excavations of the Indian Site Survey of New Jersey.* Archaeological Society of New Jersey, Leaflet no. 6.

Holmes, William H. 1890. Excavations in an Ancient Soapstone Quarry in the District of Columbia. *American Anthropologist*, o.s., 3:321–331.

———. 1892. Aboriginal Quarries of Flakable Stone and Their Bearings upon the Question of Paleolithic Man. Abstract in *Proceedings of the American Association for the Advancement of Science* 41:279–280.

———. 1893. Are There Traces of Glacial Man in the Trenton Gravels? *Journal of Geology* 1:15–37.

———. 1897. Stone Implements of the Potomac-Chesapeake Tidewater Province. In Bureau of American Ethnology, *Fifteenth Annual Report*, 13–152. Washington, D.C.: Smithsonian Institution.

———. 1898. Primitive Man in the Delaware Valley. *Proceedings of the American Association for the Advancement of Science* 46:364–370.

———. 1903. Aboriginal Pottery of the Eastern United States. In Bureau of American Ethnology, *Twentieth Annual Report*, 1–201. Washington, D.C.: Smithsonian Institution.

———. 1919. *Handbook of Aboriginal American Antiquities, Part 1.* Bureau of American Ethnology, Bulletin 60. Washington: Smithsonian Institution.

Hotchkin, Wayne, and F. Dayton Staats. 1983. The Edmunds Rock Shelter. *Bulletin of the Archaeological Society of New Jersey* 39:1–4.

Hrdlička, Aleš. 1907. *Skeletal Remains Suggesting or Attributed to Early Man in North America.* Bureau of American Ethnology, Bulletin 33. Washington, D.C.: Smithsonian Institution.

———. 1916. *Physical Anthropology of the Lenape or Delawares, and of the Eastern Indians in General.* Bureau of American Ethnology, Bulletin 62. Washington, D.C.: Smithsonian Institution.

———. 1942. The Problem of Man's Antiquity in America. *Proceedings of the 8th American Scientific Congress* 2:53.

Hummer, Chris C. 1981. A Perforated Ceramic Discoidal from Salem County. *Bulletin of the Archaeological Society of New Jersey* 37:19–20.

———. 1994. Defining Early Woodland in the Delaware Valley: The View from the Williamson Site, Hunterdon County, New Jersey. In *Recent Research into the Prehistory of the Delaware Valley*, ed. Christopher A. Bergman and John F. Doershuk, 141–151. A special issue of *Journal of Middle Atlantic Archaeology* 10. Bethlehem, Conn.: Archaeological Services.

Hunter Research. 1994. *Phase III Archaeological Data Recovery on the Western Portion of the Olt Farm Site (28-BU-104), Sagemore Multifamily Development, Marlton, Evesham Township, Burlington County, New Jersey.* Report to Davis Enterprises, Marlton, N.J.

Jones, Jean, and Everett Turner. 1975. Excavations at the Bevan Site. *Newsletter of the Archaeological Society of New Jersey* 97:4.

Jordan, Francis, Jr. 1906. *Aboriginal Fishing Stations.* Lancaster, Pa.: New Era Printing Company.

Joyce, Arthur A. 1983. Explanatory/Predictive Models in Archaeology and Their Application in New Jersey. Trenton: New Jersey Department of Transportation. MS on file.

———. 1984. A Consideration of Middle Atlantic Region Paleo-Environmental Reconstructions. Trenton: New Jersey Department of Transportation. MS on file.

———. 1988. Early/Middle Holocene Environments in the Middle Atlantic Region: A Revised Reconstruction. In *Holocene Human Ecology in Northeastern North America*, ed. George Nicholas, 185–215. New York: Plenum Press.

Joyce, Arthur A., William Sandy, and Sharon Horan. 1989. Dr. Charles Conrad Abbott and the Question of Human Antiquity in the New World. *Bulletin of the Archaeological Society of New Jersey* 44:59–70.

Kennedy, Steel M., Bertrand B. Boucher, John T. Cunningham, and Patricia S. Merlo. 1963. *The New Jersey Almanac: 1964–1965.* Upper Montclair, N.J.: New Jersey Almanac, Inc.

Kent, Barry C. 1984. *Susquehanna's Indians.* Anthropological Series, no. 6. Harrisburg: Pennsylvania Historical and Museum Commission.

Kier, Charles F., Jr. 1949. Cohansey Quartzite and the Riggins Farm. *Bulletin of the Archaeological Society of New Jersey* 2:1–7.

———. 1954. An Interesting Bone Fragment from New Jersey. *Bulletin of the Archaeological Society of New Jersey* 8:10–12.

———. 1960. As it Was—An Archaeological Study of Atlantic County, New Jersey. *Atlantic County Historical Society Yearbook 1960,* 18–23.

Kier, Charles F., Jr., and Fred Calverley. 1957. The Raccoon Point Site, an Early Hunting and Fishing Station in the Lower Delaware Valley. *Pennsylvania Archaeologist* 27(2): 1–100.

Kinsey, W. Fred, III. 1959. Recent Excavations on the Bare Island in Pennsylvania: The Kent-Halley Site. *Pennsylvania Archaeologist* 29:109–133.

———, ed. 1972. *Archaeology of the Upper Delaware Valley.* Anthropological Series, no. 2. Harrisburg: Pennsylvania Historical and Museum Commission.

Knoblock, Byron W. 1939. *Bannerstones of the North American Indians.* LaGrange, Ill.: Byron W. Knoblock.

Knowles, Nathaniel. 1941a. Comparative Petrology and Typology. In Dorothy Cross, *The Archaeology of New Jersey,* 1:153–176. Trenton: Archaeological Society of New Jersey and New Jersey State Museum.

———. 1941b. Vertical Distribution of New Jersey Artifacts. In Dorothy Cross, *The Archaeology of New Jersey,* 1:185–206. Trenton: Archaeological Society of New Jersey and New Jersey State Museum.

Kraft, Herbert C. 1969. There Are Petroglyphs in New Jersey. *Bulletin of the Archaeological Society of New Jersey* 24:13–16.

———. 1970. Prehistoric Indian Housepatterns in New Jersey. *Bulletin of the Archaeological Society of New Jersey* 26:1–11.

———. 1972. The Miller Field Site, Warren County, N.J. In *Archaeology of the Upper Delaware Valley,* ed. W. Fred Kinsey III, 1–54. Anthropological Series, no. 2. Harrisburg: Pennsylvania Historical and Museum Commission.

———. 1973. The Plenge Site: A Paleo-Indian Occupation Site in New Jersey. *Archaeology of Eastern North America* 1(1): 56–117.

———. 1974a. Canoe-shaped Artifacts. *Bulletin of the Archaeological Society of New Jersey* 30: 11–12.

———. 1974b. Canoe-shaped Artifacts of Bone. *Bulletin of the Archaeological Society of New Jersey* 31:33.

———. 1974c. Indian Prehistory of New Jersey. In *A Delaware Indian Symposium,* ed. Herbert C. Kraft, 1–55. Anthropological Series, no. 4. Harrisburg: Pennsylvania Historical and Museum Commission.

———. 1975a. *The Archaeology of the Tocks Island Area.* South Orange: Seton Hall University Museum, Archaeological Research Center.

———. 1975b. The Late Woodland Pottery of the Upper Delaware Valley: A Survey and Reevaluation. *Archaeology of Eastern North America* 3:101–140.

———. 1975c. Upside-Down Pendants. *Bulletin of the Archaeological Society of New Jersey* 32:33.

———. 1976a. *The Archaeology of the Pahaquarra Site.* South Orange: Seton Hall University Museum, Archaeological Research Center.

————. 1976b. The Rosenkrans Site: An Adena-related Mortuary Complex in the Upper Delaware Valley, New Jersey. *Archaeology of Eastern North America* 4:9–50.

————. 1977. Stone Mask Found in Elizabeth, Union County, New Jersey. *Bulletin of the Archaeological Society of New Jersey* 34:33.

————, ed. 1978. *The Minisink Site: A Reevaluation of a Late Prehistoric and Early Historic Contact Site in Sussex County, New Jersey.* South Orange: Seton Hall University Museum, Archaeological Research Center.

————. 1982. The Late Woodland Period in Northern New Jersey. In *New Jersey's Archeological Resources from the Paleo-Indian Period to the Present: A Review of Research Problems and Survey Priorities*, ed. Olga Chesler, 143–158. Trenton: New Jersey Office of Cultural and Environmental Services.

————. 1986a. Late Woodland Settlement Patterns in the Upper Delaware Valley. In *Late Woodland Cultures of the Middle Atlantic Region*, ed. Jay F. Custer, 102–115. Newark: University of Delaware Press.

————. 1986b. *The Lenape: Archaeology, History, and Ethnography.* Newark: New Jersey Historical Society.

————. 1987. A Unique Sandstone Bowl from South Amboy. *Bulletin of the Archaeological Society of New Jersey* 42:10.

————. 1989a. A Dated Meadowood Component from Fairfield, Essex County, N.J. *Bulletin of the Archaeological Society of New Jersey* 44:51–54.

————. 1989b. Minisink Phase, Animal Effigy Pottery Sherd. *Bulletin of the Archaeological Society of New Jersey* 44: cover illustration.

————. 1989c. Winakung Village at Waterloo. *Bulletin of the Archaeological Society of New Jersey* 44:72.

————. 1991. An Effigy Face from Lake Hopatcong. *Bulletin of the Archaeological Society of New Jersey* 46:1–12.

————. 1992a. Of Fish, Nets, and Sinkers. *Bulletin of the Archaeological Society of New Jersey* 47:11–19.

————. 1992b. A Platform Pipe from Morris County. *Bulletin of the Archaeological Society of New Jersey* 47:75.

————. 1992c. A Wooden Cup in a Brass Kettle. *Bulletin of the Archaeological Society of New Jersey* 47:86–88.

————. 1993. Dr. Charles Conrad Abbott, New Jersey's Pioneer Archaeologist. *Bulletin of the Archaeological Society of New Jersey* 48:1–12.

————. 1995a. A Re-examination and Re-interpretation of the Passaic River Petroglyph. *Bulletin of the Archaeological Society of New Jersey* 50:87–90.

————. 1995b. A Response to Lenik's "Indian Petroglyphs on the Passaic River: A Rejoinder to Kraft." *Bulletin of the Archaeological Society of New Jersey* 50:93.

————. 1996a. Effigy Face on Large Cobblestone. *Bulletin of the Archaeological Society of New Jersey* 40:32.

————. 1996b. The Gorman Petroglyph. *Bulletin of the Archaeological Society of New Jersey* 40:49.

————. 1998. The Rosenkrans Site: An Adena-related Mortuary Complex in the Upper Delaware Valley, New Jersey. *Bulletin of the Archaeological Society of New Jersey* 53:69–97.

Kraft, Herbert C., and Glenn A. Wershing. 1974. An Effigy Face from Mt. Arlington. *Bulletin of the Archaeological Society of New Jersey* 31:33.

Kraft, John C. 1977. Late Quaternary Paleogeographic Changes in the Coastal Environments of Delaware, Middle Atlantic Bight, Related to Archaeologic Setting. In *Amerinds and Their Paleo-Environments in Northeastern North America*, ed. W. S. Newman and Bert Salwen, 35–69. Annals of the New York Academy of Sciences, 288. New York: New York Academy of Sciences.

Kraft, John C., and Chacko J. John. 1978. Paleogeographic Analysis of Coastal Archaeological Settings in Delaware. *Archaeology of Eastern North America* 6:41–60.

Kümmel, Henry B. 1913. Annual Administrative Report of the State Geologist for the Year 1912. In Bulletin 8, 33–34. Trenton: Geological Survey of New Jersey.

————. 1941. Geography of New Jersey. In Dorothy Cross, *Archaeology of New Jersey*, 1:7–12. Trenton: Archaeological Society of New Jersey and New Jersey State Museum.

LaPorta, Philip. 1989. The Stratigraphic Relevance and Archaeological Potential of Chert Bearing Carbonates within the Kittatiny Subgroup. In *Field Trip Guide Book*, ed. Dennis Weiss, 240–269. Middletown: New York State Geological Association.

————. 1994. Lithostratigraphic Models and the Geographic Distribution of Prehistoric Chert Quarries within the Cambo-Ordovician Lithologies of the Great Valley Sequence, Sussex County, New Jersey. In *Recent Research into the Prehistory of the Delaware Valley*, ed. Christopher A. Bergman and John F. Doershuk, 47–66. A special issue of *Journal of Middle Atlantic Archaeology* 10. Bethlehem, Conn.: Archaeological Services.

Lavin, Lucianne. 1988. Coastal Adaptations in Southern New England and Southern New York. *Archaeology of Eastern North America* 16:101–120.

————. 1994. More News on Ground and Edge-Perforated Artifacts. *Bulletin of the Archaeological Society of Connecticut* 57:61–62.

Lavin, Lucianne, and Donald R. Prothero. 1987. Identification of "Jasper" Sources in Parts of the Northeast and Middle Atlantic Region. *Bulletin of the Archaeological Society of New Jersey* 42:11–23.

Lenik, Edward J. 1973. The Thom Petroglyph. *Pennsylvania Archaeologist* 43(1): 21–23.

————. 1974. The West Milford Effigy Stones. *Bulletin of the Archaeological Society of New Jersey* 31:7–9.

————. 1989. New Evidence on the Contact Period in Northeastern New Jersey and Southeastern New York. *Journal of Middle Atlantic Archaeology* 5:103–120.

————. 1990. The Mountainside Park Site: A Hilltop Procurement-Processing Camp Overlooking the Former Glacial Lake Passaic Basin. *Bulletin of the Archaeological Society of New Jersey* 45:29–41.

————. 1991. Patterns of Lithic Resource Selection in the Highlands Region of Northern New Jersey and Southeastern New York. *Bulletin of the Archaeological Society of New Jersey* 46:13–17.

————. 1992. Indian Petroglyphs on the Passaic River. *Bulletin of the Archaeological Society of New Jersey* 47:1–9.

————. 1995a. A Final Note from Ed Lenik. *Bulletin of the Archaeological Society of New Jersey* 50:93–94.

————. 1995b. Indian Petroglyphs on the Passaic River: A Rejoinder to Kraft. *Bulletin of the Archaeological Society of New Jersey* 50:90–92.

————. 1998. *Max Schrabisch: Rockshelter Archaeologist.* Wayne, N.J.: Wayne Township Historical Commission.

Levine, Mary Ann. 1999. Native Copper in the Northeast. In *The Archaeological Northeast*, ed. Mary Ann Levine, Kenneth E. Sassaman, and Michael S. Nassaney. Westport, Conn.: Bergin and Garvey.

Lilly, Eli, C. F. Voegelin, Erminie Voegelin, et al. 1954. *Walam Olum or Red Score, the Migration Legend of the Lenni Lenape or Delaware Indians: A New Translation, Interpreted by Linguistic, Historical, Archaeological, Ethnological, and Physical Anthropological Studies.* Indianapolis: Indiana Historical Society.

Lindeström, Peter M. 1925. *Geographia Americae, with an Account of the Delaware Indians, Based on Surveys and Notes Made in 1654–1656.* Trans. Amandus Johnson. Philadelphia: Swedish Colonial Society.

Lopez, Julius, and Stanley Wisniewski. 1958. Discovery of a Possible Ceremonial Dog Burial in the City of Greater New York. *Bulletin of the Archaeological Society of Connecticut* 29:14–19.

Loskiel, George H. 1794. *History of the Mission of the United Brethren among Indians in North America.* Trans. Christian Ignacius La Trobe. 3 parts. London.

Louis Berger and Associates, Inc. 1987. *A Report on Archaeological Investigations and Data Recovery in the Route 90, Section 2B Corridor, Burlington and Camden Counties, New Jersey.* Report to New Jersey Department of Transportation, Trenton.

Lutins, Allen H., and Anthony P. DeCondo. 1999. The Fair Lawn/Paterson Fish Weir. *Bulletin of the Archaeological Society of New Jersey* 54:7–11.

Macgowan, Kenneth. 1953. *Early Man in the New World.* New York: Macmillan.

MacLeod, W. C. 1922. The Family Hunting Territory and Lenape Political Organization. *American Anthropologist* (Lancaster) 56:448–63.

MacNeish, Richard S. 1952. The Archeology of the Northeastern United States. In *Archeology of the Eastern United States,* ed. James B. Griffin, 46–58. Chicago: University of Chicago Press.

Manson, Carl. 1948. Marcey Creek Site: An Early Manifestation in the Potomac Valley. *American Antiquity* (Menasha) 13:223–227.

Marchiando, Patricia. 1972. Bell-Browning Site, 28-SX-19. In *Archaeology of the Upper Delaware Valley,* ed. W. Fred Kinsey III, 131–158. Anthropological Series, no. 2. Harrisburg: Pennsylvania Historical and Museum Commission.

Marshall, Sydne. 1982. Aboriginal Settlement in New Jersey during the Paleo-Indian Cultural Period: ca. 10,000 B.C.–6,000 B.C. In *New Jersey's Archeological Resources from the Paleo-Indian Period to the Present: A Review of Research Problems and Survey Priorities,* ed. Olga Chesler, 10–51. Trenton: New Jersey Office of Cultural and Environmental Services.

Martin, John W. 1991. Prehistoric Cultural Resources at the Old Barracks, Trenton, New Jersey. *Bulletin of the Archaeological Society of New Jersey* 46:19–30.

———. 1995. A Sharpening Stone from the Abbott Farm. *Bulletin of the Archaeological Society of New Jersey* 50:61–62.

Mason, J. Alden. 1956. Henry Chapman Mercer, 1856–1930. *Pennsylvania Archaeologist* 26(3–4):151–165.

Mason, Otis T. 1904. *Indian Basketry—Studies in a Textile Art without Machinery.* New York: Doubleday, Page and Company.

Mason, Ronald J. 1957. New Jersey State Museum Excavations at the Steppel Site, Morris County. *Bulletin of the Archaeological Society of New Jersey* 14:1–20.

———. 1959. Letter to Charles F. Kier Jr., 27 March. Document on file with the author.

McCann, Catherine. 1950. The Ware Site, Salem County, New Jersey. *American Antiquity* (Menasha) 15:315–321.

———. 1957. Six Late Sites in Southern and Central New Jersey. *Bulletin of the Archaeological Society of New Jersey* 13:1–10.

McCormick, Jack. 1970. *The Pine Barrens—A Preliminary Ecological Inventory.* Report 2. Trenton: New Jersey State Museum.

McGee, W. J. 1888. Paleolithic Man in America. *Popular Science Monthly* 34:20–36.

———. 1893. Review of Man in the Glacial Period. *American Anthropologist*, o.s., 6:85–95.

McNett, Charles, Barbara A. McMillan, and Sydne Marshall. 1977. The Shawnee-Minisink Site. In *Amerinds and Their Paleo-Environments in Northeastern North America*, ed. W. S. Newman and Bert Salwen, 282–296. Annals of the New York Academy of Sciences, 288. New York: New York Academy of Sciences.

McWeeney, Lucinda. 1984. Wood Identification and Archaeology in the Northeast. *North American Archaeologist* 5(3): 183–195.

———. 1990a. Can We See the Forest for the Swamp? Paper presented at the Middle Atlantic Archaeological Conference, Ocean City, Md.

———. 1990b. The Potential of Wood and Charcoal as Environmental Indicators in Middle Atlantic Sites. *Journal of Middle Atlantic Archaeology* 6:1–14.

Menzer, Charles H. 1977. Prescribed Burning for Wildlife. *New Jersey Outdoors* 4(1): 2–3.

Mercer, Henry C. 1893. The Result of Excavations of the Ancient Argillite Quarries Recently Discovered near the Delaware River on Gaddis Run. *Proceedings of the American Association for the Advancement of Science* 42:304–307.

———. 1897. Researches upon the Antiquity of Man in the Delaware Valley and the Eastern United States. In *Publications of the University of Pennsylvania*, Series in Philology, Literature, and Archaeology, 6:1–85. Philadelphia: University of Pennsylvania.

Michels, Joseph W. 1973. *Dating Methods in Archaeology.* New York: Seminar Press.

Mid-Atlantic Archaeological Research, Inc. 1984a. *Intensive Archaeological Survey at the Larchmont Planned Unit Development, Burlington County, New Jersey.* Newark, Del.: Mid-Atlantic Archaeological Research, Inc.

———. 1984b. *Stage II Archaeological Investigations at 28-BU-165, Burlington County, New Jersey.* Newark, Del.: Mid-Atlantic Archaeological Research, Inc.

Middleton, Dorothy E. 1932. My Collection of Indian Relics. In Frank H. Stewart, *Indians of Southern New Jersey*, 48–56. Woodbury: Gloucester County Historical Society.

Moeller, Roger W., ed. 1982. *Practicing Environmental Archaeology: Methods and Interpretations.* Occasional Paper no. 3. Washington, Conn.: American Indian Archaeological Institute.

Moonsammy, Rita Zorn, Richard Steven Cohen, and Lorraine Williams, eds. 1987. *Pinelands Folklife.* New Brunswick: Rutgers University Press.

Moorehead, Warren K. 1922. *A Report on the Archaeology of Maine.* Andover: Andover Press.

Morris, George J. 1974. The Boni Site, Gloucester County, New Jersey: A Preliminary Report. *Bulletin of the Archaeological Society of New Jersey* 31:9–14.

———. 1986. Perforated Pebbles: An Evaluation. *Bulletin of the Archaeological Society of New Jersey* 40:7–9.

———. 1988. Three Ceramic Discs from Cumberland County, New Jersey. *Bulletin of the Archaeological Society of New Jersey* 43:15–16.

Morris, George J., and Wilbert F. Reed. 1990. A Pedestaled Vessel from the Ware Site. *Bulletin of the Archaeological Society of New Jersey* 45:53–54.

Morris, George J., Wilbert F. Reed, Cindy Karageanes, and Guy DiGiugno. 1996. The Ware Site Ceramics: A Proposed Chronological Sequence. *Bulletin of the Archaeological Society of New Jersey* 51:17–34.

Mounier, R. Alan. 1972a. The Blue Hole Site. *Bulletin of the Archaeological Society of New Jersey* 29:14–27.

————. 1972b. The Question of Man's Antiquity in the New World: 1840–1927. *Pennsylvania Archaeologist* 42:59–69.

————. 1974a. Aboriginal Use of Petrified Wood in New Jersey. *Bulletin of the Archaeological Society of New Jersey* 30:25–26.

————. 1974b. Archaeological Investigations in the Maurice River Tidewater Area, New Jersey. *Man in the Northeast* 7:29–56.

————. 1974c. An Archaeological Survey of a Section of the Pureland Industrial Park, Logan Township, Gloucester County, New Jersey. Unpublished report on file with the author.

————. 1975. The Indian Head Site Revisited. *Bulletin of the Archaeological Society of New Jersey* 32:1–14.

————. 1976a. *An Archaeological Survey of Portions of Galloway Township, Atlantic County, N.J.* Report to Galloway Township Municipal Utilities Authority.

————. 1976b. *An Archaeological Survey of Proposed Construction of I-676 (Alignment Scheme 1-W), Camden, New Jersey.* Report to New Jersey Department of Transportation. Trenton.

————. 1978a. The Environmental Basis of Prehistoric Occupation on the New Jersey Coastal Plains. *Man in the Northeast* 15–16:42–69.

————. 1978b. Two New Radiocarbon Dates for New Jersey. *Pennsylvania Archaeologist* 48(1–2): 16–19.

————. 1981a. *An Archaeological Survey of Portions of Cooper Street–Clements Bridge Road, Deptford Township, Gloucester County, New Jersey.* Report to New Jersey Department of Transportation. Trenton.

————. 1981b. Three Possible Middlesex Sites in Southern New Jersey. *Archaeology of Eastern North America* 9:52–63.

————. 1982. The Late Woodland Period in Southern New Jersey. In *New Jersey's Archeological Resources from the Paleo-Indian Period to the Present: A Review of Research Problems and Survey Priorities,* ed. Olga Chesler, 158–167. Trenton: New Jersey Office of Cultural and Environmental Services.

————. 1984. *Data Recovery Excavations at Prehistoric Archaeological Site 28-MO-125, Marlin Estates, Marlboro Township, Monmouth County, N.J.* Report to Schoor, DePalma & Gillen, Inc., Matawan, N.J.

————. 1985. *Archaeological Data Recovery at 28-BU-165, Larchmont Center, Mount Laurel Township, Burlington County, New Jersey.* Report to Orleans Builders and Developers, Huntingdon Valley, Pa.

————. 1987. Estimation of Capacity in Aboriginal Conoidal Vessels. *Journal of Middle Atlantic Archaeology* 3:95–102.

————. 1988. A Stage II Archaeological Survey of Rosewood Condominiums, Town of Hammonton, Atlantic County, N.J. Unpublished report on file with the author.

————. 1989a. *An Archaeological Survey of a Major Subdivision, Blocks 1, 2, 3; Lots 44–48, etc., City of Northfield, Atlantic County, N.J.* Report to Kiejdan & Trocki, Northfield, N.J.

————. 1989b. *An Archaeological Survey of Block 544.10, Lot 2, Upper Township, Cape May County, N.J.* Report to Aldon Homes, Inc., Marmora, N.J.

————. 1990a. *The Abature Site (28-MO-134): Report of Archaeological Data Recovery, Route 18, Section 3C, Eatontown Borough, Monmouth County, N.J.* Report to New Jersey Department of Transportation.

————. 1990b. *An Archaeological Survey of Greens at Galloway, Galloway Township, Atlantic County, N.J.* Report to K. C. Development Company, Mount Laurel, N.J.

————. 1991. *Report of Archaeological Data Recovery, Route 55 Freeway, Section 13A, Deptford Township, Gloucester County, New Jersey.* Report to New Jersey Department of Transportation.

————. 1996a. *An Archaeological Survey of Proposed Northeast Business Center, Logan Township, Gloucester County, New Jersey.* Report to Trammell Crow NE, Inc., Cherry Hill, N.J.

————. 1996b. *A Stage IB/II Archaeological Survey of Thomas Edison State College, City of Trenton, Mercer County, New Jersey.* Report to D. F. Gibson, Architect, Newark, N.J.

————. 1997. Archaeological Data Recovery: Avalon Golf Resort and Country Club, Middle Township, Cape May County, New Jersey. *Bulletin of the Archaeological Society of New Jersey* 52:1–23.

————. 1998a. *Data Recovery at Site 28-BU-407, Block 17, Lot 11, Evesham Township, Burlington County, N.J.* Report to Troth Associates, Marlton, N.J.

————. 1998b. *Report of Archaeological Data Recovery, Sites 28-GL-29 and 28-GL-30, Logan Township, Gloucester County, New Jersey.* Report to Liberty Property Trust, Malvern, Pa.

————. 1998c. Small Things, Considered Closely. *Bulletin of the Archaeological Society of New Jersey* 53:33–39.

————. 1999a. *Archaeological Data Recovery at Site 28-HU-200, Block 53, Lot 1, Raritan Township, Hunterdon County, N.J.* Report to DeLuca Enterprises, Newtown, Pa.

————. 1999b. *Archaeological Data Recovery at the Baseman Site, Block 18, Lots 1, 2, and 4, Evesham Township, Burlington County, New Jersey.* Report to Evecan, L.L.C., Haddon Heights, N.J.

————. 1999c. *A Stage I Archaeological Survey of Harbor Bay Square Retail and Commercial Development, Vicinity of Swainton, Middle Township, Cape May County, New Jersey.* Report to Harbor Bay, L.L.C., Bryn Mawr, Pa.

————. 1999d. *A Stage II Archaeological Survey of the Dutchtown Road Pumping Station Project, Voorhees Township, Camden County, New Jersey.* Report to Richard A. Alaimo Associates, Mount Holly, N.J.

————. 2000a. *Archaeological Data Recovery at Site 28-BU-492, Block 16, Lot 3, Evesham Township, Burlington Co., N.J.* Report to Pulaski Construction Company, Mercerville, N.J.

————. 2000b. *Archaeological Data Recovery, Site 28-BU-489, Block 119, Lots 16, 18, and 18.01, Delran Township, Burlington County, New Jersey.* Report to Atlantic Five Developers, Voorhees, N.J.

————. 2000c. *Report of Archaeological Data Recovery Sites 28-BU-225 and 28-BU-226, and Relict Charcoal Kilns in the Highbridge Lakes Development, Medford Township, Burlington County, New Jersey.* Report to Main Line Realty Group, West Berlin, N.J.

————. 2001. *A Stage II Archaeological Survey of the Tindall Homes Tract, Woolwich Township, Gloucester County, N.J.* Report to Tindall Homes, Princeton, N.J.

————. N.d.a. Aboriginal Textiles in Northeastern Archaeology. Manuscript on file with author.

————. N.d.b. Unpublished Research Notes in possession of the author.

Mounier, R. Alan, and Jack Cresson. 1988. A Case of Lachrymose Archaeology in Southern New Jersey. *Newsletter of the Archaeological Society of New Jersey* 146:5–8.

Mounier, R. Alan, Jack Cresson, and John W. Martin. 1993. New Evidence of Paleoindian Biface Fluting from the Outer Coastal Plain of New Jersey. *Archaeology of Eastern North America* 21:1–23.

Mounier, R. Alan, and John W. Martin. 1992. *Report of Archaeological Data Recovery, Route 55 Freeway, Section 2, Franklin and Elk Townships, Gloucester County, New Jersey.* Report to New Jersey Department of Transportation.

————. 1994. For Crying Out Loud! News about Teardrops. In *Recent Research into the*

Prehistory of the Delaware Valley, ed. Christopher A. Bergman and John F. Doershuk, 125–140. A special issue of *Journal of Middle Atlantic Archaeology* 10. Bethlehem, Conn.: Archaeological Services.

Myers, Albert Cook. 1970. *William Penn's Own Account of the Lenni Lenape or Delaware Indians.* Rev. ed. Somerset: Middle Atlantic Press.

Newcomb, William W., Jr. 1956. *The Culture and Acculturation of the Delaware Indians.* Anthropological Paper no. 10. Ann Arbor: University of Michigan.

Noël Hume, Ivor. 1969. *A Guide to the Artifacts of Colonial America.* New York: Alfred A. Knopf.

Oestreicher, David M. 1994. Unmasking the *Walam Olum:* A 19th Century Hoax. *Bulletin of the Archaeological Society of New Jersey* 49:1–44.

Omwake, H. Geiger. 1963. Aboriginal Nonceramic Artifacts. In *The Townsend Site near Lewes, Delaware*, ed. H. Geiger Omwake and T. D. Stewart, 11–13. *The Archeolog* 15(1). Seaford, Del.: Sussex Society of Archaeology and History.

Pagoulatos, Peter. 1992. *Phase II Cultural Resource Survey of Prehistoric Site 28-OC-100, Brick Township, N.J.* Report on file with New Jersey Historic Preservation Office.

Parris, David C. N.d. Vertebrate Faunal Remains from the Pennella Site (28-OC-80). Manuscript. Copy on file with the author.

Parris, David C., and Lorraine E. Williams. 1986. Possible Sources of Mica from the Abbott Farm Site, Mercer County, New Jersey. *Bulletin of the Archaeological Society of New Jersey* 40:1–6.

Payne, Ted M. 1990. Investigations at a Lackawaxen Generalized Hunting Settlement in the Middle Delaware River Drainage. *Bulletin of the Archaeological Society of New Jersey* 45:9–13.

Perazio, Philip. 1988. The West Parkway Site: A Late Woodland Hunting Camp in the Glacial Lake Passaic Bottom. *Bulletin of the Archaeological Society of New Jersey* 43:57–78.

Perkins, William R. 2000. Archeological, Experimental, and Mathematical Evidence Supporting the Use of the Atlatl as a Primary Big Game Procurement Weapon of Prehistoric Americas. *Bulletin of Primitive Technology* 20:69–72.

Perpillou, Aimé Vincent. 1966. *Human Geography.* New York: John Wiley and Sons.

Petrosky, Eugene R. 1983. An Unusual Spearthrower Weight from Hunterdon County. *Bulletin of the Archaeological Society of New Jersey* 39:13–14.

———. 1989. Rockshelters in Northern Hunterdon County. *Bulletin of the Archaeological Society of New Jersey* 44:6–8.

Philhower, Charles A. 1927. Indian Days in Middlesex County, New Jersey. *Proceedings of the New Jersey Historical Society*, n.s., 12(4): 385–409.

———. 1931. South Jersey Indians on the Bay, the Cape, and the Coast. *Proceedings of the New Jersey Historical Society*, n.s., 16(1): 1–21.

———. 1932. *The Art of the Lenape.* Archaeological Society of New Jersey, Leaflet no. 1.

———. 1933. *The Human Face in Lenape Archaeology.* Archaeological Society of New Jersey, Leaflet no. 2.

———. 1934. *Indian Pipes and the Use of Tobacco in New Jersey.* Archaeological Society of New Jersey, Leaflet no. 3.

———. 1935. *New Jersey Indian Celts, Adzes and Gouges.* Archaeological Society of New Jersey, Leaflet No. 4.

———. 1936. *The Semilunar Knife in New Jersey.* Archaeological Society of New Jersey, Leaflet no. 5.

———. 1952. The Earliest Report of the Lenape and Narragansett Indians. *Bulletin of the Archaeological Society of New Jersey* 5:10–12.

————. 1953. The Historic Minisink Site—Part I. *Bulletin of the Archaeological Society of New Jersey* 7:1–9.

————. 1954. The Historic Minisink Country—Part II. *Bulletin of the Archaeological Society of New Jersey* 8:1–7.

————. 1955. The Origin and Meaning of the Name Amboy and the Word Lenape. *Bulletin of the Archaeological Society of New Jersey* 10:9–10.

————. 1957. The Indians about Lake Hopatcong. *Bulletin of the Archaeological Society of New Jersey* 13:11–20.

Pietak, Lynne Marie. 1995. Trading with Strangers: Delaware and Munsee Strategies for Integrating European Trade Goods, 1600–1800. Ph.D. diss., University of Virginia, Charlottesville.

Powell, John Wesley. 1893. Are There Evidences of Man in the Glacial Gravels? *Popular Science Monthly* 43:316–326.

Printz, Johan. 1912 [1644]. Relation to the Noble West India Company. In *Narratives of Early Pennsylvania, West Jersey and Delaware*, ed. Albert Cook Myers, 103. New York: Charles Scribner's Sons.

Putnam, Frederick Ward. 1898. Early Man in the Delaware Valley. *Proceedings of the American Association for the Advancement of Science* 46:344–348.

Rafinesque, Constantine S. 1836. *The American Nations; or, Outlines of Their General History, etc.* Philadelphia: C. S. Rafinesque.

Ramenofsky, Ann F. 1987. *Vectors of Death: The Archaeology of European Contact.* Albuquerque: University of New Mexico Press.

Randolph, Larry R. 1983. A Burial from Central New Jersey, *Bulletin of the Archaeological Society of New Jersey* 39:12–13.

Ranere, Anthony, and Patricia Hansell. 1985. *Archaeological Survey in the Drainage of the Lower Great Egg Harbor River.* Report to the Office of New Jersey Heritage.

Rau, Charles. 1865. Artificial Shell Deposits in New Jersey. In *Annual Report for 1864*, 370–374. Washington, D.C.: Smithsonian Institution.

Regensburg, Richard A. 1971. The Savich Farm Site: A Preliminary Report. *Bulletin of the Massachusetts Archaeological Society* 32:20–23.

Reilly, George J. 1974b. Letter to the author. 28 March.

Rementer, James. 1987. A New Look at "Canoes of the Lenni Lenape." *Bulletin of the Archaeological Society of New Jersey* 42:32.

Richards, Horace G. 1939. Reconsideration of the Dating of the Abbott Farm Site at Trenton. *American Journal of Science* 237:345–354.

————. 1941. Petrology of Artifacts. In Dorothy Cross, *Archaeology of New Jersey*, 1:19–22. Trenton: Archaeological Society of New Jersey and New Jersey State Museum.

Ritchie, William A. 1932. The Lamoka Lake Site. *Researches and Transactions of the New York State Archaeological Association* 7(4): 79–134.

————. 1944. *The Pre-Iroquoian Occupations of New York State.* Memoir no. 1. Rochester: Rochester Museum of Arts and Sciences.

————. 1949. *The Bell-Philhower Site, Sussex County, N.J.* Prehistoric Research Series, vol. 3, no. 2. Indianapolis: Indiana Historical Society.

————. 1959. *The Stony Brook Site and Its Relation to Archaic and Transitional Cultures on Long Island.* Bulletin 372. Albany: New York State Museum and Science Service.

————. 1961. *A Typology and Nomenclature for New York Projectile Points.* Bulletin 384. Albany: New York State Museum and Science Service.

————. 1965. *The Archaeology of New York State.* Garden City: Natural History Press.

———. 1969. *The Archaeology of Martha's Vineyard.* Garden City: Natural History Press.

Ritchie, William A., and Don W. Dragoo. 1960. *The Eastern Dispersal of Adena.* Bulletin 379. Albany: New York State Museum and Science Service.

Ritchie, William A., and Robert E. Funk. 1971. Evidence for Early Archaic Occupations on Staten Island. *Pennsylvania Archaeologist* 41:45–59.

———. 1973. *Aboriginal Settlement Patterns in the Northeast.* Memoir no. 20. Albany: New York State Museum and Science Service.

Ritchie, William A., and Richard S. MacNeish. 1949. Pre-Iroquoian Pottery of New York State. *American Antiquity* (Menasha) 15(2): 97–124.

Robbins, Austin, and Chris C. Hummer. n.d. Subsistence and Dentition: A Dental Analysis of Woodland Burials from a Site in Southern New Jersey. Paper submitted for publication in *Bulletin of the Archaeological Society of New Jersey.*

Robbins, Maurice. 1968. *An Archaic Ceremonial Complex at Assawompsett.* Attleboro: Massachusetts Archaeological Society.

———. 1972. Some Early House Floors. *Bulletin of the Massachusetts Archaeological Society* 32(1–2): 1–12.

Robichaud, Beryl, and Murray F. Buell. 1973. *The Vegetation of New Jersey.* New Brunswick: Rutgers University Press.

Rothchild, Nan A., and Lucianne Lavin. 1978. The Kaeser Site: A Stratified Shell Midden in the Bronx, New York. In *Readings in Long Island Archaeology and Ethnology,* 2:367–393. N.p.: Suffolk County Archaeological Association.

Russell, Frank. 1899. Human Remains from the Trenton Gravels. *American Naturalist* 33:143–153.

Salisbury, Rollin D., and George N. Knapp. 1917. *The Quaternary Formations of Southern New Jersey.* Reports of the State Geologist, vol. 7. Trenton.

Salwen, Bert. 1962. Sea Levels and Archaeology in the Long Island Sound Area. *American Antiquity* 28(1): 46–55.

———. 1966. Cultural Inferences from Faunal Remains: Examples from Three Northeastern Coastal Sites. *Pennsylvania Archaeologist* 40(1–2): 1–8.

———. 1975. Post Glacial Environments and Culture Change in the Hudson River Basin. *Man in the Northeast* 10:43–70.

Sandy, William. 1981. The College Farm Site, 28Mi75. *Bulletin of the Archaeological Society of New Jersey* 37:6–14.

Sargent, Paul H. 1953. Perforated Net Sinkers of Gloucester County, New Jersey. *Bulletin of the Archaeological Society of New Jersey* 6:5–6.

Schmitt, Karl. 1952. Archaeological Chronology of the Middle Atlantic States. In *Archeology of the Eastern United States,* ed. James B. Griffin, 59–70. Chicago: University of Chicago Press.

Schrabisch, Max. 1915. *Indian Habitations in Sussex County, N.J.* Bulletin 13. Union Hill: Geological Survey of New Jersey.

———. 1917. *Archaeology of Warren and Hunterdon Counties.* Bulletin 18. Trenton: New Jersey Division of Geology.

———. 1926. *Aboriginal Rock Shelters and Other Archaeological Notes of Wyoming Valley and Vicinity.* Proceedings and Collections of the Wyoming Historical and Geological Society, vol. 19. Wilkes-Barre, Pa.: E. B. Yordy Company.

———. 1930. *Archaeology of Delaware River Valley.* Harrisburg: Pennsylvania Historical Commission.

Shepherd, Walter. 1965. *Archaeology.* New York: New American Library.

Sidoroff, Maria-Louise. 1991. Primitive Pottery Firing, Lenape Village, Waterloo Foundation for the Arts. *Bulletin of Primitive Technology* 1(2): 58–59.

Sirkin, Les. 1977. Late Pleistocene Vegetation and Environments in the Middle Atlantic Region. In *Amerinds and Their Paleo-Environments in Northeastern North America*, ed. W. S. Newman and Bert Salwen, 206–217. Annals of the New York Academy of Sciences, 288. New York: New York Academy of Sciences.

Skinner, Alanson. 1909. Archaeology of the New York Coastal Algonkian. In American Museum of Natural History, *Anthropological Papers* 3:213–235. New York: American Museum of Natural History.

———. 1913. *Social Life and Ceremonial Bundles of the Menomini Indians.* Anthropological Papers, vol. 13, pt. 1. New York: American Museum of Natural History.

———. 1915. *The Indians of Newark before the White Men Came.* Newark: Newark Museum Association.

———. 1921. *Notes on Iroquois Archaeology.* Indian Notes and Monographs. New York: Museum of the American Indian, Heye Foundation.

———. 1932. *The Indians of Manhattan Island and Vicinity.* Guide Leaflet Series no. 41. 5th ed. New York: American Museum of Natural History.

Skinner, Alanson, and Max Schrabisch. 1913. *Preliminary Report of the Archaeological Survey of the State of New Jersey.* Bulletin 9. Trenton: New Jersey Geological Survey.

Sloshberg, Willard. 1964. Mechanized Excavation of the Pahaquarra Boy Scout Camp Site. *Eastern States Archaeological Federation Bulletin* 23:10–11.

Smith, Benjamin L. 1948. An Analysis of the Maine Cemetery Complex. *Bulletin of the Massachusetts Archaeological Society* 9(2–3): 19–71.

Smith, Carlyle S. 1950. *The Archaeology of Coastal New York.* American Museum of Natural History, Anthropological Papers, vol. 43, pt. 2. New York: American Museum of Natural History.

Smith, Samuel. 1765. *The History of the Colony of Nova-Caesaria or New Jersey.* Burlington, N.J. Reprint. Trenton: William S. Sharp, 1890.

Snow, Dean. 1980. *The Archaeology of New England.* New York: Academic Press.

Speck, Frank G. 1931. *A Study of the Delaware Indian Big House Ceremony.* Harrisburg: Pennsylvania Historical Commission.

———. 1940. *Penobscot Man.* Philadelphia: University of Pennsylvania.

———. 1946. *Catawba Hunting, Trapping, and Fishing.* Joint Publications, no. 2. Philadelphia: University Museum and Philadelphia Anthropological Society.

Spier, Leslie. 1915. *Indian Remains near Plainfield, Union County, and along the Lower Delaware Valley.* Bulletin 13. Trenton: New Jersey Geological Survey.

———. 1918. *The Trenton Argillite Culture.* American Museum of Natural History, Anthropological Papers, vol. 22, pt. 4. New York: American Museum of Natural History.

Staats, F. Dayton. 1974. A Fresh Look at Bowmans Brook and Overpeck Incised Pottery. *Bulletin of the Archaeological Society of New Jersey* 30:1–7.

———. 1978. An Unusual Faceted Plummet from the Middle Delaware Valley. *Pennsylvania Archaeologist* 48(3): 48.

———. 1986. Bolas Stones of Northwestern New Jersey and Adjacent States. *Bulletin of the Archaeological Society of New Jersey* 40:12–14.

———. 1987. The Harding Lake Rockshelter: A Lackawaxen Phase Station of the Late Archaic Period. *Bulletin of the Archaeological Society of New Jersey* 42:24–26.

———. 1988. The Hartung Rockshelter, Warren County, New Jersey. *Bulletin of the Archaeological Society of New Jersey* 43:42–44.

————. 1990. A Deposit of Netsinkers from the Upper Delaware Valley. *Bulletin of the Archaeological Society of New Jersey* 45:17.

————. 1991a. An Archaic Adze from the Musconetcong Valley, Hunterdon County, New Jersey. *Bulletin of the Archaeological Society of New Jersey* 46:81.

————. 1991b. A Chipped Adze from the Upper Delaware Valley. *Bulletin of the Archaeological Society of New Jersey* 46:54.

————. 1991c. The Furnace Brook Rockshelter, Warren County, New Jersey. *Bulletin of the Archaeological Society of New Jersey* 46:31–40.

————. 1992a. Late Woodland Miniature Pottery Vessles from the Upper Delaware Valley. *Bulletin of the Archaeological Society of New Jersey* 47:61–62.

————. 1992b. A Spearthrower Weight from Warren County. *Bulletin of the Archaeological Society of New Jersey* 47:9.

————. 1992c. An Unusual Stone Axe Head from the Upper Delaware Valley. *Bulletin of the Archaeological Society of New Jersey* 47:92.

————. 1995. A Ceramic Effigy Face from the Upper Delaware Valley. *Bulletin of the Archaeological Society of New Jersey* 50:19.

Stanzeski, Andrew J. 1981. Quahog "Shell Tools." *Bulletin of the Archaeological Society of New Jersey* 37:15–18.

————. 1996. Two Decades of Radiocarbon Dating from the New Jersey Shore. *Bulletin of the Archaeological Society of New Jersey* 51:42–45.

————. 1998. Four Paleoindian and Early Archaic Sites in Southern New Jersey. *Archaeology of Eastern North America* 26:41–53.

Stewart, Frank H. 1932. *Indians of Southern New Jersey.* Woodbury: Gloucester County Historical Society.

Stewart, R. Michael. 1987. Middle and Late Woodland Cobble/Core Technology in the Delaware River Valley of the Middle Atlantic Region. *Bulletin of the Archaeological Society of New Jersey* 42:33–43.

————. 1990. Late Archaic Axe Manufacturing at the Shady Brook Site, Mercer County, New Jersey. *Bulletin of the Archaeological Society of New Jersey* 45:3–8.

————. 1992. A Late Woodland "Heirloom" from the Trenton Area. *Bulletin of the Archaeological Society of New Jersey* 47:79–82.

————. 1994. Stratigraphic Sequences and Archaeological Sites in the Delaware Valley: Implications for Paleoenvironmental Change in the Middle Atlantic Region. *Bulletin of the Archaeological Society of New Jersey* 49:99–106.

————. 1995. Archaic Indian Burials at the Abbott Farm. *Bulletin of the Archaeological Society of New Jersey* 50:73–80.

————. 1998. *Ceramics and Delaware Valley Prehistory: Insights from the Abbott Farm.* Trenton Complex Archaeology, Report 14. East Orange, N.J.: Cultural Resource Group, Louis Berger and Associates, and the Archaeological Society of New Jersey.

Stewart, R. Michael, Chris C. Hummer, and Jay F. Custer. 1986. Late Woodland Cultures in the Middle and Lower Delaware River Valley and the Upper Delmarva Peninsula. In *Late Woodland Cultures of the Middle Atlantic Region,* ed. Jay F. Custer, 58–89. Newark: University of Delaware Press.

Stewart, T. D. 1963. Skeletal Remains of Aboriginal Dogs. In *The Townsend Site near Lewes, Delaware,* ed. H. Geiger Omwake and T. D. Stewart. *The Archeolog* 15(1): 54–58. Seaford, Del.: Sussex Society of Archaeology and History.

Streeter, Donald. 1982. Autographed inscription to R. Alan Mounier.

Tantaquidgeon, Gladys. 1972. *Folk Medicine of the Delaware and Related Algonkian Indians.* Anthropological Series, no. 3. Harrisburg: Pennsylvania Historical and Museum Commission.

Thomas, Ronald A. 1987. Stone Effigy from the Gloucester City Site (28-CA-50), Camden County, New Jersey. *Bulletin of the Archaeological Society of New Jersey* 42:49.

————. 1990. Salvage Excavations at the Gloucester City Site, Camden County, New Jersey. *Bulletin of the Archaeological Society of New Jersey* 45:43–53.

Thomas, Ronald A., Robert F. Hoffman, and Douglas G. Sahady. 1998. Data Recovery at the Sickle Farm Site (28Mo192), Monmouth County, New Jersey. *Bulletin of the Archaeological Society of New Jersey* 53:13–27.

Thomas, Ronald A., and Nancy H. Warren. 1970. 1970 Salvage Excavations at the Mispillion Site. *The Archeolog* 22(2): 1–23. Seaford, Del.: Sussex Society of Archaeology and History.

Thorbahn, Peter F., and Deborah C. Cox. 1988. The Effect of Estuary Formation on Prehistoric Settlement in Southern Rhode Island. In *Holocene Human Ecology in Northeastern North America,* ed. George P. Nicholas, 167–184. New York: Plenum Press.

Truncer, James J. 1990. Perkiomen Points: A Study in Variability. In *Experiments and Observations on the Terminal Archaic of the Middle Atlantic Region,* ed. Roger W. Moeller, 1–62. Bethlehem, Conn.: Archaeological Services.

Tuck, James A. 1976a. *Ancient People of Port au Choix: The Excavation of an Archaic Indian Cemetery in Newfoundland.* Newfoundland Social and Economic Studies no. 17. St. John's: Memorial University of Newfoundland.

————. 1976b. *Newfoundland and Labrador Prehistory.* Archaeological Survey of Canada. Ottawa: National Museum of Man.

Tull, Stephen W., and Bernard W. Slaughter. 2001. *The Dundee Site (Native American Occupation in Northern New Jersey from 1,000 B.C.) Technical Report.* Prepared for Howard Needles Tammen & Bergendoff, Fairfield, N.J., and Bureau of Environmental Analysis, New Jersey Department of Transportation. Florence, N.J.: URS Corporation.

Twitchell, M. W. 1913. *The Mineral Industry of New Jersey for 1912.* Bulletin 11. Trenton: Geological Survey of New Jersey.

Ubelaker, Douglas H. 1976. Analysis of the Human Skeletal Remains from the Rosenkrans Site, Sussex County, New Jersey. *Archaeology of Eastern North America* 4:45–48.

————. 1996. Aboriginal Human Remains from Osborne Island, N.J. *Bulletin of the Archaeological Society of New Jersey* 51:73–74.

————. 1997a. Human Skeletal Remains from the Pennella Site, Ocean County, N.J. *Bulletin of the Archaeological Society of New Jersey* 52:92–96.

————. 1997b. The Savich Farm Site Cremations, Burlington County, N.J. *Bulletin of the Archaeological Society of New Jersey* 52:88–92.

Veit, Richard. 1993. Pierre Eugène Du Simitière (ca. 1736–1784): A Colonial Archaeologist. *Bulletin of the Archaeological Society of New Jersey* 48:71–72.

————. 1994. Contact Period Artifacts from Burlington County, New Jersey, in the Collections of the University Museum. *Bulletin of the Archaeological Society of New Jersey* 49:77–79.

Veit, Richard. 2002. *Digging New Jersey's Past: Historical Archaeology in the Garden State.* New Brunswick: Rutgers University Press.

Veit, Richard, and Charles A. Bello. 2001. "Tokens of their Love": Interpreting Native American Grave Goods from Pennsylvania, New Jersey, and New York. *Archaeology of Eastern North America* 29:47–64.

Volk, Ernest. 1911. *The Archaeology of the Delaware Valley.* Papers of the Peabody Museum of American Archaeology and Ethnology, 5. Cambridge: Harvard University.

Walker, Iain C. 1977. *Clay Tobacco Pipes, with Particular Reference to the Bristol Industry.* History and Archaeology, vol. 11c. Ottawa: Parks Canada.

Wallace, Anthony F. C. 1947. Woman, Land and Society: Three Aspects of Aboriginal Delaware Life. *Pennsylvania Archaeologist* 17(1–4): 1–35.

———. 1957. Political Organization and Land Tenure among Northeastern Indians, 1600–1830. *Southwestern Journal of Anthropology* 13:301–21.

Walwer, Gregory, and Peter Pagoulatos. 1990. Native American Land-Use Patterns on the Outer Coastal Plains of New Jersey. *Bulletin of the Archaeological Society of New Jersey* 45:77–95.

Webb, William S. 1946. *Indian Knoll, Site Oh 2, Ohio County, Kentucky.* Reports in Anthropology and Archaeology, vol. 4, no. 3, pt. 1. Lexington: University of Kentucky.

———. 1959. Letter to C. A. Weslager, editor, 11 January. Archaeological Society of Delaware. Document on file with the author.

Werner, David J. 1964. Vestiges of Paleo-Indian Occupation near Port Jervis, New York. *New World Antiquity* (London) 11:30–52.

White, Richard S., Jr. 1974. Notes on Some Archaeological Faunas from the Northeastern United States. *Archaeology of Eastern North America* 2(1): 67–72.

Widmer, Kemble. 1964. *The Geology and Geography of New Jersey.* New Jersey Historical Series, 19. Princeton: D. Van Nostrand Company.

Willey, Gordon R. 1966. *An Introduction to American Archaeology.* Vol. 1, *North and Middle America.* Englewood Cliffs, N.J.: Prentice Hall.

Willey, Gordon R., and Jeremy A. Sabloff. 1974. *A History of American Archaeology.* San Francisco: W. H. Freeman.

Williams, Lorraine, and Ronald A. Thomas. 1982. The Early/Middle Woodland Period in New Jersey. In *New Jersey's Archeological Resources from the Paleo-Indian Period to the Present: A Review of Research Problems and Survey Priorities,* ed. Olga Chesler, 103–138. Trenton: New Jersey Office of Cultural and Environmental Services.

Willoughby, Charles C. 1935. *The Antiquities of the New England Indians.* Cambridge: Peabody Museum of American Archaeology and Ethnology, Harvard University.

Witthoft, John. 1949. An Outline of Pennsylvania Indian History. *Pennsylvania History* 16(3): 3–15.

———. 1952. A Paleo-Indian Site in Eastern Pennsylvania: An Early Hunting Culture. *Proceedings of the American Philosophical Society* 96:464–495.

———. 1953. Broadspears and the Transitional Period Cultures. *Pennsylvania Archaeologist* 23(1): 4–31.

———. 1963. General Interpretations. In *The Townsend Site near Lewes, Delaware,* ed. H. Geiger Omwake and T. D. Stewart. *The Archeolog* 15(1): 59–69. Seaford, Del.: Sussex Society of Archaeology and History.

Witthoft, John, and W. Fred Kinsey III, eds. 1959. *Susquehannock Miscellany.* Harrisburg: Pennsylvania Historical and Museum Commission.

Witthoft, John, and James Miller. 1952. Grooved Axes of Eastern Pennsylvania. *Pennsylvania Archaeologist* 22(3–4): 81–94.

Wolfe, Peter. 1977. *The Geology and Landscapes of New Jersey.* New York: Crane Russak.

Woolley, Harold K. 1948. The Indians and Ocean County. *Bulletin of the Archaeological Society of New Jersey* 1:5–12.

Wormington, H. M. 1957. *Ancient Man in North America.* Popular Series 4. 4th ed. Denver: Denver Museum of Natural History.

Wren, Christopher. 1914. *A Study of North Appalachian Indian Pottery.* Proceedings and Collections of the Wyoming Historical and Geological Society, vol. 13. Wilkes-Barre, Pa.: E. B. Yordy Company.

Wright, George Frederick. 1892. *Man and the Glacial Period.* New York: D. Appleton and Co.

Wright, George Frederick. 1897. *Man and the Glacial Period.* 2d. ed. New York: D. Appleton and Co.

INDEX

Note: Page numbers in boldface denote material in illustrations.

burials (*continued*)
163, 167, 188; at West Creek site, 168,
198; at West Long Branch site, 115, 163,
185, 187
Burlington County, sites in, 23, 44, 72,
133, 149, 159, 168, 175, 199, 201, 208
Burrow, Ian, 172

caches: at Abbott Farm site, 53, 120, 137,
139; at Canton site, 181; defined, 128,
137; distribution of, 138; at Harry's
Farm site, 139; of Koens-Crispin complex, 138; at Koens-Crispin site, 169,
170; at Larchmont site, 209; of Meadowood complex, 174–175; as mortuary
furniture, 138, 163, 174; with red ochre,
83; at Red Valley site, 171, 172; ritual
use of, 137–138; at Stow Creek, 205,
208; at Williamson site, 211
Cadwalader site, 190, 213–215
Calverley, Fred, 49, 211
Camden County, sites in, 118, 126, 148,
149, 167
Canoe Place, N.Y., canoe paddle from,
114
Canton site, 181, 182
Cape May, purported wampum factories
at, 117, 142
Cape May County, sites in, 27, 113, 115,
117, 142, 143, 175, 180, 189, 217
Cape May Court House, sites near, 142;
wampum manufacturing near, 142
Carman, Alan E., 74, 84, 142, 189, 190,
206
Carpenter, Edmund S., 177
Cavallo, John, 53
Cedar Creek (Ocean County), sites
along, 145
Cedar Swamp Creek, sites along, 142
cemeteries: at Beesley's point, 175; near
Biles Island, 167, 183; at Boni Farm
site, 185, 186; distribution of, 125, 167,
168; at Koens-Crispin site, 173; at Lenhardt site, 185, 186; at Lerro Farm site,
168; of Middlesex complex, 175; Munsee cemetery, 45, 111, 115, 116, 163, 166,
184–186, 190; at Red Valley site, 173; at
Rosenkrans Ferry site, 175, 177, 178; at
Savich Farm site, 172; at Scott site,

180; near Trenton, 168; at West Creek
site, 168; at West Long Branch site,
185, 186
ceramic artifacts: beads, 103; "ceramic
cork," 104; cups, 90, 92; disks and
plates, 101, **103**; sphere, 103; various
kinds of, 85. *See also* pipes; pottery;
pottery types
chalcedony, *see under* lithic materials
Cherry Hill site, 148
chert, *see under* lithic materials
Clabeaux, Marie Striegal, 187
climate, *see* environment
Coe, Joffre L., 202
Cohansey Creek, sites along, 157, 158
Cohansey quartzite, *see under* lithic
materials
components, defined, 9
Constable Hook, sites on, 139, 145, 163
containers, of organic materials, 85
copper: artifacts, 80, 120, 137, 176, 177,
181, 184, 185, 222; source of, 176, 177
corn (maize), *see under* cultigens
cradle boards, 187
cremation: effects of, on bone, 164, 179;
temperatures required for, 173, 179
cremations, *see* burials
Cresson, Jack, 52, 133, 155, 157, 196, 209
Cross, Dorothy, 4, 46–48, **92**, 224
cryptocrystalline materials, *see* lithic materials: flint, jasper, etc.
crystals, aboriginal use of, 85, 169, 196,
197
cuesta quartzite, *see under* lithic materials
cuestas: composition of, 36; location of,
36, 157
cultigens: beans, 152; corn (maize), 13,
122, 151–153, 187; at Harry's Farm site,
152; at Miller Field site, 151; pumpkins,
151; squash, 152
cultural change, 12, 50
culture, defined, 12, 55
Cumberland County, sites in, 84, 101,
103, 104, 106, 109, 113, 114, 133, 142, 150,
157, 158, 168, 190, 203, 221

DaCosta, dugout canoe from, 113
Dalrymple, Edward S., 45
Dark Moon site, 103, 131, 139, 148, 149

ABOUT THE AUTHOR

Born in New Jersey, R. Alan Mounier has had a lifelong fascination with the archaeology and history of the Garden State and its native peoples. Over the past 35 years, he has conducted archaeological research in virtually all parts of New Jersey. He has written widely on the subject of New Jersey archaeology, particularly with respect to the prehistory of the coastal plains and Pine Barrens. His early training in archaeology was at Syracuse University, where he participated in the excavation of several Iroquois sites. He received a master's degree from Memorial University of Newfoundland and participated in the investigation of Indian and Eskimo sites in Newfoundland and Labrador. In 1976 he formed the professional consulting firm of R. Alan Mounier, Archaeologist and has been employed by that firm to the present. Mr. Mounier lives in Vineland with his wife and family. He is the current president of the Archaeological Society of New Jersey.